Edwidge Danticat

Edwidge Danticat

A READER'S GUIDE ▣ Edited by Martin Munro

UNIVERSITY OF VIRGINIA PRESS • CHARLOTTESVILLE AND LONDON

University of Virginia Press
© 2010 by the Rector and Visitors of the University of Virginia
All rights reserved
Printed in the United States of America on acid-free paper

First published 2010

9 8 7 6 5 4 3 2 1

LIBRARY OF CONGRESS CATALOGING-IN-PUBLICATION DATA

Edwidge Danticat : a reader's guide / edited by Martin Munro ; with a foreword by Dany Laferrière.
    p. cm.
    Includes bibliographical references and index.
    ISBN 978-0-8139-3021-3 (cloth : alk. paper) — ISBN 978-0-8139-3022-0 (pbk.) — ISBN 978-0-8139-3073-2 (e-book)
    1. Danticat, Edwidge, 1969—Criticism and interpretation—Handbooks, manuals, etc. 2. Caribbean Area—In literature. I. Munro, Martin.
    PS3554.A5815Z65 2010
    813'.54—dc22

2010005642

CONTENTS

SECTION THREE
Danticat & Her Peers

SECTION FOUR
Interview & Bibliography

FOREWORD

A Heart of Serenity in the Storm

DANY LAFERRIÈRE

Had she just published her first novel or was she just about to have it published? I no longer know, but I first met Edwidge Danticat at that moment in her career, at a small literary soirée that she attended with a friend who was also writing her first novel. For every young writer it is a time when the heart is like a mad horse that is impossible to control. You flit easily between dejection and exaltation. What struck me from the first time I looked at Edwidge Danticat was her composure. That calmness and serenity that she would retain as celebrity arrived some time later with its peculiar violence—it is only in America that success can take on such dimensions. I promised myself in leaving her that evening that I would read her book. Which is to say that she made an impression on me, for at the time I only read Borges. In the time it took to raise my head away from the strange fictions woven by that old blind man hidden away in Buenos Aires, the word was already out that a new voice was retelling in its own way the same old fables that have occupied the hearts of human beings since the beginning of time. One morning, at a café, I was able to examine at my leisure the face of this young prodigy featured on the front page of the newspaper's literary section. That ageless face catches the attention immediately. You feel yourself in the presence of one of those anonymous divinities from the peripheral religions. Just as Mr. Yunioshi finds Holly Golightly's likeness while traveling through Africa in Truman Capote's *Breakfast at Tiffany's*, I am convinced that I will come across one day the sculpted head of Edwidge Danticat on the Vodou altar of one of those huts placed in unstable equilibrium on the mountainsides of Haiti. It is not by chance that from the first letter of our correspondence, which has unfortunately frayed with time, I baptized her "My princess of Brooklyn."

If I recall correctly Danticat's major preoccupation at the time was Haiti. To face up to the storm that was breaking on this young novelist, a real anchorage point was needed. My impression is that Danticat chose composure and serenity. She must have remembered those old ladies from her childhood who could sit out on their porches the whole blessed day. It was a very dynamic kind of immobility, for in offering coffee to passersby they came to create a whole life all around them. It is not that far from the poetic art of Edwidge Danticat. But this sense of calm does not eliminate anxiety. I remember those times when she felt herself somewhat torn between this almost magic world that lived within her and that seemed to her at the point of plunging into nostalgia, and that New York modernity that was sending her signals ever more rapidly. How to reconcile these two worlds? The question was all the more complex in that there are two, maybe three Haitis: the Haiti that she keeps fresh in her memory, the Haiti of her parents who lived with her in Brooklyn, and the country itself that she continued to see on television and in the newspapers, always in great difficulty. What characterizes Danticat's style are human preoccupations fed by a myriad of everyday truths and presented in a style so natural that it may appear simple. It is the art of the night-time storytellers of the country of her childhood. And this very particular style (a simplicity that erases all traces of toil) is making of her nothing less than a contemporary classic.

Edwidge Danticat

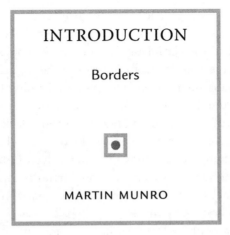

INTRODUCTION

Borders

MARTIN MUNRO

When you go to a bookstore to look for something by Edwidge Danticat, which section do you go to first? Depending on the store layout, and the country in which you live, you might look in the sections for African American, ethnic, black, Caribbean, women's, even world literature. Or you might try the regular fiction section, normally the largest part of any bookstore, where you will find those works and those authors deemed by the bookstore to require no additional classification or categorization. Maybe you will find copies of Danticat's works in more than one section, or maybe you will find none at all.

The decision to place an author's book in a particular section of the store is determined by marketing and economic concerns (in terms of the greatest potential sales), but it is also underpinned by a complex set of issues related to race, gender, sexual orientation, and identity politics: the question of *who* has written it seems to take precedence over *what* is written (and how it is written). Indeed, there is an implicit expectation that there will be a direct connection between, say, a "black female" author and the content of her works: such an author may be expected to deal primarily, if not exclusively, with issues of race and gender. In Edwidge Danticat's case, these issues seem all the more complicated as she does not fit easily into any of the standard categorizations. We may find Danticat's works in the African American section, but for a writer born in Haiti, that label is not fully applicable unless we take the American part of it to mean the Americas. In any case, the notion of African American identity has grown out of a specifically U.S. history of race, color, and class, which is different in certain important ways from that of the Caribbean, where many people "of color" may not identify themselves primarily in terms of race. Caribbean societies typically have more nuanced and complex gradations of class and color, and migrants from there to the United States might not accept the all-encompassing African American tag. The term "black literature" may be more appropriate in that it seems to be open to all authors of African origin, no matter where they find themselves. But again, it seems too restrictive to apply to Danticat and carries with it the idea that literature by blacks is a phenomenon apart from and yet defined by opposition to literature by whites.[1]

If we locate a book by Danticat in the ethnic literature section, we may feel that this is closer to its rightful home, in that this category might include authors like her who are part of minority groups in the United States, or who are not native to the country. In this section may also be found books by (nonwhite) authors from outside the United States, whose work might also be shelved in a world literature section. But again there are problems, in that these tags (and, it seems, all other labels) flatten, limit, and prescribe. They moreover carry with them connotations of exoticism.

Whose work gets the broader designation of "fiction"? Which authors can simply write without having to address a set of expectations imposed on them by readers and salespeople, or by the demographics of race, color, and class? One of the fascinating—and little-known—aspects of Edwidge Danticat's writing is that it comes out of a literary tradition that has carried out one of the most searching and sophisticated inquiries into the nature of writing and its relation to class, place, race, gender, and nation of all New World traditions. Works of Haitian literature—I would argue the tradition with which Danticat's novels can be most closely aligned—have long addressed such issues, and they seem even to have gone beyond them in calling into question the worth of all literary (and racial) categories. Danticat's great compatriot Dany Laferrière refuses all labels, including those of Haitian, Caribbean, francophone, black, and exiled author. The fact that he was born in Haiti does not, he insists, make him a Haitian writer. Laferrière turns things on their head by proposing that he comes from his reader's country. "When someone from Japan reads me," he says, "I become a Japanese writer."[2] Imagine that: a bookstore arranged according to the origins of the reader, and not the author's race or ethnicity. Laferrière's idea that the identity of the author is not "natural" or predetermined by biology but shifts and remakes itself according to the particular reader is indicative of a particularly strong thread in contemporary Haitian writing. With Haiti's history of revolution and resistance, writers from there have often taken on the role of defenders of the nation and the black race in general. Contemporary authors like Laferrière challenge and distance themselves from this prescribed role. Much like Laferrière, the Haitian Canadian author Joël Des Rosiers calls into question the idea that one's birthplace determines one's identity for life. "The real place of birth," Des Rosiers says, "is the place where one looks upon oneself through a stranger's eyes: my first homelands have been foreign countries."[3] Des Rosiers also suggests that a fixed identity and sense of belonging are something alien to island people, for to be born on an island is, he says, to know an "endless call toward the elsewhere." Island people, he believes, are "always on a journey."[4]

Haitian women authors have, if anything, been even more insistent on overturning given identities and on challenging expectations determined by race and gender. Largely eschewing political ideologies (though articulating a different kind of politics), these women tend to represent quotidian, individual reality, people living ordinary lives rather than being avatars of race or nation. In the words of the contemporary author Yanick Lahens, women writers in Haiti were the first in the Haitian literary tradition to shed "a certain number of masks, [tear] down a certain number of [ideological and political] screens," and express the "first truly individual and personal words in fiction."[5] One of the foremost examples of this personalized women's writing is Marie Chauvet's 1968 trilogy *Amour, Colère, Folie* (*Love, Anger, Madness*), a potent work written from and through the perspectives of alienated female figures, which offers a devastating critique of black nationalism in Haiti, specifically the pre-Duvalier, noiriste celebration of "black essence." In short, Haitian women writers have produced a body of work that has mapped out "new territories of the imagination" and brought into being a new consciousness in Haitian literature.[6]

Edwidge Danticat is well aware of this great and growing tradition of women's writing in Haiti, and she agrees that Haitian literature did not "get personal" before women authors came to prominence.[7] This is not to say that Danticat's work in particular or broader women's writing from Haiti in general has no political significance. On the contrary, personal lives are politicized in Danticat's work, and conversely politics is personalized, as characters seek to survive ideology-driven dictatorships, political violence, and the poverty and social damage wreaked by various regimes. Private space is often invaded by public discourse, and individuals find themselves unwittingly caught in the swirl of political retribution and the racial and nationalist thinking that perpetuates it. Danticat's characters may well be marginalized socially, but they do not and cannot exist apart from history and politics, those external forces that often drive the most vulnerable from their homes, indeed from the very nation that the political ideology venerates and glorifies.

If Danticat has much in common with this tradition of women's writing from Haiti, she is also in certain respects not entirely part of that tradition. Most important perhaps is the fact that she writes in English, while most of the great works of Haitian literature have been published in French. In this crucial regard, Danticat's works implicitly weaken the bond between French (and Kreyòl) language and Haitian literary identity, a bond that has existed since the immediate postrevolutionary period. In general terms, Danticat shares the kind of relationship to language and identity that Joël Des Rosiers ascribes to contemporary Haitian-Canadian authors, who "have come to the end of coincidences between language, culture, and identity." For these authors, Des Rosiers says, "any language is tainted, and our poetical art attempts to put a check on any kind of principle of deep-rooting."[8] From another perspective, Danticat's writing in English, and the fact that she has lived in the United States since the age of twelve, brings her work into an indirect dialogue with (African) American authors. But as we have already seen, she does not quite fit into that category, either. While this in-between situation may be seen as a loss of identity for Danticat (as for many other exiled authors), it is also a kind of liberation in that she is free from many of the constraints and expectations that direct, unambiguous attachments bring. Danticat can and does write freely, in a style that is unmistakably hers; and it is ultimately in her style, her phrasing, her imagery, her presentation of time and place, and her nuanced plots and characterizations that her identity and individuality as a writer exist and express themselves. This is how it should be.

This book extends and deepens the lines of inquiry that I have begun to open up in this introduction. Its broadest aim is to act as a guide for current and future readers of Danticat's work, not to prescribe ways of reading the work but to suggest some points of departure for further inquiries and discussions. The book also seeks to situate Danticat in relation to the various geographical, literary, and cultural contexts with which her work intersects without ever being fully incorporated into them. The book works on the premise that while Danticat's closest affinities are with Haitian writing, and that consequently any appreciation of her work must be grounded in an awareness and a knowledge of Haitian literature, readers should also be aware of how her work influences and is influenced by the broader contexts of Caribbean and American writing.

Divided into four sections, the book aims first to analyze the various overlapping contexts in which Edwidge Danticat writes. Beginning with a brief biography, the first section of the book features three critical essays by prominent scholars—J. Michael Dash, Carine Mardorossian, and Régine Michelle Jean-Charles—that situate Danticat in relation to the Haitian, Caribbean, and African American literary contexts and show how she fits into and diverges from those contexts. Dash turns the question of literary influence and heritage around and considers the possibility that Danticat, the careful reader of the classics of Haitian writing, is less the product of her precursors than a medium through which those earlier texts might be reconsidered and read differently. Mardorossian similarly calls into question the notion that Danticat can be easily placed within a pre-existing category of writers, in this case that of "Caribbean women writers." Recognizing the ways in which Danticat does echo the themes and concerns of other Caribbean women writers, Mardorossian goes on to argue that what is most significant in Danticat's fiction is the way that it reworks those same themes, radically reconceptualizing the sexual, racial, class, and national concepts that have defined understandings of women's or Caribbean literature. Mardorossian concludes that stable, discrete categories of identity are replaced in Danticat's work by a more relational model of identity that is born of the interconnected workings of difference *across* gender, race, class, and national boundaries. Jean-Charles also hesitates to categorize Danticat too narrowly, but she argues that the contemporary definition of an African American woman writer is itself fluid and expansive and that Danticat makes an important contribution to this broadening and diversification of the tradition. To include Danticat in the African American women's literary tradition is, she says, to acknowledge the "diasporic nature" of blackness in the United States and to contribute to the reworking of the notion of

Americanness to include all the peoples and nations of the Americas, as well as those like Danticat who spend their time moving between different sites within the Americas.

Indeed, this shifting, unpredictable "diasporic" group constitutes a further dimension in which we might discuss Danticat's work, one that is not dealt with directly in this book. This group is bound not so much by common racial or national bonds, but by a shared experience of displacement from places of birth to the metropolitan centers of North America and Europe. There is also a generational link, in that many of these relatively new authors are sounding out and shaping a cosmopolitan, postnational consciousness that calls into question the ideologies and revolutions that were crucial to the experiences and convictions of preceding generations. This group is also a product of the particular ways in which books are marketed in our time, the way that online booksellers, for example, send recommendations for further reading based on previous purchases and on what other readers with similar tastes are reading. Thus if one has purchased a Danticat work online, the seller might introduce the reader to the works of, for instance, Jhumpa Lahiri, Zadie Smith, Colin Channer, Adam Mansbach, Angie Cruz, Chimamanda Adichie, Joseph O'Neill, and Junot Diaz (the latter is a particularly important point of reference in that he comes from the same island as Danticat does, and he deals with similar issues of state violence and relationships between the island state and the United States). These authors, from various cultural, social, and national backgrounds, are also Danticat's peers and form an important, evolving context in which she is being read and understood.[9]

The second section of this book focuses more closely on Danticat's work itself and offers close analyses of each of her published works up to and including *The Dew Breaker*. The first essay in this section, by Nick Nesbitt, deals exclusively with Danticat's short fiction. Nesbitt considers the relationship between the personal worlds of Danticat's characters and the broader political realities of the contemporary world, arguing that Danticat's writing interweaves personal and political space and thus sets out new means and understandings of political activity. As Nesbitt's analysis of Danticat's *Krik? Krak!* shows, the personalized, testimonial intimacy of Danticat's writing emphatically does not involve a turning away from universal problems of poverty and social injustice and suggests a kind of politics that could potentially begin to address the contemporary personal and social dilemmas in what Nesbitt terms this time of expanding global imperialism. The second essay, by Kiera Vaclavik, focuses on a critically neglected element of Danticat's work: her writing for young adults. As Vaclavik argues, Danticat's two books for young adults have much in common in terms of themes and style with her other fictional work. At the same time, there are specific elements in Danticat's writing for young adults, including a didactic impulse to encourage understanding about Haiti and the particular plights of immigrant children. As Vaclavik concludes, Danticat's fiction for young adults is grounded in Haitian experience but carries important messages of tolerance and understanding for all living in multicultural societies. In the third essay, on Danticat's travel writing, Charles Forsdick deals with another less prominent genre in her oeuvre, showing how Danticat's *After the Dance* draws on and in certain ways calls into question the conventions of travel writing and at the same time sets up a dialogue with Danticat's own fictional writing.

The remaining essays in this section analyze the three novels. Mireille Rosello's essay on *Breath, Eyes, Memory* addresses the dilemmas that arise for critics in discussing a novel whose subject matter—rape, incest, and the ways that stories can belie truth and perpetuate abuse—cannot be easily incorporated into existing critical discourses. As Rosello points out, Danticat's novel invites reflection on the means of representing rape in fiction. By invoking a mother figure who is a radically disempowered narrator, controlled and eventually destroyed by the story of rape and incest, the novel makes a specifically literary contribution to the representation of rape. Myriam J. A. Chancy's essay on *The Farming of Bones* discusses the ways in which Danticat reinvokes the 1937 massacre of Haitians in the Dominican Republic to present female characters who are parts of communities but also individual actors within those communities. As Chancy shows, these women are active agents in the creation of new, less closed and oppositional ideas of nation, race, and class. Finally, in her discussion of *The Dew Breaker*, Mary Gallagher recognizes that this third novel continues many of the thematic concerns of Danticat's previous novels. At the same time, Gallagher argues, this novel shifts its focus somewhat from mother figures to the troubled eponymous father figure. By doing so, Danticat pursues her nuanced critique of masculinity in Haitian lives, both in the native country and in various sites of exile. In effect, all the essays in this section discuss and reinforce the idea that while Danticat writes with the political bit between her teeth her political engagement is always allied with an unwavering sensitivity to style. It is as if style, and Danticat's unrelenting attention to it, are themselves political acts, the textual manifestations of a sensibility that refuses to be bowed or to relinquish its quest for truth.

The third section of the volume comprises shorter, more general reflective and appreciative essays written by Danticat's peers—Haitian, Caribbean, and American authors alike. The contributors in this section are Maryse Condé, Évelyne Trouillot, Madison Smartt Bell, and Lyonel Trouillot. In her essay, Condé argues that Danticat is establishing a new set of functions for the Caribbean writer. Previously charged with speaking on behalf of the people, the Caribbean writer, Condé says, often appeared as a demiurge. In grounding her work in everyday lived reality, Danticat has brought about a shift in Caribbean writing in that she claims no special status for herself as messiah or voice of the people. Danticat has moreover effected what Condé calls a linguistic "revolution" in the traditionally francophone literature of Haiti. Breaking away from French and Kreyòl, Danticat, in Condé's opinion, creates a new language: that of the newly exiled Caribbean subject in the era of globalization. Évelyne Trouillot's essay places Danticat on the "right side of history," that is, on the side that is distinguished by a concern for historical and social truth, an openness toward the other, and an instinct to question cultural and national stereotypes. These are for Trouillot the primary strengths of Danticat's writing. In his essay, Madison Smartt Bell discusses questions of style and language, Danticat's "radical" simplicity and expressiveness that, he feels, come from her rootedness in Haitian culture. For Bell, Danticat's work gives the sense of calmness and control, of "poised equilibrium." As he argues, however, this serenity is arrived at only through great effort, unusual strength, and at "a price of pain." Lyonel Trouillot considers Danticat's work to be an individual expression of her own particular reality, and not as a contribution to "literary nationality," a concept that he dismisses as vulgar and outdated. Danticat's territory, he says, is her writing. In Danticat's work, he finds a "goodness," an attachment to and faith in the human that is manifested in characters' modest, personal, positive actions. Like the three other writers, Lyonel Trouillot is sensitive to Danticat's style and in particular to the rhythm of her phrasing, which he relates to Haitian tradition, to the tendency for Haitian writing since Jacques Roumain to have a "carnal, swinging" quality.

The fourth, and final, section of the book consists of an interview with Edwidge Danticat conducted by Renee H. Shea, in which Danticat discusses her latest work as of this writing, *Brother, I'm Dying*. A bibliography of classic and contemporary Haitian literature, compiled by Nadève Ménard, follows the interview. Apart from contextualizing Danticat and her work, this book also aims to lead readers to other Haitian authors, such as past masters like Jacques Roumain and Jacques-Stephen Alexis and modern stars like Dany Laferrière, Gary Victor, Louis-Philippe Dalembert, Lyonel Trouillot, Joël Des Rosiers, Stanley Péan, Frankétienne, and Évelyne Trouillot, all of whom are writing remarkable work in what is a golden age of Haitian writing. The work of Edwidge Danticat can be used as a bridge between previously separate literary traditions, and it can open up the rich tradition of Haitian writing to the North American and European reading and academic publics, which are, since the bicentenary of the Haitian Revolution in 2004, showing unprecedented interest in Haiti. This volume is meant to invite readers to read Danticat in her various contexts and to explore those contexts further, in particular the neglected but substantial Haitian tradition that is Danticat's closest point of reference— one she is enriching while questioning many of its most longstanding assumptions.

I wish to thank Edwidge Danticat for her generous support for this project, and Édouard Duval Carrié for providing the cover image. Special thanks to Cathie Brettschneider for encouragement and good advice throughout, to Jane Curran for meticulous copyediting, and to Raennah Mitchell and Morgan Myers for guiding the project to completion.

NOTES

1. Indeed, African American writers have long demonstrated a similar reticence by self-consciously embracing and rejecting the label of black literature.

2. Dany Laferrière, *J'écris comme je vis: Entretien avec Bernard Magnier* (Lyon: Editions La Passe du Vent, 2000), 9, my translation.

3. Joël Des Rosiers, *Théories caraïbes: Poétique du déracinement* (Montreal: Triptyque, 1997), 75, my translation.

4. Ibid., 187.

5. Yanick Lahens, "Interview," trans. Mohamed B. Taleb-Khyar, *Callaloo* 15, no. 2 (1992): 441–44 (441–42).

6. Marie-Denise Shelton, "Haitian Women's Fiction," *Callaloo* 15, no. 3 (1992): 770–77 (770).

7. Edwidge Danticat, interview with author, December 2002.

8. Joël Des Rosiers, "Joël Des Rosiers," trans. Suzanne Houyoux, *Callaloo* 15, no. 2 (1992): 427–30, 428.

9. I am grateful to my anonymous reviewer for pointing out this further dimension.

Contexts

This section begins with a brief biography that outlines Edwidge Danticat's life and work to date, and then sets out and interrogates the ways in which the author and her work relate to three key literary contexts: Haitian, Caribbean, and African American. The aim is to help readers to understand the three traditions, their key concepts and preoccupations, and to think of the ways in which Danticat fits in with or diverges from these traditions. In each case, the discrete nature of the categories is called into question, as the essays demonstrate the ways in which Danticat's work occupies a very particular place in Haitian, Caribbean, and African American literature.

INSIDE OUT

A Brief Biography
of Edwidge Danticat

MARTIN MUNRO

Edwidge Danticat was born in Port-au-Prince, Haiti, on January 19, 1969. Her parents, André and Rose, were born in the provinces, her mother in the city of Léogâne and her father in the mountains around Léogâne. Like many of their midcentury generation, the parents migrated from the provinces to the capital, Port-au-Prince, in search of better living conditions. Unlike most of Haiti's major literary figures, Danticat does not come from a middle-class or elite background; her family, she says, would have been considered lower class or poor, or at best working class due to the fact that some members of the family lived abroad. The family's standing was elevated somewhat by Danticat's uncle Joseph's position as a Protestant minister. Her grandparents had been Presbyterians, and most of the family remained Protestant, though some had become Baptists or Pentecostals or Jehovah's Witnesses. Family values were perhaps typically Protestant: hard work, honesty, and modesty. Despite the status the uncle's ministry gave to the family, they were essentially poor, with strong provincial and peasant roots. Danticat's connections to these roots were maintained through her long summer family vacations in the mountains of Léogâne. Just as it would do later in her work, the peasant, folk elements of her childhood served as a counterpoint to the more chaotic, sometimes alienating experiences of the city.[1]

One of the most significant of these experiences—and one that comes back in commuted form in *Breath, Eyes, Memory*—was the emigration of her parents to New York. When she was two years old, her father left Haiti, to be followed two years later by her mother. The parents' new migration was again motivated by economic reasons and the desire for a better life. André Danticat had left school in 1954 at the age of nineteen to work as an apprentice with a tailor. After about six months he bought his own sewing machine and began to work for himself, selling shirts to vendors for resale all over Haiti. This lasted until the early 1960s, when during the Kennedy administration American used clothing was sent directly to Haiti, and small-time businesses such as André's became unviable. On the recommendation of the boss of his brother Joseph, André found himself a new job selling shoes in the store of an Italian émigré. In 1962 André met Rose, and three years later they married, moving into a small house in the popular district of Bel Air. The 1960s was also the time when François "Papa Doc" Duvalier consolidated his political hold on Haiti, refusing to stand down or to hold new elections, even as his repression of adversaries became ever more violent. This repression was carried out chiefly through the militia he created, the Tontons Macoutes, his private army recruited from the country's urban and rural poor. Many of André's clients in the shoe store were Macoutes, who would simply take the shoes they wanted without paying. André finally grew tired of the constant fear and the struggle to feed a wife and two children on his salary, so he chose to go to New York on a one-month tourist visa, which he had every intention of extending into a permanent stay. In his absence, Danticat's mother continued her husband's work, sewing school uniforms and flags for sale, desperately trying to support her young family on the meager revenues from her sewing work. Two years after André had left, when Edwidge was four and her brother André, or "Bob," was two, Danticat's mother was approved for a one-month tourist visa, which would reunite her with her husband in New York.

Edwidge and Bob were left in the care of their uncle Joseph and aunt Denise. Reverend Joseph Nosius had moved to the Bel Air district of Port-au-Prince in 1947, had worked as a salesman for a Syrian fabric merchant, and had been a fervent supporter of Daniel Fignolé, the populist Haitian politician who founded the Mouvement Ouvriers Paysans, the Laborers and Peasants Party. Joseph's own father had been a member of the guerilla resistance against the U.S. forces that had occupied Haiti during 1915–34. Joseph appreciated Fignolé's prioritization of the plight of Haiti's neglected poor masses and his commitment to ending the Haitian elite's economic and political dominance. When on May 25, 1957, Fignolé was sworn into office, Joseph and Danticat's father André were part of the massive crowd that converged on the national palace to celebrate. However, when Fignolé was deposed after only nineteen days in office and replaced by Papa Doc Duvalier, Joseph was distraught and gave up on his own plans to run for political office. The void he felt after having his political hopes dashed was in part filled when he joined a Baptist congregation, which offered order and austerity and an outlet for his public spiritedness. Newly invigorated, he helped build his own church in Bel Air, which he named L'Eglise Chrétienne de la Rédemption, the Christian Church of Redemption.

Danticat's parents' plan was to send for the two children once they had found jobs and settled in New York. However, due to delays with U.S. immigration, the separation lasted eight years. The near decade the family was apart was filled, Danticat says, with long letters, lengthy voice messages on cassette tapes, and tearful phone calls, "all brimming with the promise that one day we would be united," not only with their parents, but also with their two Brooklyn-born siblings Kelly and Karl, whom André and Edwidge had never met. Even as they suffered through being separated from their parents, however, Edwidge and André were regularly reminded by their uncle how fortunate they were that their parents were in New York. If they raised their voices in protest, Danticat says, the "Faustian bargain" their parents had faced would be laid out before them: "They could have stayed behind with us and we could have all starved or they could have gone to New York to work so that we could not only have clothes and food and school fees, but also a future. For a future, for people like us, the *malere,* the poor, as my uncle liked to say, was not a given. It was something to be clawed from the edge of despair with sweat and blood. At least in New York, our parents would be rewarded for their efforts."[2]

New York was to Edwidge and André the "city on the hill," the "imaginary haven" of their lives. When they fantasized about New York, they imagined themselves there, "walking the penny-gilded streets and buying all the candies we could stuff into ourselves." As time passed, they came to accept the idea that New York was where they were destined to go, "as soon as the all powerful gatekeepers saw fit to let us in, and if we could help it we would never leave once we were once again at our parents' side."[3]

Danticat attended a modest private school called Collège Elliot Pierre;

"it was not fancy at all," she says. Like most schools in Haiti, it was privately run. It was here that she was first exposed to Haitian history. The students were expected to memorize key dates and information about the Haitian Revolution and to repeat verbatim famous speeches such as Toussaint Louverture's "In overthrowing me they have cut down the trunk of the tree of liberty, but it will grow back by its roots for they are deep and numerous." The emphasis at this stage was on memorizing and accepting the official version of Haitian history; it was only later in her works that she would "process" this history and call aspects of it into question, even as she would remain equally aware of the value of that history and its influence in shaping her work.

She began to write when she was about nine years old. Her motivations were simple—"I loved stories and loved to read," she says—and writing came easily for her at this early stage, without the pressures of writing for readers. She wrote for pleasure, as she still does. Moreover, writing was for her a way of being and keeping well; even today, she says, "I don't feel right or happy if I am not writing." Danticat recalls that the first book she ever read was *Madeline*, Ludwig Bemelman's classic of children's literature about a young Parisian girl's adventures. The memory of this first book has remained with Danticat, becoming a mnemonic device, something like Proust's own Madelines, and her bond with it strengthened when she discovered that Bemelman was a traveler who divided his time between Paris and New York City, and that he began to write the Madeline stories in an eatery called Pete's Tavern in New York. "Over the years," Danticat says, "as I reflected on my experiences with Madeline—when I discovered her origins, it almost seemed as though she had followed me to New York—I realized how literary encounters, be they our first or last or most recent, can metamorphose over and over again, regardless of where we go or what we do."

The language of education in Haiti was French, but the family spoke Kreyòl at home. French was, she says, "an outside language, the language of books." For this reason, she "never felt like [her]self speaking it." In this regard, questions of social class are again important, as the French language is considered a sign of prestige. For Danticat's family, French was largely a foreign language, the tool of education and a sign of class division. The lives of the Danticat family had little in common with those of what the uncle called "la société," or respectable society. Although the Danticats would not have been considered by the elite as very cultured, they aimed to be so, in their own way. The uncle, for example, always made sure that they used the correct knives and forks and refrained from putting their elbows on the table in case, she says, "we were ever invited into a high society home some day." Social class in Haiti was, however, largely based on lineage, francophilia, wealth, and family name. Somewhat ironically, for someone who has become one of the best known of all Haitian people, in Haiti the Danticat name meant nothing socially, and this anonymity determined and reflected the family's modest status. Similarly, her cultural upbringing was influenced more by popular phenomena such as storytelling (her aunt Denise's centenarian mother, Granmè Melina, would tell tales to the small children in the evenings), *rara* music, and carnival; and again, she would return to these cultural forms in her work, engaging with them in a more profound and knowing way than she was able to as a child, when she was largely a passive, if interested, observer.

Growing up in Duvalierist Haiti in the mid-1970s, Danticat was aware to some extent of the political and social tensions that infiltrated into every family and every home. Her close-knit family sheltered her from the harshest realities of that time, but she and the other children inevitably "could hear the adults talking" about events outside the home. Silence and suspicion became elements of her experience, and children were "warned to be quiet." People she knew disappeared unexpectedly, she heard of public assaults in the news, "executions were whispered about," and aspects of everyday life, such as school, were often disrupted. Again, though, the family served as a barrier that insulated her from the worst of that period's violent excesses, which were alleviated, she says, by the "efforts of loved ones at protecting me," and which were filtered "through the veil of childhood." Haiti's political violence would, however, later impact the family directly; in 1989, amid the post-Duvalier struggle for political power, Danticat's cousin Marie Micheline, a mother of four whom Danticat's uncle Joseph had adopted as a small child, was shot and killed at Joseph's clinic in Bel Air. The death was the subject of an April 17, 1989, article in *Newsday* magazine, written by the journalist Ron Howell, who wrote that Marie Micheline was "a reflection of Haiti and its potential, a flicker of light frustrated in its attempt to shine."[4]

In 1981, at the age of twelve, Edwidge left Haiti with her brother Bob to live with her parents in New York, and, again, this experience would later resurface in commuted, fictionalized form in her writing.

For Danticat's parents, it was the culmination of eight years of work and struggle, during which they would console themselves with visions of the two Haitian-born children playing together with their two New York–born siblings. Danticat's earlier dreams of leading a charmed life in New York met with the harsh reality of immigrant life in the city: the poor, she says, "were likely to be working more hours than anyone else, for less money, and with few, if any benefits." Her father had for years worked two minimum-wage jobs—one in a textile factory, one in a night car wash—to support two households in two different countries. Growing tired of irregular work and immigration raids, Danticat's father left his jobs when Edwidge and Bob arrived so that he would be able to take the youngest sibling Karl to day care and the rest of the children to school. The same year, the family car also became a Gypsy cab, an unaffiliated taxi, the name of which led Danticat to think that they "were part of a small clan of nomads and wanderers whose leader, my father, chauffeured other people around when he was not driving us." The family's financial situation was precarious: once the rent, the utility bills, and the week's groceries were paid, there was little left from her father's irregular wages. For a family without medical insurance, fear of falling ill was a constant added source of apprehension.

Apart from the financial aspects, the hardest part of adjusting to life in New York was the language barrier, even if this difficulty was eased to some extent by her integration into the Haitian community in Brooklyn. This community in many ways replicated the one she had left behind, in that it was, in her words, "cohesive and insular," and that there was a togetherness and interdependency that bonded the Haitian migrants. At this time, Danticat and her family lived on Flatbush Avenue, Brooklyn, in a six-story brick building called Westbury Court. Danticat recalls that there was a subway station beneath the building, graffiti on the walls of the building, trash piled up outside, and intermittently functioning heating and hot water. For all that, she says she never dreamed of leaving Westbury Court until fire destroyed an apartment across the hall. The fire broke out one afternoon while she was watching television in her apartment with her brothers Karl, Bob, and Kelly, and claimed the lives of two African American children.

After the burned apartment was refurbished, two blind Haitian brothers and their sister moved in. The new tenants were all musicians and were members of a group called Les Frères Parents, the Parent Brothers. Danticat would hear coming from the apartment what she describes as politically motivated, "engagée" music, which the brothers played in protest against the Duvalier dictatorship they had fled. The Parent Brothers and their sister Lydie also received religious and political leaders from Haiti and from the Haitian community in New York. Apart from the fire, Danticat recalls various other unsettling incidents—the murder of a cab driver, a burglary in the apartment, the killing of a Nigerian immigrant—but says she never felt she was living in a violent place. Westbury Court was, she says, "an elevated castle above a clattering train tunnel, a blind alley where the children from our building and the building across the street had erected a common basketball court for hot summer afternoon games, an urban yellow brick road where hopscotch squares dotted the sidewalk next to burned out, abandoned cars. It was home."

At the same time, attending secondary school in New York was difficult for Danticat; she recalls being teased for her accent, for her imperfect English, and generally for being Haitian at a time when the most prevalent international images of Haiti were related to AIDS and the boat people. Classroom readings consisted of excerpts of English classics such as Dickens. The move to New York had made her shy, more so than she had been before. It also led her to be more introverted, more of a reader, and "much more of a scribbler," writing things down that later became stories. She published her first writings in the school newspaper. Outside of class, however, Danticat never felt completely alienated from Haiti, because her family attended a Haitian church, lived in a church-owned building, and generally remained attached to the Haitian community. This connection to the Haitian community has remained a constant in her life, for even when she moved from New York to Miami early in the new millennium, she chose to live in Little Haiti and to thereby perpetuate her bond with migrant Haitian culture. Consequently, and because she can return "home" to Haiti at any time, she does not consider herself to be an exile.

As Danticat continued to write and began to consider a career as a writer, she met with some opposition from her family, who recommended that she train to become a nurse, and who were concerned about the insecurities of being a professional writer. For Haitian writers, these insecurities often involve threats to their lives, and because they had heard of many Haitian writers who had been killed or exiled, Danticat's parents considered writing to be a dangerous pursuit. Writing was something she could do on the weekends, as long as she had a more stable, settled career. Danticat's instincts, however, were toward literature, and she began to read more widely in African American and Haitian literature. The first book in English that she had read was Maya Angelou's *I Know Why the Caged Bird Sings*. Her self-education in Haitian writing took place in New York at the central branch of the Brooklyn Public Library, which was the place that "dazzled" her most in the entire city. Having only ever owned one book, which she had to leave behind in Haiti for another child before boarding the plane to New York, she was "amazed that any individual person or institution could possess more than a few, not to mention the thousands and thousands of volumes that lined the walls of the multi-storied, majestic Grand Army Plaza building." In her Haitian school they had read excerpts of French novels, but not Haitian ones. It was in New York that she first read classic Haitian authors such as Jacques Roumain, Jacques-Stephen Alexis, and Marie Chauvet.

It was also in New York that she renewed her acquaintance with *Madeline*. At first, the new encounter with the fictional French girl was a source of comfort: Danticat talks of her gratitude at rediscovering in New York "a story I had enjoyed so much in another country, another language, at a different stage in my life." In another sense, the renewed familiarity with her first book suggested to her that "stories were not static, that characters evolved and traveled and could be made to speak different languages. And if Madeline could go to London and speak English, then why couldn't I live in Brooklyn and do the same? If this book could exist in several languages, maybe I could too." If, as Danticat says, she would probably not have become a writer if she had not moved to New York, she equally would not have been such a passionate reader had she not read *Madeline* at an early age. Having grown up in a family of storytellers, whose everyday conversations were "laced with proverbs, riddles and song," she realized that nobody seemed concerned about recording the stories. For a static population, "it was taken for granted that the spirited tales that burst out of my aunts and grandmothers would be carried into the future through us, their children and their children's children." Migration, however, "broke that chain," and most of the family's children and grandchildren, nieces and nephews, moved away from Haiti, to the United States, Canada, and France. For the displaced Danticat, reading and writing became means of perpetuating those links, and reading in particular became associated with a kind of transportable homeland, a place to which to retire and feel at home for those who are forced to leave their place of birth. The cultural split created by migration opened up for Danticat a new creative space, in which she says "one is able to rewrite the book for oneself, heading off on the adventures it allows as well as one's own very real exploits." And even though she says Madeline and she were as different as they could possibly be, Danticat asserts that "during one reading moment in time, Madeline was me and I was Madeline."

Danticat's still-nascent literary instincts strongly influenced her choice of college courses. After leaving high school in the late 1980s she studied for her B.A. in French literature at Barnard College, the women's liberal arts college in New York City. Barnard was also the alma mater of Zora Neale Hurston, who became one of Danticat's favorite authors. In addition, Danticat appreciated James Baldwin, for "his commitment to social issues," Richard Wright, Ntozake Shange, Maryse Condé, Alice Walker, Toni Morrison, Paule Marshall, and Simone Schwartz-Bart—authors who inspired her, and whose influence can be sensed to varying degrees in Danticat's own work. Of all her professors at Barnard, she was most inspired by Quandra Prettyman, who still teaches English and Africana Studies at the college.

Danticat's experiences at Barnard seem to have strengthened her resolve to write professionally—even if she still did not quite think of herself as a writer—and, finally leaving the nursing option behind, she enrolled in Brown University's Fine Arts program. For her final thesis, she picked up the manuscript on which she had been working intermittently throughout her high school and college days. The thesis drew partly on her own experiences as a child living between New York and Haiti, and between two cultures and languages. While the project was initially based on personal experiences, the greater part of the writing came from her own imagination, so that the final manuscript was by her own estimation about 75 percent fictional. Before she had even completed the manuscript, it was accepted for publication by Soho Press, and it appeared in 1994 as her first novel, *Breath, Eyes, Memory.* Danticat had expected the novel to sell at most the five thousand copies of its first printing, so the runaway success of *Breath, Eyes, Memory* took her by surprise. It has subsequently been reprinted many times and translated into Spanish, French, and Dutch.

The same year, at the age of twenty-five, she returned to Haiti for the first time since leaving in 1981. Her return was preceded by that of Jean-Bertrand Aristide, who had been reinstated as Haiti's president in October 1994, backed up by twenty thousand U.S. troops and President Clinton's Operation Uphold Democracy. Aristide was a priest who had originally been elected in December 1990 and gained huge support among the nation's poor due to his bold speeches condemning the Duvaliers. His first term lasted only seven months, and then he was ousted on September 30, 1991, by a military coup. Danticat was struck on her return by the signs of the political struggle: the symbols of Aristide's Lavalas party painted on walls, the burned out shanty towns of La Saline and Cité Soleil, the destroyed offices and homes. Most striking however, was the list of casualties of violence that her uncle Joseph had kept during the political troubles, and that he showed to her on her return, the hundreds of names reading like a litany of Haiti's decline, a memorial to the forgotten, expendable lives destroyed in the rush for power.

The success of *Breath, Eyes, Memory* was immediately followed by that of *Krik? Krak!* Danticat's collection of short stories, published in 1995. Many of the stories in *Krik? Krak!* had already been published, often under different titles, in *The Caribbean Writer,* a literary anthology published by the University of the Virgin Islands.[5] Danticat's first publication in the journal was a poem entitled "Sawfish Soup" (1991), one of her rare excursions into the poetic form. The journal also published some early stories that have not been subsequently published elsewhere, and in general played an important role in nurturing Danticat's talent. Some of the stories in *Krik? Krak!* recall the focus of her first novel on Haitian migrant life in New York, while others are written from the perspective of would-be migrants, risking everything to leave Haiti. In common with other contemporary Haitian women writers—Yanick Lahens and Évelyne Trouillot, for example—Danticat remains attached to the short story form, and even in her latest full-length novel, *The Dew Breaker,* the narrative is broken up into shorter, episodic passages reminiscent of the short story. Switching between different genres—fiction, nonfiction, novel, short story—"keeps things a lot more interesting" for Danticat as a writer.

In 1998, Danticat published her second novel, *The Farming of Bones,* which was also an instant success. The second novel differs from the first in that it is not set in the contemporary period, but in 1937, the year of the massacre of migrant Haitian cane workers in the Dominican Republic. This novel is inspired in part by her great predecessor Jacques-Stephen Alexis's *Compère Général Soleil* (1955) and by

René Philoctète's *Le Peuple des terres mêlées* (1989). Danticat's work in general engages with painful moments in Haitian history, and as is the case in *The Farming of Bones*, it tends to deflate nationalist rhetoric by focusing on the dilemmas of individuals caught up in historical events. Her desire to face up to the most challenging episodes in Haitian history is further shown in her third novel, *The Dew Breaker*, which deals with the intersecting lives of a cast of Haitians, in Haiti and in the United States, and in particular with a former Tonton Macoute and his attempts to build a new life in the States. Published in 2004, the year of the bicentenary of Haitian independence, *The Dew Breaker* implicitly critiques the grand nationalist rhetoric of the Haitian state and calls attention to the urgent task of questioning and facing up to the realities of the past. In its complex thematic intersections and its restrained, elegant narration, *The Dew Breaker* represents Danticat's most accomplished work to date. Indeed, in moving through Danticat's work sequentially, the reader is aware of a steadily improving aesthetic, a growing confidence, and an increasing assertiveness. Each book for Danticat is, she says, "a master class," an attempt to move forward both in terms of improving style and sharpening insight. Writing is for her a means of learning; and even if she continues to improve as a writer, she does not feel that the creative process becomes easier. "Perhaps," she says, "the more of it you do the less intimidating it seems." But starting a new piece, a new book, she says, "is always terrifying," in that she feels the writer's fear of failing, of writing a bad book, or of being unable to complete the work. If she feels pressure, it is not from critics or from readers' expectations, but from within herself: "I don't want to repeat myself," she says. "I want to get better. I want to do better with every word, every page."

In addition to these works, Danticat has also published children's novels—*Behind the Mountains: The Diary of Celiane Espérance* (2002), *Anacaona, Golden Flower* (2005)—and travel literature: *After the Dance: A Walk through Carnival in Jacmel, Haiti* (2002). Danticat considers these ventures as breaks from her more usual mode of adult fictional writing and as opportunities to explore different genres. Her motivation in writing books for children is to create something for her young daughters (Mira, named after her father's pet name, and Leila) and her nieces and nephews to read. With these works, Danticat in a sense returns to the role of the popular narrator, the storyteller figure that was one of her own formative influences.

After leaving office in 1996, Jean-Bertrand Aristide was re-elected in 2000 for a second term. The result of the election was contested by a coalition of opposition parties, and over the next three years, the opposition grew in strength, holding mass demonstrations against Aristide's increasingly authoritarian rule. At the same time, Aristide's supporters, many of them from Bel Air, held their own mass rallies, and there were regular clashes between the two sides. Aristide was finally removed from power in February 2004, the year of the Haitian nation's bicentenary. The United Nations Security Council passed Resolution 1542, which installed the Brazilian-led MINUSTAH, the UN Stabilization Mission in Haiti, as the means by which order would be restored to the nation. After September 30, 2004, the thirteenth anniversary of Aristide's first ousting, his supporters began to protest on a daily basis in Bel Air. In late October 2004, Danticat's uncle Joseph was awakened by heavy gunfire, which turned out to be a raid led by the UN forces in collaboration with the Haitian police. Their stated intention was to root out the most violent pro-Aristide gang members, the notorious *chimères,* from Bel Air and to clear the barricaded roadways. The Haitian police forced their way into Joseph's church, where he, some of his parishioners, and others from the neighborhood were sheltering, and made their way to the roof of the building, from which they killed or injured many of the gang members. After the police and UN forces left, the church was raided by local gang members, who accused Joseph of allowing the police to use his premises to fire on their people, and who promised to kill him if he did not pay them a large sum of money, a ransom for his own life that he could never afford. The terrifying episode continued with Joseph being smuggled out of the neighborhood, leaving Haiti for Miami with his son Maxo, requesting asylum on arrival, and being held by U.S. Customs and Border Protection at the Krome Detention Center in southwest Miami. Deprived of his herbal medication, Joseph became ill at Krome and was taken to Jackson Memorial Hospital, where he died from acute and chronic pancreatitis in the institution's prison wing.

In her 2007 book, *Brother, I'm Dying,* Danticat interweaves Joseph's story with those of her entire family, in particular the account of her father's life and death and the birth of her daughter, Mira. This book has all the power and subtlety of her fiction and shares with her novels, especially *The Farming of Bones,* a testimonial quality, a function of bearing witness for people whose lives involved long, sometimes thankless struggles. In the Haitian writer Kettly Mars's 2005 novel *L'Heure hybride*, the narrator figure speaks of his society as one that "forgives a man everything, his political beliefs, his cowardice, his scheming, his vices." Everything, that is, "except his poverty" (34). In her writing in general, and in particular in *Brother, I'm Dying*, Danticat "forgives" poverty and lends dignity and meaning to the lives of people who would otherwise be too easily forgotten. This book, like a lot of her fiction, is a harrowing read, but one that humanizes poverty, gives it a face, a body, a voice, a family, hopes, and dreams. The story of Edwidge Danticat and her family as it is told in *Brother, I'm Dying* is one of living amid death and fear, of clinging stubbornly to life, of creating new life, and of living between a troubled motherland and the North American cities that are often unsatisfactory, unwelcoming havens. In these and many other ways, Edwidge Danticat's story is that of modern Haiti.

NOTES

1. Unless otherwise indicated, information in this essay is taken from interviews conducted with Edwidge Danticat in March 2007, from essays provided by Edwidge Danticat, and from the manuscript of *Brother, I'm Dying*. Grateful thanks to Edwidge Danticat for providing these resources.

2. Edwidge Danticat, "New York Was Our City on the Hill," *New York Times*, November 21, 2004, http://select.nytimes.com/gst/abstract.html?res=F70616F93A5 B0C728EDDA80994DC404482.

3. Ibid.

4. The story of Marie Micheline appears in fuller detail in Danticat's "Marie Micheline: A Life in Haiti," *New Yorker*, June 4, 2007, http://www.newyorker.com/reporting/2007/06/11/070611fa_fact_danticat

5. See http://www.thecaribbeanwriter.org.

DANTICAT & HER HAITIAN PRECURSORS

J. MICHAEL DASH

In the critics' vocabulary, the word "precursor" is indispens-
able, but it should be cleansed of all connotation of polemics or
rivalry. The fact is that every writer creates his own precursors.
His work modifies our conception of the past, as it will modify
the future.—Jorge Luis Borges, "Kafka and His Precursors"

In contrast to the often tense or conflicted relationship between Caribbean writers and their literary predecessors, Edwidge Danticat
unfailingly acknowledges her Haitian precursors. The iconic figures of
post-occupation Haitian writing—Jacques Roumain, Jacques-Stephen
Alexis, and René Depestre—invariably are cited as literary ancestors
or precursors who have indelibly marked the territory she wishes to
explore. In the acknowledgments of her novel of the Haitian-Dominican
borderlands, *The Farming of Bones,* Danticat offers the peasant saluta-
tion of "One" to Alexis for his writing of *Compère Général Soleil (Gen-*
eral Sun, My Brother, 1999). In her travel book *After the Dance* she is
careful to mention René Depestre's novel about Jacmel, whose main
character Hadriana "is one of those rare literary cases in which a novel's character becomes even more real, and more powerful, than actual
people."[1] Her preface to the English translation of René Philoctète's
novel *Le Peuple des terres mêlées (Massacre River,* 2005) describes him
as "extraordinary."[2] Her 2005 novel that deals with painful reconciliation in the wake of the Duvalier dictatorship, *The Dew Breaker,* clearly

echoes Roumain's *Gouverneurs de la rosée* (*Masters of the Dew*, 1978) in its somber reflection on the metamorphosis of a mobilized peasantry from agents of social transformation into the hired killers of the Duvalier dictatorship.

It is, therefore, tempting to situate Danticat's work in terms of a celebration of the empowering cultural traditions of her homeland. In particular, the cultural nationalism that was provoked by the U.S. occupation appears to be a literary legacy to which Danticat is strongly attached. For instance, in her first novel, *Breath, Eyes, Memory*, the main character Sophie ultimately finds a restorative wholeness when her grandmother puts a hand on her shoulder and says to her, "There is a place where women are buried in clothes the color of flames, where we drop coffee on the ground for those who went ahead, where the daughter is never fully a woman until her mother has passed on before her. There is always a place where, if you listen closely in the night, you will hear your mother telling a story and at the end of the tale, she will ask you this question: '*Ou libere?* Are you free, my daughter?' "[3]

It is easy to relate these final words of the novel with their affirmation of place as cultural ground and ancestral wisdom to the Indigenist movement in Haiti and its celebration of Haitian peasant traditions. Haiti's cultural hinterland, which was conceived during the U.S. occupation as the zone of resistance against neocolonial rule and modernizing materialism, becomes in Danticat's first novel the site of a lost plenitude in which the protagonist's identity is grounded. Similarly in the epilogue to the collection of short stories *Krik? Krak!* ancestral voices are invoked as the sources of inspiration, responding with affirmation to the author's queries. "And over the years when you have needed us, you have always cried 'Krik?' and we have answered 'Krak!' "[4]

Indeed, as Carine Mardorossian perceptively notes, the novel not only activates the idea of redemptive periphery against the present dystopia of the United States but also uses a monolithic racial solidarity to subvert the nation state in both its Haitian and American manifestations as it "constructs a diasporic black identity based on a common link to Africa and the history of slavery and opposes this inclusive notion of blackness to white America's racist and purist ways."[5] In this regard, Danticat's work can be seen as a throwback to the longing for an ideal of a grounded folkloric identity that is central to post-occupation Haitian writing and the negritude movement as a whole. The diasporic attachment to geographical specificity and an anti-assimilationist racial solidarity do not make for an unproblematic creolization or happy hybridity in the case of the Haitian migrant. Danticat's world is one of loss, trauma, and displacement. But Danticat is careful not to freeze this cultural specificity in time or to construct it as an immutable idea of home. As Mardorossian again observes, while reifying a cultural past, Danticat's work "paradoxically revises the concept of Haitian tradition to signify a hybrid and changing space that is open to incorporating other aspects of the other culture."[6]

This idea of mobile traditions is almost literally evoked by Danticat in the image of being housed in dislocated cultural space in her 1995 lecture *Haiti: A Bi-cultural Experience* when she describes the building in which she lived in 1981 after having just moved to New York to join her parents:

> The building had a very large population of Haitian families because we would draw one another in. If there was a vacant apartment, one person would tell another, and the other person would tell another until we had created this little haven of Haiti in most of the building . . . When I was teased at school, I would dream of that building and I would run home as though it were a leap into the past, a leap into the familiar, a leap into the loving arms that understood me and knew how I functioned . . . The elders of that building were all our elders . . . they knew of places in Haiti that even the new arrivals among us didn't know about . . . When they closed their eyes, they saw the past, deep into the past, like a well.[7]

Haiti is therefore temporarily housed in Flatbush, Brooklyn, where an ideal cultural wholeness is sustained while the actual homeland drifts into greater and greater chaos. This new relocated Haitian national space allows for a leap into the past and sustains the displaced Danticat, who knows that it is a construct doomed to disappear even as her future takes her further away from having a single cultural inheritance into a bicultural world. This, then, is more about strategic and provisional cultural positioning than about celebrating national identity as Danticat avoids being assimilated into either state-derived identity. This precarious dwelling with its detachable roots evokes resistance and impermanence. Danticat's complex strategy of cultural recovery and adaptation could be applied to her reverence for Haiti's literary past as well. Arguably, we should not see her writing as the simple passing on of literary tradition from one generation to another but as a process of recovery and rewriting.

As Borges's seemingly outrageous but deeply perceptive essay on Kafka argues, the writer creates his or her precursors, meaning that each text allows us or obliges us to read earlier texts differently. In this regard, Danticat's writing might be seen not simply as the fated product of a Haitian narrative tradition to which she owes a literary debt but a site from which we read differently the writing that preceded her. Perhaps the complexity of Danticat's relationship to the modern fathers of the Haitian narrative can be sensed in her 2004 novel *The Dew Breaker,* which begins with the startling line "My father is gone."[8] In this book of interconnected stories she depicts the terror inflicted on Haiti by the Duvalier dictatorship, displaces the true beginning of the events that connect all the chapters to the end of the text, and begins with the story of a Haitian-American artist who adores her father and uses him as the subject of her sculpture. On the way to delivering the carving, the father throws the sculpture into a lake and reveals to the daughter that he was the torturer, not the tortured. In the final title story the horror of the arrest and torture is narrated in a stark yet understated way. It is indeed a cautionary tale of reverence and disillusion, reactivating a glorious past and deflating it at the same time. Ka must bear the weight of her father's problematic legacy as a Duvalierist Macoute. Her involuntary bond with the past surfaces when, as her father rubs the scar on his face, the sign of his complicity with violent repression, she says "out of a strange reflex, I scratch my face in the same spot" (32). Most importantly, the story is about how to represent the troubling ambiguities of this past, which reaches beyond the opposition of victim and torturer, father and daughter, past and present. As Ka reflects, "maybe my father was wrong in his own representation of his former life [. . .] maybe his past offered more choices than being hunter or prey" (24). Notwithstanding the strangeness and uncertainties of the diasporic Haitian community in the United States, racked as it is with memories of recent horrors, it still "offers more choices" and creates the possibility of rethinking the space of a literary home and the complexity of belonging.

The grand narratives of the dead iconic fathers of Haitian literature mark Danticat's fictions. An image in *The Farming of Bones* might serve to illustrate the precarious weight of the literary past. Sebastien talks about carrying his father's body during the hurricane: "You can see it before your eyes, a boy carrying his dead father from the road, wobbling, swaying, stumbling under the weight. The boy with the wind in his ears and pieces of the tin roofs that opened the father's throat blowing around him. The boy trying not to drop the father, not crying or screaming like you'd think, but praying that more of the father's blood will stay in the father's throat and not go into the muddy flood, going no one knows where."[9]

Trying to preserve the martyred father from muddy anonymity means having to deal with the dead weight of the body. Reverence for this body causes the son to stagger under its weight, but his response is neither self-pity nor protest but a dry-mouthed perseverance in the face of lethal flying debris. On the national level the father becomes the uncaring patriarch as *The Farming of Bones* invokes "the old dead fathers of [Haitian] independence" who remain deaf to the cries of the victims of the 1937 massacre in the Dominican Republic. For the main character the weight of the Haitian past manifests itself in the figure of Henry Christophe and the ghost-filled Citadelle, which was built to defend the newly created nation and loomed over her parents' house. When the protagonist Amabelle visits this monument turned tourist attraction seeking the solace of the familiar, she finds herself among a group of Spanish-speaking tourists. She is faced with the reality of the king's excesses, a past stripped of its grandeur, a monument built on human blood yet still casting its giant shadow. "The giant citadel, Henry I's treasure [. . .] leaning down towards the city from inside a wreath of sun filled clouds" (219). The decaying relic of the Haitian past, its wreathed glory, and the flawed father suggest an ambiguous relation to the national past. For Amabelle it was once a place from which to view the world. "As a child I played in the deserted war rooms of Henry I's citadel. I peered at the rest of the world from behind its columns and archways." But now Christophe's kingdom is one of tired ghosts, displaced victims of state terror. "And from the high vaulted ceilings I could almost hear the king giving orders to tired ghosts who had to remind him that it was a different time—a different century—and that we had become a different people" (46). It is that "different people" that artificially constructed a house in exile in Flatbush, in which no father figure looms large. It provides solace, a transitory plenitude for "tired ghosts" un-housed in the monumental Citadelle. In the same way that the national historical past is flawed, the Haitian literary past with its grand narratives of collective action and utopian dreams are inadequate for the "tired ghosts" of the present.

Danticat can be situated between two traditions in post-occupation Haitian literature. On one hand, there was the protest fiction of the U.S. occupation, which summoned writers to assume their responsibility before history. It broke with the defensive literary nationalism that dominated the nineteenth century and the idea of high culture that often sought technical sophistication as an end in itself. Instead, the American neocolonial military occupation gave a new purpose to literary activity. Words were valued by their ability to have an effect, as a form of action. Leftist politics also promoted a reluctance to identify with a territorially defined nation, focused on the migrant worker as revolutionary, and heralded the birth of a postnational proletariat. The grand vision of writers such as Jacques Roumain and Jacques-Stephen Alexis was to conceive of the peasantry as agents of social change and to reconnect them to the revolutionary Haitian past as well as to global proletarian resistance. For instance, in *Gouverneurs de la rosée,* the *coumbite,* the traditional collective work system, is reconfigured as a form of rural resistance, shadowing the protest strike of collective mobilized labor on the cane fields of Cuba. The novel is essentially about founding a project of peasant modernity, Fonds Rouge as Front Rouge. Similarly Alexis's *Compère Général Soleil* is a novel of displacement and transformation from rural Haiti as the protagonist Hilarion's political awareness grows in Port-au-Prince, where he is imprisoned, and later intensifies in the Dominican Republic, where he goes to cut cane and is caught up in the 1937 massacre. As in Roumain's novel, the end focuses on the passing on of the protagonist's revolutionary consciousness, in this case to Hilarion's partner Claire Heureuse, as the mortally wounded revolutionary migrant makes it back to Haitian soil. In *L'Espace d'un cillement* (*In the Flicker of an Eyelid,* 2002) the promotion of a hybrid worker culture is even more apparent as Fonds Rouge becomes "Sensation Bar" in the outskirts of the Haitian capital, the hub of a circum-Caribbean imagined community in a deterritorialized new world of *gringos, manolitas, horizontals,* and *chulos.* This literary practice comes to an end in the 1960s with what amounts to a postmodern turn in Haitian fiction after the repressive measures of the Duvalier regime begin to silence writers and call into question the utopian dreams of an earlier generation. As Chris Bongie puts it, postmodernism in the Caribbean "takes as its point of departure the collapse of the heroic dreams of modernism—and of the aesthetic and political revolutions and/or resolutions that such dreams promised."[10] In a reaction against being silenced by the Duvalierist state, writing becomes an existential act of authenticity. Literature reinvents itself as a kind of moral daring, an unauthorized form of expression. It is the expression of internal exile, unthreatening yet underground, inaccessible yet resistant. The later writing of Marie Chauvet and the *Spiraliste* group shows evidence of these changes from which literalism has been banished and ideology is absent. To some extent Edouard Glissant speaks for this new valorization of the literary when he says, "Literature matters more than making testimonies and taking sides, not because it exceeds all possible appreciation of the real, but because it is a more profound approach and, ultimately, the only one that matters."[11]

Elements of the postmodern turn abound in contemporary Haitian writing. For instance, Dany Laferrière, inter-American wanderer, as much a Québécois as a Haitian novelist, depicts in *Pays sans chapeau* (*Down among the Dead Men,* 1997) the native land of Haiti as not awaiting the fiery ideological inscription of the returning visionary but as defiantly opaque. Realism as much as magical realism is abandoned in this novel of return, and the effect of the real is explained as the dream of a primitive painter. Similarly the narrative breakdown and scrambling of time in Lyonel Trouillot's *Rue des pas perdus* (*Street of Lost Footsteps,* 2003) turns on the questions of representation and the uselessness of old literary codes. Similar issues are raised in Emile Ollivier's *Passages,* a novel that presents various Haitian figures wandering across seas and cities, and in which the intersecting journeys are articulated through multiple voicings. Its narrative echoes with intertextual references, "passages" as it were, from Aimé Césaire to Victor Segalen.

Danticat, however, harks back to the earlier experience of literature, one that is more historically bound, where the writer has a social responsibility, yet one from which the element of the author as transcendental modernist visionary and the ideological mission of literature have been removed. In an interview with Renee Shea, Danticat openly admits her admiration for Alexis. "I have always liked this about Alexis, that he believed that art should have a purpose. His writing was part of an overall engagement. He was killed during the Duvalier dictatorship, trying to unseat the dictatorship. . . . There are so many wonderful levels to this book. It's didactic, erotic, but always novelistic."[12] The idea of purposeful writing, of "overall engagement," is precious to Danticat. The author's raison d'être becomes the work, which has the value of testimony, of a kind of catharsis for an embattled community. However, unlike the ideologically driven narratives of political commitment, Danticat's fictions are not about speaking on behalf of the masses but attempt to establish a space where the voices of the disempowered victims and their persecutors are allowed to speak.

Downplaying the image of the writer as the "kitchen poet," as she put it in the epilogue to *Krik? Krak!* she must establish a narrative space in which communication is initiated between voices, histories, and places that were never previously connected. In an almost direct reference to Roumain's image of marking the world, literally through Manuel's machete, the blades of the hoes during the *coumbite* raised in unison and the blade of water at the end of *Gouverneurs de la rosée*, she declares: "Writers do not leave any mark on the world. Not the world where we are from. In our world writers are tortured and killed if they are men. Called lying whores, then raped and killed, if they are women. In our world if you write you are a politician and we know what happens to politicians" (221).

If writing cannot leave a mark, it can perhaps resurrect lives. In the absence of truth and reconciliation committees, there is a need for a literature of testimony. Danticat assumes a new literal referentiality in her narratives that is unlike the underground esthetic of the Duvalier years, and that recognizes the importance of writing in the blind spots of the grand narratives of the post-occupation era. This is startlingly present in *The Farming of Bones*, where the epigraph is attributed to Amabelle Désir, thereby undermining the hierarchy between author and narrator, and whose opening line is "His name is Sebastien Onius." The borders between fiction and reality blur, as the literary text becomes the testimony that Amabelle never manages to give to the Justice of the Peace. Instead, the hegemonic Haitian state in complicity with its Dominican counterpart silences the voices of the victims. "The soldiers of the Police Nationale, wearing the same uniforms as the Dominican soldiers—a common inheritance from their training during the yanki invasion of the whole island" (234)—chase the witnesses away, and the police station where President Vincent's portrait is boldly displayed, wearing the Order of Merit given to him by Trujillo, is burned down. Individual testimony, not collective mobilization, replaces the idea of providential history as Danticat responds to the nation's amnesia and the state's negation.[13]

The ground on which Danticat situates her narrative is neither that of absolute belonging nor that of postcolonial placelessness, but the in-between spaces of the displaced Haitian nation. In *The Farming of Bones*, that ground is the Massacre River, located on the border between Haiti and the Dominican Republic, and a space of memory. This novel can be read as a rewriting of the famous novel by Jacques-Stephen Alexis, *Compère Général Soleil*, which also traces the history of the massacre of Haitian cane cutters in the Dominican Republic. Instead of Alexis's apocalyptic denouement, where the hero greets the rising militant General Sun at the frontier of his native land, Danticat's protagonist Amabelle, with her ambiguous ancestry, as much Dominican as Haitian, describes herself as "half submerged, the current floating over me in a less than gentle caress, the pebbles scouring my back" (310). Hovering between life and death, belonging and uprooting, past and present, Amabelle, whose name epitomizes her own ambiguous identity, represents not glorious return but an unvoiced imagined community. This borderland river that marked the massacre of the Tainos by the Spanish and later Haitian *braceros* by the Dominican military is not the hinterland space of Haitian national memory. In this fictional scene, a new idea of Haitian identity emerges, with the creation of a new diasporic self. In her preface to Philoctète's *Massacre River*, Danticat describes visiting the river in 1995 and finding that this waterway "filled with ghosts" had become "simply a tiny braid of water." The diminished nature of the river makes Danticat's image of it as a birthplace, a kind of amniotic fluid bloodied by history, even more forceful, as she envisions a new people "fluid as the waters themselves" (8) attempting to emerge despite the policed nature of this space.

If the world of Roumain involved reviving the zombified peasantry of the Haitian interior, Danticat's new community is a world of living dead wandering in liminal extra-national spaces. Danticat does not write foundational fictions in which, as Doris Sommer says, romance fiction is used to construct national allegories. *Gouverneurs de la rosée* is to this extent a classic example of such a "fictive discourse."[14] However, you only have to compare the eroticism of Manuel and Annaïse's fertile coupling to the grim copulation of Yves and Amabelle, which yields only "a flashflood of tears, tears that rolled down my forehead, stung my eyes, made me sneeze when they slipped into my nostrils and tasted like my own when they fell on my tongue" (250). The hidden spring where Manuel and Annaïse's sexual union takes place holds the key to transcending the divisions of the feuding families in Fonds Rouge. However, the grotto where Sebastien and Amabelle first make love is ambiguous, wet, mossy, oddly illuminated by a trapped light, with no connection to outside reality, "no crickets no hummingbirds no pigeons," just the echoes of the sounds of "water sliding off the ledge and crashing in a foamy white spray into the pool below." The scene seems to evoke death more than life as their lovemaking takes place in a crook "where you feel half buried" (100). Unlike in Roumain's fiction, where nature is saturated with signifiers, in *The Farming of Bones* "Nature has no memory" (309). Amabelle is not the gendered creation, the "femme jardin," of Roumain's allegorical text. She is not fertile ground, will have no children but, as a midwife, helps others to be born. She helps her employer give birth in demonstration of unity among different races and classes. For a while the ideal of the fluid people of the borderlands is manifested, but before long reality intrudes, and the mother, Valencia herself, resorts to the racial mythmaking of the Dominican Republic by describing the twins as "my Spanish prince and my Indian princess" (29).

The writer is not unlike Amabelle in that she is able to bring others to life, to farm the bones of the dead for a harvest of testimonies. In her later works Danticat farms the bones of an "orphaned" people of wounded drifters. Far removed from the purposeful migrants of Marxist narratives, her subjects are the homeless victims of the vagaries of history. "They say some people don't belong anywhere and that's us. I say we are a group of vwayajè, wayfarers" (56). They are shunned as other, embarrassing relics of the recent genocidal nightmare. "Some of the merchants and shopkeepers and their workers moaned as we moved among them. They recognized us without knowing us. We were *those* people, the nearly dead, the ones who had escaped from the other side of the river" (220). In her introduction to *The Butterfly's Way*, Danticat dwells on the problematic identity of the Haitian diaspora. When members of this community are criticized for "having fled during difficult times," "shamefacedly," she says, "I would bow my head and accept these judgments when they were expressed, feeling guilty for my own physical distance from a country I had left at the age of twelve years during a dictatorship that forced thousands to choose between exile or death."[15] The burden of guilt is one of the defining features of Danticat's "tired ghosts." Guilt at having survived while others were massacred. Amabelle, for instance, is haunted by the trauma of her parents' drowning. She remembers her mother's raised hand and is unsure whether she was inviting her to join them or warning her to sit where she was. Just as her personal past is traumatizing and unknowable, so, having survived the Trujillo genocide, she also feels survivors' guilt. She never gets to know how Sebastien died. She can only alleviate the trauma of not knowing by bearing witness to the unspeakable.

Danticat is very aware of the historical roots of the disrupted lives of the Haitian underclass. In *The Farming of Bones* we are given the sequence of Sebastien's family's displacement that began with the U.S. occupation. He and his sister ended up in the Dominican Republic after a series of tragedies that combined natural and historical forces. As their mother explains, "Their father was killed in the hurricane. . . . After the hurricane, this house was taken from us by the yankis; they wanted to make a road of this house. It was given back to us only after they left" (239). Both children go off to the Dominican Republic, and their mother goes to live in Port-au-Prince. The house was returned, but the children never knew. The displaced peasantry has been a theme in Haitian writing since the U.S. occupation, and in the novels of political engagement the journeys are linear and progressive, as in the case of Manuel or Hilarion. In contrast, Danticat's characters are condemned to crossing and recrossing from one country to another, between the past and the present without ever finding answers. There is no guide such as Manuel or Pierre Roumel (Alexis's Roumain-inspired figure) who can bring political consciousness to the unenlightened revolutionary migrant. Instead, a madman who is given the nickname Pwofesè (Professor) stares blankly at Amabelle at the end of the novel. We do not have political resolution but a tragicomic scarecrow that can profess nothing. He disappears into the night, his sanity surrendered to Massacre River. This scene is perhaps echoed in the epigraph to *The Dew Breaker*, which states, "Maybe this is the beginning of madness," a phrase taken from the Polish writer Osip Mandelstam, who was executed by Stalin.

In the only story set entirely in Haiti in this novel, Danticat cleverly tackles iconic narratives of return in Haitian and Caribbean literature. She also seems to slyly invoke Laferrière's novel of return *Pays sans chapeau* by naming the protagonist Dany, whose name is shortened to Da, the term of affection for Laferrière's grandmother, and by naming another character Old Zo, which is the name Laferrière's grandmother gives him. The village to which Dany returns is called Beau Jour, which suggests the romanticized space of home that the migrant cherishes. However, it is in truth the space of the brutal murder of Dany's parents. Dany, who has been living in Brooklyn, is haunted by the past and the traumatic memory of his parents' death. His return to Beau Jour is motivated by his discovery of the perpetrator of their murder, a barber in Brooklyn. Seeking some kind of closure, he pesters his blind aunt who survived the attack with questions about the murder, but she only replies "m pa konnen" (I don't know) (109). She has managed to get over the past. He is still paralyzed by mourning its horror. In the story another returnee, named Claude, who is a deportee and dope addict who killed his father, has found solace among the people of Beau Jour who have taken him in even though he was not even aware of their existence. Claude is healed by the community's unexpected embrace while his double, Dany, insists on seeing Beau Jour as a lost paradise, a place of traumatic memory. The village is marked by a nightmare and fixed in time for Dany as Haiti is for many "dyaspora" but for Claude, who has never known it as a home from which he was exiled, it is a space that allows a non-creolophone Haitian, with a criminal past, to start again. Dany needs to bring himself to see Beau Jour the way Amabelle sees Massacre River, that is, as a site of horror and healing. She does so by rethinking space as liminal and borderless, marginal locales that have become relational crossroads. Danticat identifies with Claude, a "palannit" or night talker who sees Beau Jour in its role of creating new lives as an extension of Dany's Aunt Estina, who was a midwife. In the night before her burial, he does not just voice the nightmares of the past in his sleep but, awake beyond dream, like Amabelle, he gives testimony to the living, thereby becoming an unwitting agent of change for a traumatized contemporary Haiti.

NOTES

1. Edwidge Danticat, *After the Dance* (New York: Crown, 2002), 66. Subsequent references are to this edition and are given after quotations in the main body of the text.

2. René Philoctète, *Massacre River*, trans. with note by Linda Coverdale (New York: New Directions, 2005), 9.

3. Edwidge Danticat, *Breath, Eyes, Memory* (New York: Soho, 1994), 234. Subsequent references are to this edition and are given after quotations in the main body of the text.

4. Edwidge Danticat, *Krik? Krak!* (New York: Vintage, 1996), 224. Subsequent references are to this edition and are given after quotations in the main body of the text.

5. Carine Mardorossian, *Reclaiming Difference: Caribbean Women Rewrite Postcolonialism* (Charlottesville: University of Virginia Press, 2005), 133.

6. Ibid.

7. Edwidge Danticat, *Haiti: A Bi-cultural Experience* (Washington, DC: Inter-American Development Bank Lecture Series, 1995), 7.

8. Edwidge Danticat, *The Dew Breaker* (New York: Knopf, 2004), 3. Subsequent references are to this edition and are given after quotations in the main body of the text.

9. Edwidge Danticat, *The Farming of Bones* (New York: Soho, 1998), 34. Subsequent references are to this edition and are given after quotations in the main body of the text.

10. Chris Bongie, *Islands and Exiles: The Creole Identities of Post/colonial Literature* (Stanford: Stanford University Press, 1998), 354.

11. Edouard Glissant, *Faulkner, Mississippi* (New York: Farrar, Strauss and Giroux, 1999), 64.

12. Renee H. Shea, "Bearing Witness and Beyond: Edwidge Danticat Talks about Her Latest Work," *Journal of Haitian Studies* 7, no. 2 (Fall 2001): 14.

13. The need for testimony is evident as well in Jean-Robert Cadet's autobiography of domestic child servitude, *Restavec: From Haitian Slave Child to Middle-Class American* (Austin: University of Texas Press, 1998).

14. Doris Sommer, *Foundational Fictions: The National Romances of Latin America* (Berkeley: University of California Press, 1991), 37.

15. Edwidge Danticat, ed. *The Butterfly's Way: Voices from the Haitian Dyaspora in the United States* (New York, Soho, 2001), xv.

DANTICAT & CARIBBEAN WOMEN WRITERS

CARINE MARDOROSSIAN

Discussing Edwidge Danticat in relation to the category of "Caribbean women writers" feels, paradoxically, both like a natural extension of her work and a misrepresentation of it. Indeed, on the one hand, her preoccupation with issues of femininity and mother-daughter relationships and her powerful fictionalizing of the matriarchal nature of the family in the Caribbean and of the external and internal struggles faced by women in the diaspora are recognizable tropes that seemingly place her within the boundaries of this literary community we call "Caribbean women writers." On the other hand, while it is true that her writing has helped expand the critical parameters through which the Caribbean and its literature have traditionally been represented, this is not to say that her contribution can be subsumed under a category that risks wrongly suggesting a uniformity about contemporary women's writings. If by "Caribbean women's fiction" we mean a revision and extension of predominantly male configurations of subjectivity and nationality in Caribbean literature, then Danticat's work certainly qualifies as one of the best examples of this expanding perspective. If, however, what we have in mind are thematic and stylistic patterns that suggest a uniformity about contemporary women's writings and identities, then we would be hard pressed to fit Danticat's stories into this paradigm.

This essay therefore does not engage in the futile exercise of trying to ascertain how Danticat's fiction fares in relation to a pre-existing category of Caribbean women's literature. Rather, I highlight how one of the defining features of her fiction is precisely its ability to simultaneously inhabit a category such as Caribbean women's fiction while stepping outside the category to expand its premises. Indeed, Danticat belongs to a new generation of Caribbean writers who have radically reconceptualized the workings of the sexual, racial, class, and national concepts through which postcolonial studies has traditionally configured difference. Her revisionary intervention questions the categorical affirmations of identity that have heretofore defined our understanding of women's or Caribbean literature. Instead, she offers a new formulation of gender, race, or class as categories whose meanings do not precede their interaction with one another so much as derive from it. In this context, the stable, discrete categories of identity that scholars typically posit in order to analyze cultural, gender, or racial difference in Caribbean fiction are replaced by a form of relational identity that accounts for the contingent workings of difference *across* gender, race, class, and national boundaries.

Postcolonial scholars have traditionally (and understandably) emphasized issues such as voice and voicelessness as key to understanding Caribbean women's writing. In their pioneering anthology *Out of the Kumbla,* for instance, Carol Boyce Davies and Elayne Savory Fido discuss the imperialist "master discourses" that have historically shut out Caribbean women's voices as a kind of multilayered "voicelessness" against which Caribbean women authors have to write. They define "voicelessness" both as a lack of or misrepresentation in texts and as silence, that is, the inability to speak and be heard, the consequence of an "articulation that goes unheard."[1] Similarly, in "On the Threshold of Becoming: Caribbean Women Writers," Lizabeth Paravasini and Barbara Webb argue that an incomplete sense of history and lack of closure are key to understanding contemporary Caribbean women's writing and an inevitable outcome of the kind of "unhearing" Davies and Savory highlight in their work.[2] In *The Daughter's Return: African American and Caribbean Women's Fiction of History,* Caroline Rody echoes Paravasini and Webb's conclusions by tracing contemporary women writers' creation of an allegorical and magic "returning black daughter," an archetype that serves to reclaim the matrilineage that has been occluded due to women's exclusion from the historical record.[3] Nevertheless, as critics such as Selwyn Cudjoe or Newson and Strong-Leek have pointed out, in the last few decades, a strong Caribbean female presence has established itself in the literary canons of the United States and Canada, where Caribbean women's writing is increasingly received with wide acclaim. The Dominican Jean Rhys and the Guadeloupean Maryse Condé are two of the most revered and canonized figures in postcolonial studies, while Edwidge Danticat, along with Condé, Elizabeth Nunez, and Julia Alvarez, has long been affiliated with North American institutions of higher learning. Authors such as Julia Alvarez and Danticat have even succeeded in bridging the high-low cultural divide that continues to define approaches to literature by producing novels that are bestsellers both among the general public and in academic/university circles.[4]

The privileged position of contemporary female Caribbean authors complicates their attempts at giving a voice to history's unheard. In light of their newly anointed status in the field on the one hand and the institutionalization of postcolonial studies on the other, their engagements with "voicelessness" are necessarily problematic, especially in relation to the Caribbean people represented in their fiction. In her review of Belinda Edmondson's *Making Men: Gender, Literary Authority, and Women's Writing in Caribbean Narrative*, for instance, Kathleen Balutansky takes issue with the way Edmondson's theorizing of a Caribbean feminist aesthetics obscures the privileged position of contemporary women writers such as Michelle Cliff and Jamaica Kincaid. In her book, Edmondson makes a distinction between male writers such as George Lamming or Claude McKay, who based their literary authority on the intellectual labor/capital that attracted them to the West on the one hand and women who migrated to the States to find jobs and support their families on the other. For Balutansky, however, this distinction between intellectual exile and laboring immigrant conveniently overlooks Caribbean women's affiliation with universities and "fails to accommodate important differences between the female writers she discusses and the vast number of struggling women immigrants from the Caribbean who do toil at physical labor."[5]

I argue that the involvement of writers such as Danticat in Western literary and academic circles is significant insofar as it leads not to the invalidation of their engagement with suppressed modes of expression but to an anxious recognition of the mediated nature of such a process. As Danticat's fiction exemplifies, rather than unproblematically linking voice and agency, or literary and social authority, contemporary Caribbean women authors attend to the complexities of "finding a voice" and "breaking the silence" in the context of the conflicting legacies of colonialism. Issues of voice and representation remain an imperative in Danticat's postcolonial narratives, but they are no longer seen as necessarily tantamount to possessing historical or narrative authority. Partly because of her "relational positionality,"[6] she is generating narratives where female agency and the metaphor of voice are sites of contradiction rather than unidirectional tropes of power and authority. Instead of narratives whose central preoccupation is the unproblematic because decontextualized coming to voice of women, her novels generate questions surrounding the fraught process of voicing, self-determination, agency, and the production of cultural and national identity.

It is no coincidence, for instance, that the process of self-determination of the heroine Sophie Caco in *Breath, Eyes, Memory* is hampered not by her relationship with men but with her mother and grandmother, who are mediating the patriarchal scripts of femininity that so brutally constrain their lives. Indeed, "testing," the "virginity cult" and cultural practice that consists of probing the vagina to check that the hymen is still intact, is passed on in the novel "like heirlooms," through generations of women who, having suffered from it themselves, nonetheless go on performing it on their own daughters.[7] This representation of the transgenerational violation perpetrated against women's bodies by women thus challenges the matriarchal/patriarchal binary that the novel's focus on matriarchal lines might evoke. So does her focus on the importance and implications of the father figure's absent presence in her later novel *The Dew Breaker.*[8] Indeed, *The Dew Breaker,* like *Breath, Eyes, Memory,* powerfully exposes the history of colonial and neocolonial violence that defines Haitian society by challenging facile oppositions between nurturers and torturers without, however, ever obscuring the distinction between them. Both novels are powerful stagings of the historical, cultural, and gendered contexts through which the tortured become agents of suffering and the torturers in turn become tortured beings who are prisoners of their own conscience or of recurring nightmares.

This ability to represent the forces that channel violence and to identify without opposing them the contingent workings of victimization in Haitian society also defines Danticat's nuanced approach to issues of cultural and historical identity. Indeed, her work consistently challenges the facile oppositions through which cultural identity has traditionally been discussed and celebrated. What distinguishes Haitian and Caribbean cultural practices from their Western hegemonic counterparts for Danticat is neither their radical difference nor sameness but the reconceptualization of difference itself. The "difference" of Caribbean culture is one that radically revises Western logocentric paradigms because it recasts difference as a fluid, relational, and kaleidoscopic process that is open to change. It is, in other words, the syncretism of "traditional" Haitian cultural practices that constitutes the nexus of Caribbean "difference" and that distinguishes it from the totalitarian, monolithic, and identitarian views of "difference" in the West. This "play of difference" is also what grounds the interconnectedness of cultures such as African American and Caribbean cultures that, unlike the dominant Euro-American ethos, remain open to the ceaseless process of refraction that characterizes the workings of culture.

For instance, in an interview with Vintage Books, Danticat explained that the source of testing virginity in *Breath, Eyes, Memory,* which many critics treat as a purely Haitian tradition, can in fact be traced back to the Virgin Mary: "If you look at the apocryphal gospels, after the Virgin Mary gives birth to the Christ child, a midwife comes and tries to test her virginity by insertion, if you can imagine. The family in [*Breath, Eyes, Memory*] was never meant to be a 'typical' Haitian family, if there is ever a typical family in any culture. The family is very much Haitian, but they live their own internal and individual matriarchal reality and they worship the Virgin Mary and the Haitian goddess Erzulie in many interesting forms."[9] In other words, the novel's emphasis on the convergence of Christian and Afro-Caribbean practices checks any attempt at opposing or ranking the two traditions, which remain inextricably linked in the narrative.

The use of "doubling" in the novel fulfils a similar function since it too is represented both in the language of the folktale of the *Marassas* and in biblical terms. Doubling refers to the split identity that characters such as Sophie Caco generate in order to cope with trauma in their lives. Sophie learns "to double," that is, to have her mind leave her body during painful or threatening episodes such as testing or sex. On the one hand, this coping mechanism is ascribed to "the *vaudou* tradition" (156) in the novel, while on the other, it is also overlaid with biblical imagery, yet again emphasizing the syncretism of the cultural forces at work in the Haitian context. When Sophie asks why she has a mother and no father, her Tante Atie offers her a tale of Immaculate Conception according to which she was born out of "rose petals, the stream, and the sky" (47). This image, which identifies Sophie's mother Martine with the Virgin Mary, is then sustained in the rest of the narrative. When the young protagonist is tested for the first time, she combines the Vodou tradition of doubling with prayers to the Virgin Mother, thus again invoking her own mother's spirit through a hybrid religious form. Later, when she resorts to doubling during sex, it is again to return to her mother as "a shadow on the wall" (200). As Martine's *Marassas*, she in turn becomes identified with the Virgin Mary, as confirmed by her husband's name: Joseph.

Danticat represents Haitian culture as a "tradition" that is open to reinterpretation and transmogrification rather than as an inert and immutable condition that women, the "authentic body of national tradition," are in charge of transmitting across generations.[10] As Anne McClintock points out, most nationalist discourses equate women with an "atavistic and authentic body of national tradition (inert, backward-looking, and natural), embodying nationalism's conservative principle of continuity," while they identify men as "the progressive agent[s] of national modernity (forward-thrusting, potent, and historic."[11] By contrast, Danticat's conception of national culture is reminiscent of Frantz Fanon's discussion of oral traditions as dynamic and changing rather than as "set pieces" and "inert episodes" transmitted by women. In his discussion of national consciousness, Fanon explains that "the oral traditions—stories, epics, and songs of the people—which formerly were filed away as set pieces are now beginning to change. The storytellers who used to relate inert episodes now bring them alive and introduce into them modifications that are increasingly fundamental. There is a tendency to bring conflicts up to date and to modernize the kinds of struggle which the stories evoke."[12] While acknowledging women's role as repositories of the traditional past in her novels, Danticat also, however, revises the conventional alignment of tradition with a pure and stable precolonial past. She thus re-aligns women, that is, the "bearers of the nation" and its culture as sites of both continuity and change, modernity and tradition.[13] In *Breath, Eyes, Memory*, Haiti becomes the place where Sophie can dress her mother's corpse in red even though, in the traditional context of Haiti, it is "too loud a color for burial" (227) and almost makes Grandma Fé "fall down, in shock" (231). Yet it is the same Grandma Fé who then recuperates this very transgressive act and incorporates it into Haitian "tradition" through her storytelling: "There is a place where women are buried in clothes in the color of flames, where we drop coffee on the ground for those who went ahead, where the daughter is never fully a woman until her mother has passed on before her. There is always a place where, if you listen closely in the night, you will hear your mother telling a story and at the end of the tale, she will ask you this question: 'Ou libéré?' Are you free, my daughter?" (234). In this context, Haiti's "cultural traditions" are vital and dynamic sites of syncretism and transformation where Caribbeanness is as much a function of its "difference" from Western values as it is of its recasting of difference itself as a site of ceaseless transformation.

In his influential essay "Cultural Identity and Diaspora," the post-colonial critic Stuart Hall emphasizes the importance of rethinking cultural identity as a split formation rather than as a site of unity, authority, and authenticity. According to Hall, there have been two ways of thinking about cultural identity. The first one is "in terms of one shared culture, a sort of collective 'one true self,' hiding inside the many other, more superficial or artificially imposed 'selves,' which people with a shared history and ancestry hold in common."[14] The second conception, by contrast, sees identity not as "being" but as "becoming," as a process that entails discontinuous points of identification that are subjected to the "continuous 'play' of history" and constant transformation. Indeed, to use Hall's own words, "We cannot speak for very long, with any exactness, about 'one experience, one identity,' without acknowledging its other side—the ruptures and discontinuities which constitute, precisely, the Caribbean's 'uniqueness.'"[15] What is particularly striking about the way Hall distinguishes between these two approaches to cultural difference, however, is how he resists discussing them as opposed to one another. Even though he proclaims his preference for the second view of culture as constructed and shifting over the "act of imaginary reunification" and coherence that the first conception represents, he nonetheless emphasizes the "dialogic relationship between these two axes."[16] In other words, he emphasizes the importance of both the common history of slavery and colonization that unifies Caribbean societies and the "play of 'difference' within identity" that makes each island stand in a different relation of otherness to (neo)colonial powers. This "'doubleness' of similarity and difference" is, for Hall, what positions people from various Caribbean islands as "*both* the same *and* different" in a dialogic dynamic that challenges the typical dyad of authenticity versus hybridity through which postcolonial studies has traditionally debated issues of cultural identity.[17]

Edwidge Danticat's fiction stages a similar and powerful challenge to the dichotomization of unity/difference that has too often mobilized discussions of cultural identity in postcolonial studies. For instance, her portrayal of the Haitian cultural heritage revalorizes the black diasporic experience as, paradoxically, an inherent aspect of the creolization process that defines Caribbeanness. On the one hand, she celebrates the process of unceasing cultural transformation and intermixing that the prominent thinker Edouard Glissant has called Relation, while on the other, she highlights the regenerative black ethos whose roots/routes can be traced back to the experiences of slavery and oppression that define black history and collective memory. In this context, the kind of intervalorization of cultures outlined by the proponents of creolization is then a process that defines the black Atlantic and ultimately distinguishes it from the dominant (exclusionary) Euro-American culture. It is in this light that Danticat's confession to "relishing the role of permanent outsider" with which her fragmented identity endows her should be read.[18] Indeed, her model of cultural integration maintains a strong sense of the cultural differences that separate the fluid cultural heritage of the black Atlantic from the dominant U.S. culture in a form of divided consciousness that has important implications for our conceptualizations of identity.

In an essay entitled "AHA!" Danticat claimed having—at least temporarily—endorsed the label of "AHA, African-Haitian-American." This term, she explained, has "the following elements: African to acknowledge our ancestral roots deep in the African continent; Haitian, because of course most of us were either born in Haiti or were first generation born of Haitian parents; and American because we were from the Americas, living in the other 'America,' the United States of America."[19] Such a spirited endorsement of a doubly hyphenated identity both reflects and diverges from other Caribbean writers' emphasis on the fragmented nature of their cultural heritage. Whereas the Dominican Julia Alvarez, for instance, argues that in calling herself neither Dominican nor *una norteamericana*, she is "mapping a country that's not on the map," Danticat makes no excuses for identifying Haiti as the physical or cultural space through which she re-envisions a regenerative and relational model of identity.[20] Throughout her writings, Haiti paradoxically remains her chosen foundation in this "equally a-geographical and poly-geographical" world.[21] It is unequivocally the place, culturally or physically, where her heroines need to return in order to come to terms with their fragmented self and empower themselves. On the one hand, she claims that "these days, I feel less like an immigrant and more like a nomad" and that there is "no longer a singular harbor" to which people's bodies and shadows can be anchored exclusively in our interdependent world, while on the other, she affirms that "the more cultures I experience, the more Haitian I feel."[22] She thus deliberately develops a "poetics of location" in which one's privileging of a particular and "coherent" cultural space does not hinder Relation but provides the very condition for it. In this process of identification, the opposition between nation and transnationalism dissolves to reveal the inextricable imbrication of the two.

Just as culture in Danticat's work functions both as a site of reconfigured roots and interdependent routes, of unity as well as discontinuity, so are gender, racial, and class identities revealed as categories whose normative stability paradoxically depends on their shifting articulation with other categories of identity. Instead of treating racial, gender, religious, national, and ethnic identities as discrete and preexisting categories that define and divide groups of people in predictable ways, Danticat exposes them as categories that come into being and get naturalized *through* rather than *prior to* their interrelationships with one another. In *The Farming of Bones*, a novel about the tragic history of the massacres of black Haitians in 1937, the "naturalized" meanings of race identity that grounded this murderous rampage are exposed as sites where the production of categorical alterity is not a function of the epistemology of visibility we have come to associate with "race" but of its articulation with class and linguistic competence. In pursuing *blanquismo,* the Dominican dictator Rafael Trujillo had ordered his troops to massacre fifty thousand dark-skinned Haitian sugar cane workers, who were murdered by the truckload if they could not pronounce and roll the letter *r* in *perejil,* the Spanish word for "parsley." In other words, the a priori racial difference that supposedly separated Dominican from Haitian workers was produced not through its anchoring in "natural" difference but through its association with the trope of linguistic incompetence. In highlighting the role linguistic mastery played in justifying the genocide of dark-skinned Haitians, the novel thus reveals how attempts at fixing racial difference repeatedly and necessarily slip into references to other categories such as dirt, animality, incomprehensible speech, and so forth. Far from being a site of stable and essentialized difference, race is thus revealed as a complex of social meanings that exposes the symbolic nature of identity and challenges its yoking to the body. Difference, in other words, is exposed as a product of language rather than of "visible" or "natural" otherness.[23]

This symbolic economy replaces the facile separatism of an identitarian approach, that is, the tendency to analyze the meanings of social categories of identity such as race, class, and gender in isolation from each other. It also helps elucidate passages in Caribbean novels, which might appear puzzling to a North American audience trained to think of gender or race as the determining, more visible sites of difference rather than of identities as sites of inextricable and sometimes unexpected entanglements. For instance, in *The Farming of Bones*, at the very moment when one might expect a commentary on the horrors of racism, that is, on the epidermic difference that mobilized the campaign of hatred carried out against Haitian workers in the Dominican Republic, the characters bemoan instead the terrible price they have to pay in the name of class and class inequities. In a context in which black Dominicans who were routinely mistaken for black Haitians were also killed (217), it is nonetheless poverty not race that the victims of the massacre identify as the source of the genocide: "The ruin of the poor is their poverty. . . . The poor man, no matter who he is, is always despised by his neighbors" (178). What might strike one as an incongruous slippage is actually a jolting reminder that racial hierarchies cannot be understood outside of their articulation with class, and that crossings of class or national boundaries are at the heart of the "blackening" through racialization of a whole population whose "categorical" difference is produced rather than pre-existing and stable.[24]

Like other Caribbean women authors writing today (Julia Alvarez, Nola Hopkinson, Maryse Condé, Erna Brodber, Michelle Cliff, and Jamaica Kincaid), Danticat reformulates the old affirmations of identity (gender, race, nationality, class) through which postcolonialism has traditionally configured difference.[25] Instead of identities that are supposedly fixed within biological or epidermic visibility (gender, race), she highlights the interdependence of categories such as race, class, gender, and nationality, which are generated through their interrelations rather than through "real" or "natural" differences. Her work consistently exposes the ways in which class and gender dynamics are inextricably articulated with racial meanings and vice versa. As such, identities as social categories of belonging are always necessarily unstable since it is through their articulation with other categories of social identity that they acquire their meaning.

This is also why the process of identifying Danticat's relation to the body of work we identify as "Caribbean women writers" is both eminently fraught and extremely rewarding. While an attention to gender and "voicelessness" continues to characterize the writings of the contemporary authors we identify as "Caribbean women writers," what distinguishes women writers such as Danticat, Kincaid, or Mootoo from their predecessors is the recognition that gender and sexuality matter in ways that exceed our dichotomous understandings of masculinity and femininity. Extending the work of the heretofore predominantly male theorists of creolization and hybridity, contemporary Caribbean women authors have brought the issue of gender to the forefront of discussions of racial and cultural hybridity. More specifically, they have done so by revealing how the very meanings of mixed races and cultures are dependent on a structural interdefinition of gender with racial, national, and class identities. This new logic exposes categories of difference and identity for what they are, namely naturalized but contingent ways of seeing that are both constraining and productive.

NOTES

1. Carole Boyce Davies and Elaine Savory Fido, *Out of the Kumbla: Caribbean Women and Literature* (Trenton, NJ: Africa World Press, 1990), 1.

2. Lizabeth Paravisini and Barbara Webb, "On the Threshold of Becoming: Caribbean Women Writers," *Cimarron* 1, no. 3 (Spring 1988): 106–31.

3. Caroline Rody, *The Daughter's Return: African American and Caribbean Women's Fictions of History* (New York: Oxford University Press, 2001). For further discussions of Caribbean women's writings, see Selwyn Cudjoe, ed., *Caribbean Women Writers: Essays from the First International Conference* (Wellesley, MA: Calaloux, 1990); Evelyn O'Callaghan, "Early Versions: Outsiders' Voices/Silenced Voices," *Woman Version: Theoretical Approaches to West Indian Fiction by Women* (London: Macmillan, 1993), 17–35; Maryse Condé and Thorunn Lonsdale, eds., *Caribbean Women Writers: Fiction in English* (New York: St Martin's Press, 1999). In a 2005 essay, Ifeona Fulani addresses the politics of publishing, i.e., the "unavailability resulting from poor distribution and inadequate publicity [that] . . . becomes another way to silence Caribbean women's voices and texts." "Caribbean Women Writers and the Politics of Style: A Case for Literary Anancyism," *Small Axe* 17 (March 2005): 64–79 (65).

4. For a discussion of the ways in which postcolonial studies ironically seems afflicted with the kind of hierarchy of literary value it set out to challenge, see Chris

Bongie's essay "Exiles on Main Stream: Valuing the Popularity of Postcolonial Literature," *Postmodern Culture* 14, no. 1 (September 2003), *Project Muse*, 12 March 2007, http://muse.jhu.edu/journals/pmc/. Bongie emphasizes the tensions between cultural studies and postcolonial studies that explain why postcolonial novels that are bestsellers (especially in the Caribbean) do not usually join the postcolonial academic canon.

5. Kathleen Balutansky, "Review of Belinda Edmondson's *Making Men*," *Signs: Journal of Women in Culture and Society* 27, no. 2 (Winter 2002): 580–583 (582).

6. Susan Stanford Friedman coined the term "relational positionality" to refer to scripts that "regard identity as situationally constructed and defined and at the crossroads of different systems of alterity and stratification." *Mappings: Feminism and the Cultural Geographies of Encounter* (Princeton, NJ: Princeton University Press, 1998), 47.

7. Edwidge Danticat, *Breath, Eyes, Memory* (New York: Vintage Books, 1994), 233. Subsequent references are to this edition and are given after quotations in the main body of the text.

8. Edwidge Danticat, *The Dew Breaker* (New York: Knopf, 2004). Subsequent references are to this edition and are given after quotations in the main body of the text. For examples of the pervasiveness of the trope of the absent present father in Caribbean fiction, see Julia Alvarez, *Yo!* (New York, Plume 1997) and *In the Name of Salomé* (New York: Algonquin Books, 2000); Maryse Condé, *Célanire Cou-Coupé* (Paris: Robert Laffont, 2000) and *La Migration des Cœurs* (Paris: Robert Laffont, 1995); Edwidge Danticat's story "Caroline's Wedding" in *Krik? Krak!* (New York: Vintage, 1996); Simone Schwarz-Bart, *Un plat de porc aux bananes vertes* (Paris: Seuil, 1967); and Joseph Zobel, *La Rue Cases-Nègres* (Paris: Distribooks, 2000). For a critical discussion of the father's absence as symptom and consequence of matrifocality in plantation societies, see Fritz Gracchus, *Les lieux de la mère dans les sociétés afro-américaines* (Paris: Editions caribéennes, 1986). Many writers in the Americas, as Gracchus notes, have turned to writing as a means of procreating and engendering their own identity, thus substituting themselves for the father figure whose physical presence paradoxically also comes to signify absence and indifference.

9. Edwidge Danticat, "Interview," *Behind the Books*, 10 January 2004, http://www.randomhouse.com/catalog/display.pperl?isbn=9780375705045&view=auqa.

10. Anne McClintock, "'No Longer in a Future Heaven': Gender, Race, and Nationalism," in *Dangerous Liaisons: Gender, Nation, and Postcolonial Perspectives*, ed. Anne McClintock, Aamir Mufti, and Ella Shohat (Minneapolis: University of Minnesota Press, 1997), 89–113 (92).

11. Ibid.

12. Frantz Fanon, *Black Skin, White Masks*, trans. C. L. Markham (London: Pluto, 1986), 240.

13. McClintock, "'No Longer in a Future Heaven,'" 90.

14. Stuart Hall, "Cultural Identity and Diaspora," in *Contemporary Postcolonial Theory: A Reader*, ed. Padmini Mongia (New York: Arnold, 1996), 110–22 (111).

15. Ibid., 112.

16. Ibid., 113.

17. Ibid., 114.

18. Edwidge Danticat, "AHA!" in *On Becoming American: Personal Essays by First Generation Immigrant Women,* ed. Meri Nana-Ama Danquah (New York: Hyperion, 2001), 39–45 (44).

19. Ibid., 39–40.

20. Julia Alvarez, *Something to Declare* (New York: Plume, 1999), 173.

21. Danticat, "AHA!" 44.

22. Ibid.

23. Edwidge Danticat, *The Farming of Bones,* New York: Penguin Books, 1998. Subsequent references are to this edition and are given after quotations in the main body of the text.

24. Similarly, in Austin Clarke's *The Polished Hoe* (New York: Harper Collins, 2003), the young protagonist Mary-Mathilda's recounting of the first instance of sexual abuse and humiliation she experienced at a young age in the hands of the plantation owner Mr. Bellfeels unexpectedly triggers not the narrator's commentary on the horrors of racism and sexism but a commentary on the consequences of poverty: "From that Sunday morning, the meaning of poverty was driven into my head. The sickening power of poverty. Like the smell of leather, disintegrating from animal skin into raw leather. . . . From an animal" (12).

25. In *Reclaiming Difference: Caribbean Women Rewrite Postcolonialism* (Charlottesville: University of Virginia Press, 2005), I argue that this kind of reformulation of difference by Caribbean women writers such as Maryse Condé, Danticat, Julia Alvarez, and Jean Rhys actually represents a third phase in postcolonialism and thus extends Anthony Appiah's two-staged model for the field.

DANTICAT & THE AFRICAN AMERICAN WOMEN'S LITERARY TRADITION

RÉGINE MICHELLE
JEAN-CHARLES

In "AHA!" her contribution to *Becoming American: Personal Essays by First Generation Immigrant Women,* Edwidge Danticat reflects on the Kreyòl expression *map we lonbraj ou la.* Roughly translated as "I will see your shadow there," the phrase is the equivalent of "being there in spirit." When a person cannot be in one location, her shadow can still be there, meaning that she is there in spirit even if she cannot be physically present. "These days," Danticat writes, "my shadow is more often in Haiti and my body in the United States."[1] By explaining her relationship to migration in these terms, she conveys at once a sense of continual absence or longing in relation to her homeland and a spiritual connection to the place of her birth. The separation of her shadow from her physical body captures the dilemma the she faces as an African-Haitian-American (AHA) woman, one who is neither always or only Haitian nor always or only U.S. American.

I begin here in this discussion of Edwidge Danticat's relation to the African American women's literary tradition because the dynamic she articulates in her reference to shadows and bodies speaks to the difficulty with which one is faced when attempting to position her within a single literary tradition, whether it is African American, Caribbean, or Haitian. As we attempt to situate her body of work within one tradition, the shadows of others inevitably seep out from the sides of those canons. On the other hand, the unification of her shadow and her body potentially exists exclusively within Danticat's carefully crafted literary universes where her belonging to multiple traditions is abundantly apparent. It comes forth in the multivalence of her prose, the dimensions of her characters, and the diversity of her narrative strategies. Because her writing so faithfully expresses the experience of bodies severed from their own shadows manifested through characters who seem to be living in two places at once, to contextualize her in terms of a single literary tradition requires either the momentary suppression of the shadow or the union of the body and the shadow. Any consideration of her work according to one tradition requires that we simultaneously acknowledge the shadows present elsewhere.

This essay seeks to account for the association of a body whose shadow is elsewhere, as it situates Danticat's work in relation to African American women's literature. To do so means locating those spaces where we can glimpse continuities with African American women's writing, while simultaneously acknowledging the writer's claim to being an AHA writer and teasing out the discontinuities that such a framing may suggest. There is a natural back and forth to this practice, a swaying motion as one looks back to what the shadow suggests while the body is anchored in one place. Ultimately this motion will help to raise critical questions about the implication of placing Danticat in the category of African American women's literature. I first discuss how Danticat's work fits into definitions of African American women's literature put forth by several critics within the field and then explore ways in which she is in dialogue with other African American women writers, especially those who have most influenced her. Throughout this discussion, I make references to black feminist theoretical models that will elucidate some of the conceptual divergences and convergences that Danticat's work brings forth. It is my hope that this methodology will not only help to contextualize Danticat according to African American women's writing but also to analyze and problematize this practice as it relates to the black Atlantic or African diasporic frameworks. To address these issues I have divided this essay into three segments: definitions, dialogues, and diasporas, each of which is essential to understanding Danticat's unique contribution to African American literature.

Definitions

The category of African American women's literature can trace its beginnings to the eighteenth-century poetry of Phyllis Wheatley or, later on, Harriet Wilson's *Our Nig* (1859) and Frances Harper's 1892 novel *Iola Leroy*.[2] Notwithstanding the appearance of these earlier works, one of the most important formative periods in African American women's literature occurred during the 1970s, continuing into the 1980s with the landmark publication of novels such as Toni Morrison's *The Bluest Eye* (1971) and Alice Walker's *The Third Life of Grange Copeland* (1970), as well as Toni Cade Bambara's anthology *The Black Woman* (1970), which included creative and critical writing by African American women. At this time a principal objective was to establish an archive of African American women's writing as a counterpoint to the dominant representation of African Americans and women (written by African American men and white women) that inscribed the silencing of black women in both tacit and overt ways. As a result of this overarching project of excavation, a major theme that arises in the literature as well as in the criticism recognizes efforts to redress silences that previously obscured and denied the voices of African American women. Titles of collections such as *All the Women Are White, All the Blacks Are Men, But Some of Us Are Brave* capture this effort to account for the previous exclusion of black women. While this practice was an overarching theme evinced in the literature, scholars have attempted to delineate the African American women's literary tradition with more explicit definitions. Careful not to marshal all the works of African American women into a totalizing category based solely on racial and gender difference, literary critics sought to identify concrete aspects of this tradition.

Following critics such as Karla Holloway, I agree that "texts by black women writers are those which are most likely to force apart the enclosed spaces of critical inquiry"; thus to confine the category to specific themes and narrative strategies would be a problematic enterprise.[3] Yet looking at some of the terms according to which this literature has been defined helps us to set up a relation between Edwidge Danticat and African American women writers. For example, Mary Helen Washington offers the following definition: "If there is a single distinguishing feature of the literature of Black women . . . it is this: their literature is about Black women; it takes the trouble to record the thoughts, words, feelings, and deeds of Black women, experiences that make the realities of being Black in America look very different from what men have written. . . . Women talk to other women in this tradition, and their friendships with other women—mothers, sisters, grandmothers, friends, lovers—are vital to their growth and well-being."[4]

The characteristics that Washington outlines are identifiable in Danticat's corpus: from the publication of her first novel through the short stories, essays, children's and adolescent literature she writes extensively about "Black [Haitian] women." Her first novel is an intimate portrait of the lives of three generations of women living in Haiti and in the United States. The collection *Krik? Krak!* contains stories such as "Night Women," "New York Day Women," "Caroline's Wedding," all narratives that focus on women's thoughts, words, feelings, and deeds. She has penned forewords for nonfiction texts like *Walking on Fire: Haitian Women's Stories of Survival.* Her essay "We Are Ugly But We Are Here" accounts for the perceived absence of Haitian women in politics, culture, and the media. Even her adolescent novel *Anacaona: Golden Flower* relays the story of a forgotten Haitian queen.

Before *Breath, Eyes, Memory* begins, Danticat uses the novel's paratext to signal her commitment to all types of Haitian women by dedicating the novel to the "brave women of Haiti, grandmothers, mothers, aunts, sisters, cousins, daughters, and friends on this shore and other shores. We have stumbled but we will not fall."[5] The invocation of women in their different relational contexts (mothers, sisters, etc.) echoes the tendency that Washington specifies; one in which women are "vital to [each other's] growth and well-being." Yet, the presence of Danticat's Haitian shadow lurks here—the last half of the dedication makes use of another Haitian proverb "we have stumbled but we will not fall." Gestures such as these persist in Danticat's work, as she writes herself into the African American literary tradition with one hand, but then with another slight turn, through the use of a proverb, an expression, or a Kreyòl word, she asserts the presence of Haitian tradition. What emerges is a dance of words, languages, and cultures where African American literature can include African-Haitian-American writing as well.

If fraught mother-daughter relationships depicted in Danticat's work can be seen as a convergence with African American women's writing, a major difference can be seen in the development of female friendships. The relationships between and among women are significant in Danticat's texts, as they are in the African American works that Washington discusses. At the same time, however, few of Danticat's texts contain the intensity and intimacy of the female friendships we see in Hurston's Janie and Phoebe, Morrison's Sula and Nel, or Walker's Celie and Shug Avery. The women who are friends in Danticat's oeuvre are brought together by their common identity as immigrants. When Rézia, Mariselle, and the narrator in "The Funeral Singer" develop a close friendship in the course of their ESL classes, it is because "[they] didn't always understand what was going on in the classroom and, being the only Haitians, [they] thought [they] might explain certain lessons to one another."[6] What bonds these women and deepens their friendship are the shadows—the stories from Haiti they have carried with them to the United States. The funeral singer shares her own narrative of traumatic memories, purposefully thinking to herself: "I thought exposing a few details of my life would inspire them to do the same and slowly we'd parcel out our sorrows, each walking out with fewer than we'd carried in" (170). The caution with which her characters proceed in their relationships demonstrates one of the difficulties of migration for people whose past is populated with shadows, as they struggle between wanting to forget and needing to remember.

A brief sketch of Danticat's protagonists displays a few more of the continuities with Washington's definition of African American women's literature. For Sophie Caco in *Breath, Eyes, Memory*, the lives of women who came before her—in the form of her mother, her grandmother, and her aunt—are as integral to her daily struggles and inform her journey into selfhood. Sophie's journey is intimately entwined with her mother's experience in particular, and as the narrator she takes on the role of telling her mother's story as well as her own. The process of discovering her mother's story is acknowledged as Sophie confesses, "It took me twelve years to piece together my mother's story. By then, it was already too late" (61). The role of the storyteller is potentially life saving: Sophie's comments suggest that by taking on the role of storyteller, she could have helped to save her mother's life. For her, sharing her story is an act of triumph, and telling the stories of others acts in the same way.

Positioned as storyteller for the generations before her, Sophie mirrors the author's stance since this is also a role into which Danticat steps in her attempts to share the stories passed down by her own ancestors. The final chapter of *Krik? Krak!* can be read as a similar attempt to use literature as a medium for relaying the stories of women's lives, as Danticat expresses her desire to write the stories of previous generations of women. In this section, the narrator collects and disseminates the stories of the women in her family, despite the cultural refusal to accept Haitian women as writers. For women,

> writing was forbidden as dark rouge on the cheeks or a first date before eighteen. It was an act of indolence, something to be done in the corner when you could have been learning to cook. . . . When you write, it's like braiding your hair. . . . Your fingers have still not perfected the task. Some of the braids are long, others are short. Some are thick, others are thin. Some are heavy. Others are light. Like the diverse women in your family. Those whose fables and metaphors, whose similes, soliloquies, whose diction and *je ne sais quoi* daily slip into your survival soup, by way of their fingers.[7]

The survival soup the narrator pours out is a collection of stories and folklore transmitted by mothers, aunts, and grandmothers she gathers to concoct her narratives. Through her mention of the women in her family, she identifies the significance of a feminine space and how it influences her writing. The history of Haitian women at times whispers in pages of Danticat's writing as in characters with names like Défilé, an often overlooked figure of the Haitian Revolution, or in the invocation of queens like Anacaona. Through naming she pays homage to the women of Haitian past as well as of her own personal past. Although the stories that unfold in *Krik? Krak!* are those of both men and women, the presence of female characters and narrators dominates the text's movement as it culminates in this narrative of kitchen poetry.

The Farming of Bones also features a female protagonist in the figure of Amabelle Désir, who recounts the history of the Dominican Vespers Massacre of Haitians from the perspective of a victim, a survivor, and a historical witness. This novel subversively intervenes with historical narrative by privileging the voice of a *Haitian woman* to tell the story of the Massacre. As a Haitian, as a woman, and as a domestic servant in the Dominican Republic, Amabelle occupies a position of multiple oppressions. For early African American women writers, the situation of "double jeopardy"—to be black and female—was a constant backdrop for their writing. Later on this develops into the race, class, gender triad and the multiple jeopardy of race, class, gender, and sexuality paradigms, each of which informs various subject positions. While she is certainly attentive to class and gender, race per se does not function as prominently in Danticat's work as it does in much African American women's writing. Other factors that inform subjecthood such as ethnicity, nationality, and language are privileged modes through which her characters process their identities. *The Farming of Bones* is especially significant for how it enters into racial discourse. When Amabelle helps her employer through the birth of fraternal twins, the latter is disturbed by the children's color. The boy favors his mother's white skin while the girl is "deep bronze, between the colors of tan Brazil nut shells and black salsify."[8] The mother says to Amabelle, "My daughter favors you. . . . She's [my daughter has] taken your color from the mere sight of your face" (11). Later on she asks, "Amabelle do you think my daughter will always be the color she is now? . . . My poor love, what if she's mistaken for one of your people?" (12). To the upper-class white Dominican woman, the worst possible fate for her daughter would be to be mistaken for a darker-skinned Haitian. It is interesting to note that *The Farming of Bones* could be considered the only text in which any kind of racial discourse is explicitly relevant. This suggests that Danticat's attentiveness to the race-gender-class nexus so revered in African American women's literature should constantly be measured in relation to the other locations of identity such as ethnicity, language, and nationality.

While Danticat's 2004 work of fiction, *The Dew Breaker*, departs from the female protagonist model, the man upon whom the story is centered is portrayed in relation to his daughter and his wife as well as to a number of victims both male and female. The theme of reconciliation is powerfully rendered through the title character's complicated family relationships to his wife and daughter. In *The Dew Breaker*, as in *Krik? Krak!* there is also frequent use of female characters, which once again illustrates the author's commitment to "the brave women of Haiti." In each case, as these women circulate in the texts, what binds them together is how they translate Haitian culture and traditions into their daily lives as well as how they interact with Haitian history, politics, and economics. Their subjectivity is informed by the multiple positions they occupy as women who are usually poor, black, immigrant (or migrant in the case of Amabelle), second generation, and inhabitants of a country that is not their own. All of these characters struggle to unite their shadows and their bodies, whether those shadows are hidden secrets of traumatic pasts (Sophie), loved ones lost in the bowels of Massacre River (Amabelle), or the fraught legacy of a terror-filled regime that somehow brought forth a loving marriage (Anne). Their bodies as black women are equally significant to their experiences in the text as the complexity of the shadows they leave behind in Haiti.

Along with the frequent use of female protagonists, many thematic parallels with African American women's writing inevitably surface in Danticat's oeuvre. These include healing from sexual violence, close-knit female relationships, silence and voice, the transformative power of reading and writing, the legacy of traumatic memory, preoccupations with the female body, mothering, sexuality, spirituality, vernacular, the constitution of the self, and the use of storytelling and folklore. In *The Changing Same: Black Women's Literature, Criticism, and Theory* Deborah McDowell calls for a clearly outlined methodology to define black feminist theory as well as rigorous textual analysis to read black women's literary tradition. She posits "the journey" as a recurrent theme in black women's writing that is also present in writing by black men but approached differently by each. "The Black female's journey, though at times touching the political and social, is basically a personal and psychological journey, the state of becoming part of an evolutionary spiral moving from victim to consciousness."[9] The trajectories of both Sophie in *Breath, Eyes, Memory* and Amabelle in *The Farming of Bones* are consistent with this "evolutionary spiral." While Sophie's journey is psychological, its psychic power is inextricably bound to its physicality, that is, the experience of migration from and return to Haiti. Amabelle, on the other hand embarks on a treacherous physical journey as she attempts to flee the Massacre, a plight that is also psychological because the Dominican Republic is the only home she has ever known and she shares a close bond with her Dominican, Trujillo-partisan employers. Again, these examples indicate that while indeed Danticat's work can be linked to African American women's literature through the use of certain tropes, a complete reading of her texts necessitates distinguishing how these similarities are impacted by Haitian contexts and subtexts.[10]

If, as Henry Louis Gates Jr. explains, "part of what distinguishes Black women's writing in the contemporary scene is a sense of historical community and its peculiarities—sometimes antic, sometimes grim, but never quite reducible to the master plot of victim and victimizer," then *The Dew Breaker* could stand out as an exemplar of how

Danticat writes into the African American literary tradition.[11] From the moment that Ka's father confides in her, "One day for the hunter, one day for the prey. Ka, your father was the hunter, he was not the prey," the text destabilizes the dichotomous relationship between victim and victimizer as these played out during the Duvalier regime and its aftermath (21). Through a complex weaving of multiple narratives that climaxes with the final chapter in which the title character finally relays his entire story, *The Dew Breaker* illustrates the far-reaching effects of historical and political trauma upon generations of Haitians living abroad. The text reflects the development of the African American aspects of her African-Haitian-American positionality in a number of ways. Its form makes it difficult to classify; it can be read as a collection of short stories, but because each one is related to another and the narratives are interconnected, the stories could also be read as separate chapters of one novel. Thus Danticat experiments with the two genres of fiction rather than choosing one as she has done in the past. The text comments on various aspects of the Haitian identity in the United States in a way that differs from her previous work, especially through the author's incorporation of current events and popular culture into different stories. In *The Dew Breaker* Haitians are haunted by the past even as they dwell in relative safety in the United States; they are continuously assaulted by the severity of the past in a country that seems to mock their pain by subjecting them to violence and protecting perpetrators of violence. This is the case for Patrick Dorismond, a Haitian immigrant killed by the NYPD, and "Toto Constant," who lives comfortably among New York's Haitian community despite his participation in the rape, torture, and murder of countless Haitians under the *machin enfenal.*

Despite the attention she gives to "the lives of women," Danticat does not trace exclusively female genealogies. Her 2007 work *Brother, I'm Dying* is a memoir based on the lives and deaths of her father and uncle as well as the birth of her own daughter. In that work Danticat takes on the role of family storyteller and displays yet another facet of her AHA identity, thus conveying that she is interested in more than the stories of women. Early in the book she explains her objectives: "I write these things now, some as I witnessed them and today remember them, others from official documents, as well as the borrowed recollection of family members. But the gist of them was told to me over the years, in part by my uncle Joseph, in part by my father. . . . This [book] is an attempt at cohesiveness and at re-creating a few wondrous and terrible months when their lives and mine intersected in startling ways, *forcing me to look forward and back at the same time.* I am writing this only because they can't."[12] These words demonstrate the extent to which Danticat acts as a chronicler and an advocate for her own family. The story she tells is of two male relatives (her father and uncle) and their female descendants (Danticat and her daughter Mira), indicating a genealogy that is not based in gender. These introductory words of this recently published piece of nonfiction are consistent with Danticat's vision of shadows and bodies, as she uses her writing to "look forward and back at the same time." *Brother, I'm Dying* departs from previous works that were centered on female genealogies but is attentive to documenting the stories of family members, whose experiences in Haiti and as immigrants in the United States consistently inform Danticat's work.

Dialogues

Rather than merely estimate the category of African American women's writing based on stylistic, thematic, and aesthetic conventions, we should also consider how Edwidge Danticat can be situated *in dialogue with* both early and contemporary writers. To begin this inquiry we can look to the work of Zora Neale Hurston, an often cited literary foremother for contemporary African American women writers and one for whom Haiti also served as a site of inspiration.[13] Although there are obvious examples of how different Danticat is from Hurston, as the former's problematic account of her encounters with Haitian Vodou in *Tell My Horse* indicates, the place of honor that she occupies in African American women's writing demands that we explore the relationship between the two writers. As is the case for the African American women writers she precedes, "all of Hurston's writings," according to Lorraine Bethel, "can be epitomized as her commitment to expressing the lives and thoughts of Black women who have been *silenced* for too long."[14] The dialectics of voice and silence are virtually omnipresent in African American women's literature as they have been in Caribbean and African literature written by women. In both her fiction and nonfiction writing Danticat expresses a desire to base her narratives on the untold stories of Haitian and Haitian American women.[15] Her article "We Are Ugly, But We Are Here" points out Haitian women's invisibility in different contexts: "Watching news reports, it is often hard to tell whether there are real living and breathing women in conflict-stricken places like Haiti. The evening news broadcasts only allow a brief glimpse of presidential coups, rejected boat people, and sabotaged elections. The women's stories never manage to make the front page. However, they do exist."[16] Her determination to show that they exist is one way that Danticat overcomes the silence that seems to surround Haitian women.

For African American women writers the question of silence is often formulated in relation to writing and artistry. Zora Neale Hurston's story—the loss and rediscovery of her work as well as the subsequent claiming of it by African American women writers—is representative of the struggles black women face as artists. Alice Walker has often turned to Hurston as the object of fascination, inspiration, and critical inquiry, and in her collection *In Search of Our Mothers' Gardens* she makes numerous references to Hurston as a tortured and forgotten artist reclaimed by contemporary black women writers.[17] The search upon which Walker embarks is one for the art, the writing, and the intellectual enterprises of African American women. Danticat's position on the woman as artist differs here because rather than framing the absence of these voices in terms of silence, or focusing on their suppression, she accounts for their presence and positions herself as a scribe in their translation. In *Krik? Krak!* Danticat also explores the idea of "black woman as suppressed artist" through her characterization of "women who write and cook."[18]

Like African American women writers, Danticat has identified her own matriarchal literary heritage.[19] But rather than tracing hers back to one central figure such as Zora Neale Hurston, she names several women who influence her work, establishing a lineage in which Haitians such as Marie Vieux-Chauvet and J. J. Dominique, as well as African Americans such as Paule Marshall and Maya Angelou and Caribbean writers like Maryse Condé, coexist. Although she openly acknowledges her great admiration for Chauvet, it was not until Danticat arrived in the United States that she read fiction written by black women, so it is not surprising that she intimates a particularly close relationship to African American women writers.[20] There are connections to be made between Danticat and writers such as Alice Walker and Toni Morrison, but the author in whose lineage we can place her most effectively is Paule Marshall. Her continuous invocation of Marshall, the

United States–born daughter of immigrants from Barbados, is explicit in *Krik? Krak!* as she echoes Marshall's concept of "kitchen poets" writing: "Kitchen poets, you call them. Ghosts like burnished branches on a flame tree. These women, they asked for your voice so that they could tell your mother in your place that yes, women like you do speak, even if they speak in a tongue that is hard to understand" (222).

Both Marshall's and Danticat's first novels are narratives of young girls raised in immigrant communities in New York. Like Danticat, Marshall has often addressed the various positions she occupies due to her Caribbean and African American heritage, and how these afford her a different perspective. Marshall explains,

> I am in a unique position. I know that people have trouble defining me as a black American or Caribbean writer. I fall between two stools, I'm neither West Indian nor black American. My parents are from the West Indies and they gave me a very strong sense of the culture out of which they came. That was one of the things that molded me as a person and a writer. Yet on the other hand I was born in Brooklyn, went to public schools, and I am very much a black American. I have got my feet in both camps.... This is what my work is about: to bring about the synthesis of two cultures, and, in addition, to connect them up with the African experience.[21]

Like Marshall, Danticat acknowledges that her position as a Haitian American offers her unique insight into the different spaces she inhabits. This is clear in her critique of the American dream, as she depicts journeys full of hopes that dissipate into disillusionment for Haitian immigrants. Beyond the problems of language, belonging, and longing for homeland, the immigrants in Danticat's texts find themselves confronted by the demons of their past no matter how much distance they seek to place between the traumatic experiences from home and their new lives in the United States. This is the case for Martine in *Breath, Eyes, Memory*, such that when her daughter sees her for the first time her appearance is haggard, and it "was as though she had never stopped working in the cane fields after all" (42). In *Krik? Krak!* the story "Caroline's Wedding" begins with the narrator-protagonist obtaining American citizenship papers and a passport, what should be a symbol of accomplishment. Instead, she sees these materials in the following grim terms: "It was like being in a war zone and finally receiving a weapon of my own, like standing in a firing line and finally getting a bulletproof vest" (213). The deliberate use of war imagery here assigns a belligerent undertone to the experience of immigration.

In *The Dew Breaker,* the critique points to the complicated relationship between the United States and Haiti. To readers the similarities between the dew breaker's anonymous existence in New York and that of Emmanuel "Toto" Constant, former prominent leader of the Haitian Liberation Front, do not go unnoticed (at least for those familiar with the history after the first coup that unseated Jean-Bertrand Aristide and Haitian current events).[22] Danticat anticipates that concern by inserting Constant's story into the text. The title character's family attend Christmas Mass and see a man resembling Constant, causing them to discuss the Haitian community's outrage at the criminal's unhampered presence in New York. There is mention of the lamppost on which community activists have pasted Constant's photo with the heading in bold, "wanted for crimes against the Haitian people . . . torture, rape, and murder of 5000 people" (22). When Anne (the dew breaker's wife) removes the sign it is "not out of sympathy for Constant but out of fear that even though her husband's prison work and Constant's offenses were separated by thirty plus years, she might arrive at her store one morning to find her husband's likeness on the lamppost rather than Constant's" (80). The pairing of the two men who escape their violent pasts serves as another reminder of patterns of violence that cycle through time. It is also an overtly political gesture condemning Constant's ability to remain above the law through collusion with the U.S. government. Danticat manages to deftly integrate the contemporary concerns of Haitians living in the United States through the use of current socially relevant content.

When Alice Walker wonders in the story titled "In Search of Our Mother's Gardens," "[What] is my literary tradition? Who are the black women artists who preceded me? Do I have a ground to stand on?" she expresses yearning for a literary space that is African American and female.[23] Walker's effort to locate her own creative foremothers surfaced at a historical moment when black women seemed to be absent as writers and intellectuals. For African American intellectuals like Alice Walker, Barbara Christian, and Barbara Smith, much of the work of African American women's writing involved a project of unearthing voices that were silenced, hidden, or inaccessible. On the other hand, Danticat's first novel surfaced at a time when African American women were present as literary giants, from the Pulitzer ranks of Alice Walker to the Nobel Prize grandeur of Toni Morrison. As a black woman, Edwidge Danticat writes in a moment characterized by the post-1980s explosive acceptance of black women as writers, but as an African-Haitian-American her writing inhabits a space that was previously uncharted on such a popular level.

Black feminist theoretical discourses used to explicate African American women's literature have often relied on multiplicity and diversity as formative concepts. By employing critical strategies that emphasize plurality, black feminist literary critics account for the diversity of writing and experience among black women writers. Mae Gwendolyn Henderson contends that "what is at once characteristic and suggestive about black women's writing is its interlocutory, or dialogic, character, reflecting not only a relationship with the other(s), but an internal dialogue with the plural aspects of the self that constitute the matrix of black female subjectivity."[24] A figure like Danticat, then, could be considered the ultimate black woman writer since her work cannot be contained by literary categories or national boundaries. In fact, the notion of shadows and bodies that has guided this discussion fits well into analytic systems privileging multiplicity and plurality; it could be taken a step further to be used as a framework for reading Danticat's work.

The Dew Breaker's Anne experiences having her body in one place and her shadow in another as she rides in the car with her family one evening. From the streets of Brooklyn, she contemplates her past and the traumatic death of her brother. As she relives the accident that drowns her brother, she is neither present in the car nor for the conversation that her family is having. Anne's mind takes her to Haiti, and as she recognizes that a part of her also died right along with her brother, we come to understand how an element of her spirit/shadow will always remain on the island. That she does not share the details of the event with her family further distances her physical self in the present from the memories of the past: "Anne closed her eyes without realizing it. Her daughter knew she reacted strongly to cemeteries. Anne had never told her why, since her daughter had already concluded early in life that this, like many unexplained aspects of her parents' life, was connected to 'some event that happened in Haiti'" (72). The silence that dominates Anne's relationship with her daughter is mostly borne from the secret she and her husband keep from Ka for years. Because of the secret they constantly live between two worlds, measuring the past against the present in fear that their secrets from the past will come to inhabit the present. By breaking the silence to his daughter, the father invites an avalanche of memories to rush into his life; his speaking these words can be seen as the act that unleashes the entire text since it is expressed in the beginning and at the end of the work. Again in this relation we see that the experience of every character within the text is mediated by how they relate to their memories of the regime.

Diasporas

Throughout this essay I have used the term *African American women* as a synonym for *black women,* a move informed by the criticism on African American women's literature where black and African American often collapse into one. Perhaps this difficulty of naming is wherein lies the challenge of the project to situate Danticat in relation to African American women's literature. Unless African American women's literature broadens in scope to make comfortable room for immigrant writers such as Danticat, placing her within that tradition cannot sufficiently account for her contributions. Without such an opening, Danticat will be marginalized within that tradition, unable to be named without extensive qualification in the same way that Paule Marshall was before her. Perhaps instead of attempting to make her fit into a category that can contain neither her body nor her shadow, we could look at her as a black Atlantic or an African diasporic writer. Certainly this is what Danticat herself attempts by embracing the term *African-Haitian-American.* This category with its hyphens flanking the word *Haitian* acknowledges three distinct yet connecting categories that are fluid. As the term indicates, Haitians in diaspora are the recipients of multiple heritages from Africa, the Americas, and Europe. Ultimately Edwidge Danticat embodies a multifarious politics of location that does not privilege one location over the other. She writes, "My country . . . is one of uncertainty. When I say 'my country' to some Haitians they think of the United States, when I say 'my country' to some Americans, they think of Haiti."[25]

Writing about Danticat as an African American woman writer might suggest a certain level of co-optation, but contemporary understanding of the vicissitudes of black literature allow Danticat to be seen as a black woman writer, an African diasporic writer, or an African-Haitian-

American woman writer. Danticat's contribution to these traditions should be viewed as a broadening of the literary landscape, because her work redefines the contours of what qualifies as African American. Because she embraces this "uncertainty," her work should be located at the interstices of the space where black America empties into and converges with black Atlantic. To include her in the African American women's literary tradition is to acknowledge the diasporic nature of blackness in the United States. In fact, the acceptance of this diversity is consistent with how black feminist theorists have approached literature by black women. I want to conclude with the comment of Haitian writer Dany Laferrière, who has mused that he is more "American" than Americans themselves, because he was born in Haiti, currently resides in Canada, and has lived in the United States as well as parts of the Caribbean. The same could be said of Edwidge Danticat, whose Americanness accounts for the breadth of the Americas as well as the multiplicity of voices that make up its various countries, including those as disparate as Haiti and the United States.

NOTES

1. Edwidge Danticat, "AHA!" *Becoming American: Personal Essays by First Generation Immigrant Women,* ed. Meri Nana-Ama Danquaah (New York: Hyperion, 2000), 39–45 (44).

2. Deborah McDowell, *The Changing Same: Black Women's Literature, Criticism, and Theory* (Bloomington: Indiana University Press, 1995), xiii.

3. Karla Holloway, "Revision and (Re)membrance: A Theory of Literary Structures in Literature by African American Women Writers," *African American Literary Theory: A Reader,* ed. Winston Napier (New York: New York University Press, 2000), 392.

4. Mary Helen Washington, "The Darkened Eye Restored: Notes toward a Literary History of Black Women," *Reading Feminist, Reading Black: A Critical Anthology,* ed. Henry Louis Gates (New York: Penguin, 1990), 35.

5. Edwidge Danticat, *Breath, Eyes, Memory* (New York: Vintage, 1994), iv. Subsequent references are to this edition and are given after quotations in the main body of the text.

6. Edwidge Danticat, *The Dew Breaker* (New York: Knopf, 2004), 169. Subsequent references are to this edition and are given after quotations in the main body of the text.

7. Edwidge Danticat, *Krik? Krak!* (New York: Vintage, 1995), 219–20. Subsequent references are to this edition and are given after quotations in the main body of the text.

8. Edwidge Danticat, *The Farming of Bones* (New York: Soho Press, 1998), 11. Sub-

sequent references are to this edition and are given after quotations in the main body of the text.

9. McDowell, *Changing Same*, 13.

10. Interestingly, Danticat's use of the journey motif is closer to that of African American women writers than Caribbean writers. In her study of this trope Elizabeth Wilson observes that for Caribbean women writers the journey trope typically ends in failure of a quest for self-actualization, usually ending in "withdrawal and isolation and/or flight and evasion, rather than confrontation." Elizabeth Wilson, "*Le voyage et l'espace clos*"—Island and Journey as Metaphor: Aspects of Women's Experience in the Works of Francophone Caribbean Women Novelists," *Out of the Kumbla: Caribbean Women and Literature*, ed. Carole Boyce Davies and Elaine Savory Fido (Trenton, NJ: Africa World Press, 1990), 45.

11. Henry Louis Gates Jr., ed., *Reading Feminist, Reading Black* (New York: Penguin, 1990), 16.

12. Edwidge Danticat, *Brother, I'm Dying* (New York: Knopf, 2007), 26 (my emphasis).

13. Hurston wrote *Their Eyes Were Watching God* and *Tell My Horse* while conducting anthropological research in Haiti.

14. Lorraine Bethel, "The Infinity of Conscious Pain," *All the Women Are White, All the Blacks Are Men, But Some of Us Are Brave*, ed. Gloria T. Hull, Patricia Bell Scott, and Barbara Smith (New York: Feminist Press, 1982), 186 (my emphasis).

15. This project to redress silence is relevant to reading Danticat's work, although, as Myriam Chancy aptly points out in *Framing Silence: Revolutionary Novels by Haitian Women* (New Brunswick, NJ: Rutgers University Press, 1997), Haitian writers such as Danticat noticeably problematize the idea of silence, using it to forge positions of power.

16. Edwidge Danticat, "We Are Ugly But We Are Here," *Caribbean Writer* 10 (1996), http://www.thecaribbeanwriter.org/toc/tocvolume10.html.

17. Alice Walker, *In Search of Our Mothers' Gardens: Womanist Prose* (San Diego: Harcourt Brace, 1983).

18. Mary Helen Washington, "Teaching Black-Eyed Susans: An Approach to the Study of Black Women Writers," *Reading Black, Reading Feminist*, ed. Henry Louis Gates (New York: Penguin, 1990), 209.

19. Gates writes in his introduction to *Reading Black, Reading Feminist* that "black female authors often claim descent from other black women literary ancestors, such as Zora Neale Hurston and Anne Petry" (5).

20. With regards to Chauvet, Danticat shares the following in an interview: "I remember reading an excerpt of one of Marie Chauvet's books (*Love, Anger, Madness*), and I just loved her. Her whole story, how she fought and fought to be published, was just amazing to me, and she has become one of my favorite Haitian writers." "The Dangerous Job of Edwidge Danticat," Interview with Renee H. Shea, *Callaloo* 19, no. 2 (1996), 382–389.

21. 'Molara Ogundipe-Leslie, "'Re-creating Ourselves All over the World': A Conversation with Paule Marshall," *Moving beyond Boundaries: Black Women's Diaspo-*

ras, vol. 2, ed. Carole Boyce Davies and 'Molara Ogundipe-Leslie (New York: New York University Press, 1995), 23–24.

22. The Haitian Liberation Front is more commonly known as FRAPH (Front Révolutionnaire Pour l'Avancement du Peuple Haitien).

23. Walker, *In Search of Our Mothers' Gardens*, 233.

24. Mae Gwendolyn Henderson, "Speaking in Tongues: Dialogics, Dialectics, and the Black Woman Writer's Literary Tradition," in *Feminists Theorize the Political*, ed. Judith Butler and Joan W. Scott (New York: Routledge, 1992), 145.

25. Edwidge Danticat, *The Butterfly's Way: Voices from the Haitian Dyaspora in the United States* (New York: Soho Press, 2001), xiv.

Texts & Analyses

This section presents original, close readings of each of Danticat's published works up to and including *The Dew Breaker.* By engaging as rigorously with Danticat's writing for children and travel writing as with her fiction, the section treats individual works as part of the overall oeuvre and thus offers readers insights into the ways in which common Danticat themes are treated in the different genres. Themes analyzed include the relationship between personal lives and the political world; the treatment of issues of poverty and social justice; Haitian history and personal and collective memory; the experience of migration and the experience of return; issues of state and familial violence and the difficulty of representing it in fiction; masculinity; and ideas of nation, race, and class. In addition to the thematic analyses, each essay in this section pays close attention to Danticat's style and the ways in which her style is infused with a political edge, the tender obstinacy that courses through the entire work.

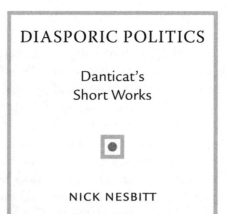

DIASPORIC POLITICS

Danticat's
Short Works

NICK NESBITT

*In our world if you write you are a politician, and we know what
happens to politicians.*—Edwidge Danticat, *Krik? Krak!*

Critical reception of Edwidge Danticat's writing has foregrounded
two aspects that distinguish it from the prose of previous Haitian
authors. On the one hand, it has been interpreted as a retreat from
the epic narratives of anticolonial, populist, Negritude, or Marxian
liberation that characterized the work of earlier Haitian authors such
as Jacques Roumain and Jacques-Stephen Alexis. Yanick Lahens has
rightly observed that for Haitian women writers such as Danticat and
her predecessor and inspiration Marie Chauvet, this involved tearing
down "a certain number of masks, . . . certain [ideological and politi-
cal] screens," the infamous "grand narratives" of Western Modernity,
in order to articulate "truly individual and personal" works of fiction.[1]
Secondly, her work can be understood as a Haitian American example
of the turn toward the genre of the testimonial, that is, the narration
(whether fictional or not) by subaltern subjects of individual experiences of social injustice. Superficially, such processes might be taken to
mark a retreat away from a more programmatic politics geared toward
the macro-transformation of society and into an intimate sphere (of
the "truly individual and personal") devoid of any claim either to comprehend or transform society as a whole.

Instead, I think Danticat's writing points to a new way of intervening at the juncture between cultural production and political praxis (in the traditional sense of the word). Following the collapse of Cold War bilateralism and the hegemonic rise of global capitalism and transnational, imperial interventionism, Danticat's writing cuts across previous demarcations of both personal and political space and narrative genre (novel, short story, memoir, op-ed editorial) to chart the course of new modalities and conceptualizations of political activity. Even the most superficial consideration of her work makes obvious that Danticat's turn to the personalized intimacy of testimonial writing and its formal corollary, the small-scale piece, does not turn its back on universal problems such as social injustice and their construction within discursive regimes of social, political, historical, and linguistic production.

For Martin Munro, Danticat's writing constitutes not a retreat from the political, but just such a development of a literary praxis that "explores *both* the personal and the political, so that she personalizes politics, and conversely, politicizes the personal."[2] Her recourse to both personalism and testimonial are understood by Munro to constitute a thoroughly complementary symbolic intervention: "The testimony is a means of validating personal experience and of exploring the effects of [social injustice] on individual lives."[3] In his study of Danticat, Munro goes on to show in insightful and nuanced readings how Danticat sustains this imperative throughout her two novels *Breath, Eyes, Memory* and *The Farming of Bones.* One goal of this essay, then, is to prolong Munro's reflection on this juncture of the political and personal to consider its implementation in her short story cycle *Krik? Krak!*[4] This leads me to propose an interpretation of the political rationality of her project: while it is clear to all her readers that Danticat is profoundly and intimately concerned with the plight of Haiti, Haitians, and contemporary migrants in general, it is less so how her authorial interventions might constitute a meaningful response to the injustice she witnesses for us. In other words, while I think it is relatively clear how her mixing of the personal and political cultivates readers' attention to the former, it remains to be seen in what way Danticat's testimonialism might begin to outline a politics that could start to address the contemporary dilemmas of social injustice in this period of expanding global imperialism.

● ●

Danticat's collection of short stories *Krik? Krak!* was the author's second book-length publication, following the wide-spread critical acclaim that accompanied *Breath, Eyes, Memory.* Of the nine short stories contained in the volume, five had been previously published between 1991 and 1995: "Nineteen Thirty-Seven," "The Missing Peace," "Seeing Things Simply," "New York Day Women," and the collection's longest piece, "Caroline's Wedding." Taken together, the stories collected in *Krik? Krak!* form a complexly interwoven whole that Rocio Davis has revealingly analyzed as a contemporary contribution to the millennial tradition of the short story cycle. Story cycles, from Homer, Bocaccio, and Chaucer to Hemingway and Carver, create a more supple interaction of elements within and between various stories than the short story form. In the story cycle, "connective patterns on all levels draw these [elements] together into a totality strengthened by varying types of internal cohesion: a title, the development of a central character, the delineation of a community, or an explicit theme."[5] The reappearance of thematic elements serves to bind narrative diversity in a literary form that remains fundamentally indebted to oral storytelling traditions.

The collection's title immediately appeals to this tradition in its invocation of the Caribbean storyteller's rhetorical call and response to her real or (in Danticat's case) implied readership: "Krik?" she calls out to us. Her inscription of our assumed response ("Krak!") then allows the storyteller to begin the cycle. From its inception, *Krik? Krak!* proceeds in the complex process of a symbolic weaving together—of voices, of experiences, of genres, of themes, of images—that the author will condense in her beautiful closing image: "When you write, it's like braiding your hair. Taking a handful of coarse unruly strands and attempting to bring them to unity" (220). This weaving that her cycle will undertake is to be a linking up, a drawing together, of diverse singularities within a series of totalities: the book itself, as well as transnational communities of readers—Haitians, immigrants, women, mothers and daughters—all of whom sympathetically react to various dimensions of the experiences of these characters. In its inscription of the oral storyteller's vocal incitement to participation, *Krik? Krak!* will strive to bring together these diverse singularities that are its readers into a whole, one that will maintain a furtive balance between the need for community and the imperative to foster diversity. The cycle itself will stand as the cypher of this process: if the successful novel would swallow us into the life-world it creates, the far briefer interjections of each short story within the cycle will allow the reader to plunge into its world, and to emerge just as quickly, and yet to be carried along by the underlying coherence and dynamic of the cycle itself.

The invocation of such a community-to-come is itself already a political act: Danticat's various addressees all suffer to some degree in isolation. The isolation of a country rich in hidden historical and cultural legacies reduced by the outside world to its status as the "poorest nation in the Western Hemisphere," immigrants isolated in the detention cells of the U.S. Immigration authorities who took the life of the author's own uncle, the isolation of those who suffer their individual plights alone, all can come to know that, in fact, they are not alone. Through the storyteller's invocation of community, each reader who thought herself alone can begin to realize the force shared in discovering common voice. The extraordinary response to Danticat's writing testifies anew that a gifted storyteller is not speaking in place of others, but voicing the intersubjective experience of a community of diverse, singular beings, testifying to the absence and voicelessness of those who have passed on, those who have been eliminated, those who have not yet found the means or courage to speak their singular experiences, those "people in this world whose names don't matter to anyone but themselves" (3).

The opening story of Danticat's cycle, "Children of the Sea," presents the cycle's model in reduction, impelling the reader irresistibly into the world of Haitian ultra-violence. Twice-ten diary entries of a young couple, separated from one another by the violence of the Macoutes, writing in unswerving devotion, are reunited beyond death through the author's summons. Brought face to face on opposing pages, it is our reading of these undelivered texts that carries their missives from one to the other with undiminished passion. First published in 1993, the exchange is set amid the violence that followed the 1991 CIA-supported coup against Haiti's first democratically elected president, Jean-Bertrand Aristide.[6] In those months, the infamous FRAPH (Front Révolutionnaire Pour l'Avancement et le Progrès Haïtien), led by Emmanuel "Toto" Constant, terrorized the vast majority of the Haitian population sympathetic to Aristide and his Lavalas political movement and any who dared to resist the postcoup military government.

Writing from the epicenter of the postcoup violence in Haiti, the young woman describes this violence to her beloved—one of the nameless whom the outside world called "boat-people"—as he drifts between the island and the far-off dream of Miami. The young man is a student who has only just passed his university entrance exams, and who has been forced to flee Haiti after comments he and his colleagues made on their radio show against the government attracted the violence of the Macoutes. The woman describes to her lover how "a group of students got shot in front of Fort Dimanche prison today. They were demonstrating for the bodies of the radio six. That is what they are calling you all" (7). The five colleagues he had left behind were all murdered, and the mother of one, "our neighbor Madan Roger[,] came home with her son's head and not much else.... By the time we saw her, she had been carrying the head all over Port-au-Prince. Just to show what's been done to her son" (7). The climate of violence and intimidation around her is total; "they [the Macoutes] are always watching you, like vultures. At night I can't sleep. I count the bullets in the dark" (8).

As the young man drifts on the boat, he gradually descends into a complementary world of violence, that of extreme physical conditions—sunstroke, thirst, seasickness, lack of hygiene—fear of impending death, and nostalgia for the country and woman he has been forced to leave behind. The focus of the migrants is on one among them in particular, a pregnant young woman named Célianne, who "stares into space all the time and rubs her stomach" (10). At night, she awakes the other passengers, screaming from her nightmares. Eventually, Célianne's child is stillborn, yet the mother holds on to her dead child, day after day. Bit by bit, as the diary entries proceed, their boat lets in ever-increasing amounts of water, till they run out of tar to patch the cracks and can hardly bail the water out fast enough to stay afloat. After writing his last entry, the narrator throws his diary overboard as the boat begins to draw them under, to rest "among the children of the deep blue sea, those who have escaped the chains of slavery to form a world beneath the heavens and the blood-drenched world where you live" (27).

These forms of violence that each narrator describes to the other weave in and out of their stories. First, the woman describes in the third person in her fourth entry how "they have this thing now that they do.... They make the son sleep with his mother" (12). It is only toward the end of the story, in his eighth entry, that the man describes a more intimate version of this same outrage, this time more directly related to him by Célianne. She tells him the terrible story of her pregnancy; how soldiers broke into her family home, forcing her brother into sexual relations with his mother, then gang-raping Célianne. "The same night, Célianne cut her face with a razor so that no one would know who she was. . . . She is fifteen" (24). Back in Haiti, the violence grows ever more terrifying. Father and daughter vent their frustration in verbal, then physical violence against each other. Eventually, the Macoutes come to Madan Roger, who screams at them, "You killed him already. We buried his head. You can't kill him twice" (15). And so they will kill her, the female narrator and her parents forced to listen, hiding in their latrine, as the sound of the soldier's blows rain down upon their defenseless neighbor.

The violence is horrific, yet at every moment Danticat's shining prose rescues shards of beauty from this wreckage. Never long, her phrasing captures such moments like the butterflies that flutter throughout her volume, to shine beyond all bestial violence. Dazed and short of breath, those who must attempt not only to survive but to continue to live fully human lives have no time for the epic proportions of Proustian reflection and phrasing. In the face of human possibilities constantly denied, Danticat's narrators recover the broken remnants of the happiness that life had promised them, "our silly dreams" (21): "I see you crying like a crushed snail, the way you cried when I helped you pull out your first loose tooth. Yes, I did love you then" (3); "I used to read a lot about America" (6); "At times I feel like I can just reach out and pull a star down from the sky as though it is a breadfruit calabash" (9); the promise of life that was Célianne's child; the university exams that "you passed" (24). Above all, a moment of love, of fully shared human emotion at its most intense, something that no violence can deny: "All anyone can hope for is just a tiny bit of love, manman says, like a drop in a cup if you can get it, or a waterfall, a flood, if you can get that too" (12). The love of the young woman for her father—who, she discovers, has sacrificed everything to preserve her from the Macoutes, and her love for the young man, the knowledge she holds onto that "I have loved someone else besides only my mother and father in my life." "I love you," she writes him, "until my hair shivers at the thought of anything happening to you" (22).

Image after searing image remind us of our own stunted potential for humane existence, of the possible depth of feeling and heights of expression we might share with others. They remind us of our own *poverty* of feeling in comparison with a country we too quickly call poor, and with individuals so rich in having known the fullest beauties and horrors of life. Danticat's writing to us, to those who have the potential to testify along with her, is precisely a condemnation of our own paucity of experience, one that prohibits us from sharing the richness of that of the so-called boat people and those they left behind. It is an invocation as well of our own enormous, underdeveloped potential for humanity, to the point where our outrage would rightfully overflow when confronted with the scandalous crimes of our government (whether Haitian, French, American, Canadian, or other) and their minions, crimes perpetrated against such individuals, crimes that have caused such sickening destruction of human potential again and again and again since 1804.

In the face of a world overcoded by highly policed borders and limitations, violence and suffering circulate freely from one story to another in *Krik? Krak!* across generations, across regimes, across borders. The formal concatenations of the story cycle instantiate a world without borders in the very process of representing their terrifying effects. A daughter visits her mother in Fort Dimanche prison in Port-au-Prince sometime during the Duvalier regime, after the latter was incarcerated following an accusation of "witchcraft" ("Nineteen Thirty-Seven"). One generation after another is subject to such renewals of violence. At each visit, the daughter witnesses death approaching closer to her mother. Her mother, in turn, had seen her own mother killed ("she could still see the soldiers chopping up *her* mother's body and throwing it in the river") in the 1937 massacre of Haitian migrants that becomes the theme of *The Farming of Bones* (40). In "The Missing Peace," a young Haitian girl and the American academic she is guiding suddenly witness two soldiers "dragging the blood-soaked body of a bearded man with an old election slogan written on a T-shirt across his chest: ALONE WE ARE WEAK, TOGETHER WE ARE A FLOOD" (117). The reader recognizes the electoral slogan of Aristide's Lavalas party and recalls, once again, the brutal aggression FRAPH members visited upon anyone openly calling for Aristide's return after 1991. In "A Wall of Fire Rising," a son and wife stand in a field, watching the father crash to the ground from the balloon he has taken to escape the gravitational forces limiting his existence.

Other themes weave their way through Danticat's prose, gradually accruing depth and richness in what she will call, in her closing epilogue ("Women Like Us"), her "survival soup" (220). Above all is the theme of the intensive interaction and interdependency of mothers and daughters. The narrator of "Nineteen Thirty-Seven" is no longer psychologically able to speak to her mother when visiting her with food in prison, after seeing her mother's beaten, broken body as she "drags herself across the clay floor on her belly" and her bestialization at the hands of the prison guards who had shaved her head "to make [the women prisoners] look like crows" (39). Each time the daughter returns, one senses that she renews the mother's hope that her daughter will escape from the pervasive climate of ruin. A woman, abandoned by her companion, devastated by repeated miscarriages, and visited in her dreams by her dead mother, brings home a child she has found left to die on the street, holding it close to satisfy her shattered dreams of motherhood. There she hides it jealously, until the corpse putrifies in the rank atmosphere of devastated human relations ("Between the Pool and the Gardenias"). A daughter is raised by her grandmother, after her own mother died in childbirth ("The Missing Peace"). Another daughter suddenly sees her mother walking down the street in Manhattan and follows her, curious about this part of her mother's life that had long remained hidden from her ("New York City Day Women"). And finally, in the volume's longest tale, "Caroline's Wedding," a mother and her daughter negotiate the complex passage from childhood to the marriage disapproved of by the mother. Across these generations, a variegated sorority takes shape, in which women affirm their solidarity in the face of disaster. "You remember while braiding your hair that you look a lot like your mother. Your mother who looked like your grandmother and her grandmother before" (219). This shift to second-person address in the volume's final pages carries this invocation to sisterhood beyond the pages of the volume itself, to interpellate the reader within this community of sustenance.

Butterflies drift across Danticat's pages, shadows of hope and mortality that appear and disappear just as quickly, fluttering freely above the wounded, suffering human bodies, while characters dream of joining them to fly into freedom. Characters and names (Célianne, Ville Rose, Lili, Eveline, Jacqueline) reappear furtively, and Danticat leaves it to her readers to speak the name of a girl who had drowned herself at sea ("Célianne") when her plight is recalled in a church in Brooklyn. Images are increasingly interwoven, not merely between individual stories in Danticat's cycle, but within a single story. The author thematizes this process in the mise en abyme that is the word game Caroline plays with her sister: "'Who are you?' Caroline asked me. 'I am the *lost* child of the night.' 'Where do you come from?' 'I come from inside of the *lost* stone.' Where are your eyes?' 'I have eyes *lost* behind my head, where they can best protect me'" (164). Stars reappear again and again, flashing across the sky to signal hope, love, and impending death. As the stories progress, they gradually open out from the Dante-esque confines of the island/boat to encompass the hope that the outside world, America in particular, continues to hold for Haitian immigrants despite the worst actions of a U.S. Department of Homeland Security not subject to constitutional legal restrictions.[7]

The cycle's final story, "Caroline's Wedding," underscores the author's call for universal social justice in the face of such unrelenting destruction of human possibility. This radical egalitarianism unambiguously places Danticat's entire oeuvre, fictional and nonfictional, within the great contributions of Haitian political culture to modernity. The signal, epoch-breaking intervention of the Haitian Independence of 1804 was to have shown the contemporary world system of slave-based agrarian capitalism (sustained with violent force across the North Atlantic states that fashioned themselves "democracies") the true universality of the human right to freedom and equality and to have created for the first time a society in which all, without distinction or differentiation, were free and equal (all humans, without exception, within Haitian territory, were to be free from slavery and racial discrimination; they were "black," whatever their skin color, in the famous words of the 1805 constitution).

Danticat's political intervention sustains this legacy, calling again and again for the implementation of an undivided, universally egalitarian regime of rights and the rule of law, a regime that in turn would allow for the fullest flourishing of the human singularity that each of us possesses. "Caroline's Wedding" is a parable of Haitians' *Vor dem Gesetz*, of former immigrants and boat people who stand before the law in absolute equality and freedom. "It was a cool September day," this closing gesture begins, "when I walked out of a Brooklyn courthouse holding my naturalization certificate" (157). In contrast to this triumphant process of subjectivation under the universal equality of law, the narrator Grace recalls on the following page the vulnerable status of the illegal immigrant, trapped outside the rule of law and subject to the whims of immigration authorities: "When my mother was three months pregnant with my younger sister, Caroline, she was arrested in a sweatshop raid and spent three days in an immigration jail" (158). Her father, in turn, had obtained a U.S. visa by "a false marriage with a widow who was leaving Haiti to come to the United States" (190).

The formal recognition of subjectivity in marriage echoes this concern for immigration documents and legal status. Grace talks with her mother about the latter's own engagement and marriage and its old-fashioned formality: "The proposal, it was all very formal, and sometimes, in some circumstances, formality is important" (163). As Grace observes, "In my family, we have always been very anxious about our papers" (158). As "Caroline's Wedding" and *Krik? Krak!* itself draw to a close, Grace triumphantly receives her American passport, securely placing her beyond the whims of immigration authorities and, above all, the total deformalization of the rule of law and ubiquitous state of exception in Haiti that underwrites the brutality witnessed in these stories (along with its unabated continuation to this day beyond the pages of Danticat's fiction). "For the first time in my life," Grace celebrates, "I felt truly secure living in America. It was like being in a war zone and finally receiving a weapon of my own, like standing on the firing line and finally getting a bullet-proof vest" (213).

Edwidge Danticat's political intervention is no programmatic manifesto. Instead, she brings the compelling force of an unrivalled poetic sensibility and micrological sensitivity for suffering to testify to the destruction of human possibility and to recover the persistent splinters of hope lodged in the wreckage of post-Duvalierist society. This she does in any genre necessary: the story cycles of *Krik? Krak!* and *The Dew Breaker,* her novels, and the interviews and nonfiction that have appeared in forums such as the *Nation* and the *New York Times.* She sustains a practical fidelity to the testimonial that is the only possible rebuttal to the observation that the genre constantly risks standing as no more than what Aberto Moreiras has called "a sort of methadone in the absence of effective literary critical practice." We can only overcome this risk, the risk of merely reading Danticat for our own "aesthetic fix," if the force of her language draws us out of the interiority of literary contemplation to what Moreiras calls "an active affirmation of solidarity."[8]

Such a politics of solidarity would erase distinctions of the personal and political that have historically allowed for various forms of injustice to continue unabated in the "private sphere" (domestic violence, etc.). It would overwrite distinctions between those who enjoy and those who remain devoid of all legal rights, to redirect our attention to the injustices done to immigrant fathers who are "casualties of [the] Department of Homeland Security."[9] It is a political interventionism beyond parties and programs, one that begins to build a complex apparatus of articulation between the singularity of any personal experience and the abstract juridical and political structures that enable and promote both injustice and its negation. Instead, Danticat uses the pre-existing means of a transnational public sphere of discussion to bring forward new subjects of political right; her interventions constitute within an English- and French-language speaking community a previously impossible formulation: call it the universal, egalitarian humanity of the (Haitian) people. Heretofore, Haiti has only ever been conceived by the world beyond its borders as lawlessness, savagery, chaos, brutality. Haiti, if it existed at all in North Atlantic perception, has been unthinkable in its radical humanity and democratic, egalitarian compass.[10] While the vehicles of Danticat's intervention pre-existed her (the novel and story cycle, the *New York Times* and *New Yorker*), she has intervened within these spaces to help to constitute a new political subaltern subject in this era of the globalized destruction of international law and human rights, a destruction that ranges from Kosovo and Guantánamo to the emblematic treatment of Haitian "boat people" themselves.

Danticat constructs this politics of solidarity out of a radical investment in language itself, gifted as she is with the capacity to fashion poetic signifiers that whisper to us the truth of their unsubstantiated promise from within their sedimentation in histories, cultures, and personalities. The "mother" and "father," a butterfly, a star, a passport, heaven and the sea, the "silly dreams" of a democratically elected president (Aristide) who tried for the first time in Haitian history to implement social justice for the *moun andeyo*. She passes these privileged signifiers to us, signifiers she has shined to reveal their fullest potential for production (of reflection, of emotion, of experience, of sympathy, of intersubjective awareness), and we receive them at once full of promise and empty, awaiting their substantial realization in an egalitarian democracy-to-come. When we will respond to her interpellation, Danticat will have begun the construction of a sequence of equivalence obtaining between all of her readers in their utter singularity. To read Edwidge Danticat successfully is to participate in the communal construction of a community-to-come inflected with a Haitian *aksan*. The meaning of the signifiers she invokes is never fully determined; instead, her poetic voice allows each of us to animate them with experiential content, while drawing us out of any possible merely aesthetic interiority (our own definition of "dream" or the sea) by grounding that signifier in the content of Haitian experience. To be faithful to her appeal, Danticat's transnational readership must participate in the formation of this simultaneously differential (in its cultivation of singularity) and equivalential (in its fidelity to undivided right, justice, and potential for humanity) system of political articulations. Danticat's poetry is no less than the petition for a system of universal justice beyond any national political structure. Her poetry and prose are in essence a sketching out—in both full negative relief and the blank positivity of a promising image—of the concretion of this dream-world.

The function of the poet in such a political sequence is to crystallize in pregnant image latent experiences of frustrated justice that draw us as individuals beyond the parochialism of our immediate, subjective demands. The exacting rhetorical justice of her poetic polemics allows for the crystallization of these various demands for a just society within a signifier (say, the abstract promise of "flight" beyond the impasse of all national borders). It is the openness of such a process of crystallization that we bring to fruition in the act of reading and reacting that can constitute the politics of a community beyond program, race, and nation. This is the crystallization of our own understanding that the system in which we participate has already and continues to this day unashamedly to destroy human lives and potentialities in the name of the imperialist nation-state and *its* client-states (the attempt to make Haiti safe for North Atlantic capital investment in neo-feudalized labor). Beyond any essentialist political logic (of a subservience to a formal dogma of, say, bureaucratic socialism or our current oligarchies of representative parliamentarianism) Danticat's writing heralds the initiation of a populist politics in the true sense of the word,[11] one that fully expresses and sustains the heterogeneity of any contemporary transnational community within the universal imperative to achieve social justice and an egalitarian, democratic community in the twenty-first century.

NOTES

1. Lahens, cited in Martin Munro, *Exile and Post-1946 Haitian Literature: Alexis, Depestre, Ollivier, Laferrière, Danticat* (Liverpool: Liverpool University Press, 2007), 219.

2. Ibid., 220.

3. Ibid., 231.

4. Edwidge Danticat, *Krik? Krak!* (New York: Vintage, 1996). Subsequent references are to this edition and are given after quotations in the main body of the text.

5. Rocio Davis, "Oral Narrative as Short Story Cycle: Forging Community in Edwidge Danticat's *Krik? Krak!*" *Melus* 26, no. 2 (Summer 2001): 65–81 (71).

6. Extensive documentation of this period appears in Alex Dupuy, *The Prophet and Power: Jean-Bertrand Aristide, the International Community, and Haiti* (Lanham: Rowman and Littlefield, 2007), and Peter Hallward, *Damming the Flood: Haiti, Aristide, and the Politics of Containment,* (London: Verso, 2007), ch. 2.

7. See Edwidge Danticat, "Impounded Fathers," *New York Times,* op-ed article, June 17, 2007.

8. Alberto Moreiras, *The Exhaustion of Difference: The Politics of Latin American Cultural Studies* (Durham, NC: Duke University Press, 2001), 216.

9. Danticat, "Impounded Fathers."

10. On the "stateless egalitarianism" of Haitian *Bossale* society since 1804, a social system that functioned for a century and a half until Duvalier as a highly articulated, systematic, and unassimilable negation of the dominant North Atlantic model of liberal individualism and consumerist subjectivity, see Gérard Barthélemy, *L'Univers rural haïtien: Le pays en dehors* (Paris: L'Harmattan, 1990).

11. A populist politics that, in comparison to the mere sketch I have made here, Ernesto Laclau describes systematically in his *On Populist Reason* (London: Verso, 2005).

WRITING YOUNG

Danticat's
Young Adult Fiction

KIERA VACLAVIK

omewhat to her surprise, Danticat's work has attracted a young readership from the first. "People often say I look young. Maybe I also write young," she muses in a 2005 interview. Yet the "crossover" appeal of her work is in fact readily understandable. Her very first novel, *Breath, Eyes, Memory* (1994), for example, combines simple syntax with the first-person narration of a young protagonist who experiences emotions and problems (such as first love and an eating disorder) with which many teenage readers can easily relate. The nature of her writing and its proven ability to transcend age barriers made Danticat an obvious choice for editors of series targeted specifically at young readers. To date, she has published two full works in English: *Behind the Mountains* (2002) and *Anacaona, Golden Flower* (2005).[1]

There is a great deal of common ground between these two works and Danticat's other writing. The only somewhat conspicuous absence is any mention of the sexual relations that figure so prominently in her adult works. On the other hand, exile and departure, brutality, violence, sadness, and death are as apparent in her works for young readers as in those for adults. For Danticat, the demarcation between adult and children's literature "can sometimes feel artificial," and her aims in writing for either audience are identical: "I hope to tell a good story that's both fulfilling and entertaining for my readers."[2] If, then, there is so little difference between her works for adults and for young readers, it may seem somewhat wrongheaded to consider the latter as a separate category, as is proposed here. Yet while it is undoubtedly important to recognize the continuities apparent within the various parts of her oeuvre, it is also essential that sufficient weight is given to the specificity of the writing for young readers, if for no other reason than that Danticat herself has evoked a particular role and function for this work. According to the writer, such texts provide a precious opportunity to shape first impressions and form mindsets: "I don't think young readers are more malleable than other readers but these encounters are perhaps the first for them, so they count a lot because they can add layers to the way they look at a particular group" (203).

All of which begs the question: *whose* impressions, and *whose* mindsets? Which young readers specifically does Danticat have in mind in her writing? In an interview with Katherine Capshaw Smith, Danticat is loathe to commit herself to a specific audience—a fairly common reflex among writers wary of fencing themselves in. But what she does reveal opens up important avenues concerning *what* as well as for whom she writes: "I never really think about an audience outside of myself when I write. If anything, I think of writing for the girl I was when I was fifteen, a girl who was looking for images of herself" (198). That girl was Haitian born, had spent the majority of her life in Haiti, but had been living in the United States for three years. She was multilingual, familiar with French, Kreyòl, and English. This statement, combined with the fact that she writes in English and publishes in America, suggests that she is writing, not for all Haitians, but specifically for English-speaking Haitian Americans. At the end of the same interview she reiterates the need for such readers to have texts that can serve as mirrors, providing "complex images of themselves, images that reflect their own reality" (205).

Yet we should perhaps be wary of a statement so reluctantly issued, and indeed it becomes clear in other parts of the interview and elsewhere that Danticat has a much broader audience in mind. The following three statements, all regarding *Behind the Mountains*, deal with the nature and function of the works but also reveal a great deal about their intended readership:

> it occurred to me that this was a rare chance to write something about Haitian immigration for an audience that might not be familiar with a character like Celiane Espérance, so I jumped at the chance.

My hope for the book, for the whole series in general, is that it will make children more understanding with immigrant children in their schools, give them a sense of what they went through before they came to this country, and what they still go through when they get here.[3]

I hope my books do that for the readers, introduce them to a Haitian character that they might find surprisingly like themselves.[4]

Clearly, then, Danticat's intended readership may include but is in no way limited to Haitian Americans.[5] Indeed, far from targeting such an audience, the division between children and immigrant children specifically, the use of "introduce" and "surprisingly," all imply that it is *non-Haitians* who are in fact foremost in Danticat's mind. In what follows, the extent to which the texts themselves bear out the implications of these citations is examined. In her writing, does Danticat appear to prioritize the numerically dominant non-Haitian reader, or is she able to write for several audiences simultaneously, without privileging one over the other? Does Danticat provide windows providing access to the lives of others, or mirrors, or both? Does the familiarization of the unknown inevitably entail the alienation of the known? Is it possible to write of "here and there" adequately when, for some, "there" has only been "here"?

Behind the Mountains

Forming part of the *First Person Fiction* series, which features "authors from a variety of backgrounds writing about the experience of coming to America," *Behind the Mountains* (2002) tells the story of a Haitian child, Celiane Espérance, who gets caught up in political turmoil on the island of her birth before leaving for a new life in New York.[6] According to one review by Marya Jansen-Gruber on a website for young readers, the text provides "a grim reminder of how people in other parts of the world have to live their lives day after day."[7] It is certainly the case that Danticat portrays the limitations, difficulties, and oppressiveness of daily life in Haiti. Poverty, illiteracy, and political violence are all evoked: in her rural village, Celiane shares a bed with her mother, writes by lamplight, eats food cooked on a fire, and serves as amanuensis to an illiterate woman whose daughter is in Canada. Later, in the capital, power cuts accompany the bloody and violent grappling for political power.

In more general terms, a current of didacticism concerning Haiti runs through the entire text. More or less passing references provide readers with information about the existence of a Haitian diaspora, about Haitian cuisine and produce, religious customs and traditions. Readers also learn a great deal alongside Celiane, who frequently records in her diary what she has learned in class, or by listening to the radio, speaking with people, and so on. It is in this way that readers are informed about the etymology of the country's name, the impact of Columbus's arrival, the Haitian Revolution, and the complexities of contemporary politics, especially the career of Jean-Bertrand Aristide.

But although Haitian hardships are certainly in evidence, the country and its people are by no means monolithic and uniform in *Behind the Mountains*. Both urban and rural environments are depicted, and although the heroine's preference is for the countryside, which receives lyrical eulogies on more than one occasion, this is not allowed to monopolize or push out alternatives. Celiane's own attitudes evolve; her initial dislike of the anonymity of the city is tempered by her appreciation of the cultural activities—movies and street concerts—it encompasses. Nor are her initial sentiments unanimous: Celiane's brother, Moy, "loves the city. When he is there, he looks at everything as though with new eyes."[8] In addition to leaving room for personal preferences and tastes, Danticat also portrays contrasting attitudes toward politics, as well as diametrically opposed interpretations of political events. She writes that "some thought President Aristide's party was responsible for the violence. Others thought the opposition was to blame." (53) Typically, Danticat avoids adjudication; the issue remains uncertain and unresolved. While certain characters retain their belief in the political process, venturing out to vote despite the dangers, others are confused or disenchanted. Aunt Rose's commitment is thus contrasted with her sister-in-law's bitter disillusionment with the politicians, who, she believes, ignore the country's rural communities: "Don't waste your time, Rose," Manman said. "None of those politicians are going to do anything for the country. . . . They never think about the people in the mountains. Victor had to leave so we would not eat dust up there. I vote for Victor, my husband. He is my president" (58–59).

It is thus a multifaceted country that Danticat portrays and about which she teaches her readers, but the didacticism is by no means limited to Haiti. There is also a great deal of information concerning the United States, and the interrelationship between the two countries.

Indeed, when Danticat states, "I hope to change the way the reader defines Haiti as well as the way he or she defines America," the syntax suggests that it is the revisioning of the *United States* that is primary.[9] Danticat evokes the economic power of America, which supplies the work that in turn provides the remittances sent back to Haiti, and fully acknowledges the differences between the two countries. Celiane repeatedly contrasts the size and scale of New York and Port-au-Prince and relishes the luxuries and opportunities newly available to her: "What an indulgence not to have to wash our clothes by hand! This was a great relief because I worried about washing my new heavy clothes myself" (99). Yet America is by no means portrayed as the unequivocal heaven to the Haitian hell. Celiane's comparisons are not always favorable to the United States (e.g., American neon signs are "not as colorful as the ones that Bòs Dezi made or as brightly embellished as the ones in Carrefour" [92]). Moreover, Danticat is at pains to show just how much Haiti and the United States have in common. As one journalist has observed, Danticat is "insistent on the deep, often obscured, ties between her two countries."[10] In *Behind the Mountains,* she evokes the struggles for independence with which both countries have been engaged. Similarly, in contemporary society, children are shown to be the victims of violence in New York as well as Port-au-Prince, and electoral disputes can occur in the home of democracy as much as in Haiti. Above all, the positive contribution of Haitians to the United States is conveyed in the same way as much of the information concerning Haiti. In class in New York, Celiane (and Danticat's readers) learn that the first settler in Chicago was Jean Baptiste Point du Sable and that Haitians, including future king Henri Christophe, fought alongside Americans in the latter's War of Independence. They also learn about other greats of Haitian birth (such as the naturalist John James Audubon) as well as Americans—like Lincoln—having taken an interest in Haiti. The importance of this material to Danticat is indicated by its reappearance in the *Selavi* essay. In both texts, the spin is entirely positive: there is no indication whatsoever that this relationship is, or has ever been, anything other than amicable and supportive. Apart from the benevolent protection of Aristide, there is no suggestion of American intervention, still less interference in, or exploitation of, Haitian affairs. In a multiply oriented text, the agenda is clearly not to put the United States on trial but instead to combat negative stereotypes of parasitic (Haitian) immigrants.

The whole issue of immigration is also approached with an emphasis on variety and multiplicity. In Haiti, the heroine has mixed feelings about her imminent departure: although she relishes the prospect of being reunited with her father, she is apprehensive about this very reunion since she worries about whether he has changed beyond recognition and stopped loving her. A series of interrogative statements suggest the considerable trepidation with which she views the country and experiences that await her: "Was America a prison that once you entered you were never allowed to leave? Would we be 'legal' when we got there?" "What if the plane falls out of the sky? What if we never make it to New York? What if we hate New York? What if we all hate each other when we get to New York?" (77, 83). Although her fears are for the most part unfounded, the settling-in process is by no means an easy one for Celiane, or for any member of her family. The reconfiguration of a family unit is shown to be a highly complex process. By giving due weight to the difficulties of (re)adjustment and integration, the myth of immigration as entry into the Promised Land is effectively debunked: thus, Manman's acquisition of a stove is not a source of unalloyed joy but one of arguments and tension.

In addition to the varied emotions and experiences of an individual family, Danticat also gives a sense of the multiple permutations of the immigrant experience. If the main focus is on a family in which the father leaves for America, followed by his wife and children five years later, we are also made aware of other possible patterns. Celiane's friend, Faidherbe, is adopted by his aunt and uncle in America, leaving the rest of his family in Haiti. A further example that echoes the author's own experience (outlined in the autobiographical essay at the end of the text) is provided by Celiane's other friend, Immacula, who could not join her parents in America until nine years—and three new siblings—after their departure. Observing an embrace between mother and daughter, Celiane notes: "There is awkwardness between her and Immacula, like two strangers who are just getting to know one another" (153).

In addition to relational difficulties, one of the biggest challenges for a newly arrived immigrant is, of course, assimilation of a new language, and this is repeatedly underlined in *Behind the Mountains*. With a Creolophone narrator and focalizing consciousness, Danticat conveys the difficulties and dangers of the language barrier when Celiane gets lost on her way home after her first day at school in New York: "Finally, a black car stopped. The driver rolled down the window and asked me something in English. I handed the driver the piece of paper Papa had given me. The driver said something that sounded like a command, which I did not understand. He repeated it a few times, his voice growing louder each time. I did not move. The driver got impatient, handed me back the paper and drove away" (110).

Linguistic issues are, in fact, foregrounded throughout the text. In the second part, the mass and school classes Celiane attends, as well as the radio programs to which she listens, are all, explicitly, in Kreyòl, and her fledgling acts of communication using the English language are noted (96, 126). All of this is, of course, written by Danticat in English. This incongruity is flagged in the aforementioned essay that follows the novel: the reader is asked to "imagine that Celiane wrote these words in her native tongue and that I am merely her translator" (166). Danticat's employment of English has attracted considerable criticism and does, of course, preclude access to the text by a vast number of Haitians.[11] Yet her deployment of language shows consideration for, and respect toward, both Haitian and non-Haitian Anglophones. Opening with a Kreyòl expression, and quickly incorporating French-language words such as "pensées" (2), Danticat's novel is happily heteroglossic. This does not in itself denote concern for a Haitian audience since foreign-language words could be incorporated as a form of exoticization signaling the priority of a non-Haitian audience. But Danticat's approach is very different: via a range of strategies, due attention is paid to the needs and competencies of the various parts of her readership. A frequent pattern is the use of italicized Kreyòl words immediately followed by their English equivalent, as in the opening words: "*Ti liv mwen*, my sweet little book." This strategy, which in a Kreyòl-French configuration is equally apparent in the work of Patrick Chamoiseau, achieves a compromise between the need to explain and the need to maintain the narrative flow. In several other instances, the use of apposition means that explanations or definitions of Kreyòl terms are seamlessly incorporated within the text, e.g.: "Manman will make her delicious coconut drink, *kremas*"; "Moy will finish his *fanal*, a cardboard lantern built in the shape of a *tap tap*" (71). But there are also several occasions where Kreyòl words stand alone, leaving the non-Creolophone reader to determine their signification from the surrounding context, such as in the following passage: "The first thing we did . . . was call Tante Rose to wish her *Jwaye Nowèl*" (95). This process of decryption is at times far from straightforward, as in the following example near the beginning of the text: "Some of my classmates were playing hopscotch, marbles, jumping rope, and singing while they twirled themselves to near dizziness in a *won*" (12). Here, Haitians are entirely relieved of unnecessary explanation while non-Haitians find themselves (however briefly) in a situation not dissimilar to that of Celiane dumbly holding out the paper to the driver of the black car.

All in all, then, *Behind the Mountains* is much more than a young American's crib sheet to the hardships of Haitian life and goes far beyond merely bolstering or engendering a sense of superiority. While it is certainly didactic, the didacticism by no means denotes a privileging of a non-Haitian readership. Nor does the use of English imply disregard for, and exclusion of, all Haitians. Danticat relates a story about what it is like to leave one place and to arrive in another in such a way that it has something to offer the various constituent parts of her audience. For those with no knowledge of the point of departure, or the experience of departing—the non-Haitian readers without knowledge or experience of Haiti or of immigration—the text serves as a window. It enables insight into a specific set of conditions and circumstances and, by humanizing what is frequently a dehumanized menace, encourages empathy and understanding. It also serves to defamiliarize the known; to see the surrounding world afresh and to see America, its snow, major leagues and projects, again for the first time. For readers who do know Haiti or the upheaval of immigration, the text serves as a mirror, offering depictions of lived experience. It provides the validation and comfort of self-recognition and solidarity. In short, *Behind the Mountains* is a far more complex text than is suggested in the aforementioned review by Jansen-Gruber, who focuses entirely on the first half of the text. Indeed, it is precisely Danticat's introduction of complexity, nuance, and multiplicity in all areas of the text that means she is able to provide for the needs of the different parts of her readership.

Anacaona, Golden Flower

Published just three years later, Danticat's second text specifically targeted at young readers bears many similarities to her first. It too employs an intimate first-person narration and an epistolary form. It also forms part of a series, in this case the "Royal Diaries" series encompassing some twenty texts, each of which features the fictional diary of a real princess from a range of geographical and historical contexts supplemented by a range of documentary evidence.[12] In *Anacaona,* as in *Behind the Mountains,* language issues are also foregrounded from the first. The text begins: "I am Anacaona. In my language, the Taíno language, *ana* means 'flower' and *caona* means 'golden'. Thus I am called the 'golden flower.'"[13] Italicized foreign-language words are incorporated throughout and are handled in much the same way as the previous text (e.g., "when I will be a *siani,* a married woman" (6); "whether we are *nitaínos* or *naborías,* whether we were born of high or low stature" [47]). Two and a half pages of Taíno words with their English translation are included in the extensive paratextual apparatus that follows the novel. As in *Behind the Mountains,* this includes author-based material: here, a section written in the third-person but involving extensive quotations deals with Danticat's own background, her connection with the subject matter, and her approach to the writing of the book. In addition to the lexical and biographical components, there is also a historical note that takes the form of a short essay, as well as a genealogical tree accompanied by a brief description of eleven key Taíno figures. The dossier is completed with a series of sixteenth-century and contemporary images as well as a map of modern Hispaniola, with a large-scale inset showing the island's location between the two American continents.

All this clearly has a strong didactic function, but the didacticism goes well beyond the paratext. Throughout the fictionalized account, a whole range of information is conveyed: customs and rites, legends, dress, agriculture, geography, flora, and the climate are all touched on. But as in *Behind the Mountains,* the *utile* is pegged onto the *dulce;* the reader ingests the information as she or he is drawn into, and carried along by, the story of Anacaona, which also resembles that of Celiane in several ways. It too tells of a young woman's departure from her place of birth and arrival in a new home and the difficulties—of loneliness and homesickness—associated with such a shift. Although there is no mention of the rape that Danticat foregrounds in a discussion of the figure of Anacaona some years before, the text does, like its predecessor, portray violence, death, and bloodshed.[14] Indeed, the accounts here are much more detailed, graphic, and harrowing than in *Behind the Mountains:* "All around us, burial plots had been dug up, bones thrown aside, and golden objects removed from sacred soil. Nearby, a pregnant woman lay dead, her still bulging belly leaning slightly away from her body. Corpses were strewn all along our path, heads separated from bodies. The body of one dead child was leaning against a post, as if he had been carefully hooked there" (148).

As here, or with the catastrophic effects of the hurricane upon Anacaona's world, much of the text has a great deal of contemporary relevance. Such an observation is, of course, predicated on the one major difference between Danticat's two works for young readers, namely, that *Anacaona* adopts a historical rather than modern-day setting. Thus, the heroine leaves her home after the tactical (but also desired) marriage that allies the tribes of Xaraguá and of Maguana. The violence portrayed consists in the raids of Xaraguan villages by the Kalinas (Caribs) and in the arrival of the Spanish, seen—like snow in *Behind the Mountains*—for the very first time: "The pale men have reached our shores. We were awakened at dawn by their clamorous voices like none I have ever heard and the sight of men unlike any I have ever seen. They were tall, nearly twice our size. Their heads were round as the full moon and what we could see of their skin—for they were covered in dark, heavy-looking material from their shoulders down to their hide-clothed feet—was indeed pale, though not as pale as I had imagined. Their hands and faces were slightly pink, as if only recently singed by the sun" (128). It is with "hollowed-looking metal sticks" that "fired bursts of lightning" (128) that these men wreak much of the havoc that is described in detail. In addition to the atrocities committed by the Spanish, the Taíno attempts to resist and retaliate are also portrayed.

Danticat thus elaborates upon a moment referred to fleetingly in *Behind the Mountains.* Although much less explicitly in the second text, the connectedness of past and present is apparent in both books. But while in *Behind the Mountains* Danticat historicizes the present by, for example, emphasizing the longstanding U.S.-Haitian interactions, in *Anacaona* she facilitates access to the past. The challenges of this second text are not inconsiderable: without written sources, Danticat must project into and (re)create the past, as well as conjuring up a language appropriate to her subject. But Danticat clearly relishes such linguistic challenges: her solution in this case is, as we have seen, to weave Taíno terms into a form of English that, especially in its syntax, is frequently formal and archaic.

Danticat thus brings to her readers a modern reconstruction of the past. The latter being a foreign country, her text is necessarily a window rather than a mirror. This is true for each of the parts of her audience. A Haitian reader may, arguably, be more curious about the text and better able to relate past and present, yet on the whole the alterity of the past serves here as a leveling device. The subject matter effectively places *all* Danticat's readers—Haitian and non-Haitian—in the same boat. *Anacaona* thus makes boat people of Haitians and Americans alike.

Yet within a text whose historical setting thus brings a certain unification, multiplicity continues to be promoted. We have already noted the incorporation of Taíno terms. Another example is the portrayal of nature. Like the Port-au-Prince of *Behind the Mountains,* which is both exciting and frightening, aesthetically pleasing and dangerous, so nature is shown here to be both positive and negative, benevolent and cruel. Anacaona is given a stone pierced by lightning, and as she holds it she reflects: "Perhaps this almost transparent rock acquired its beauty during the same hurricane that took the lives of my friends. But nature, as Simihena tells me, is as marvelous a carver as she is a destroyer" (95). However, by far the most important manifesto for multiplicity comes in the closing pages. Anacaona is not only a ruler but also a poet and storyteller, and after a battle with the Spanish, which this time results in victory for the indigenous peoples, she recites a long tale, "an account of our season of war" (155). In addition to the battle itself, the heroine also relates her marriage, arrival in Maguana, and the birth of her daughter, as well as many of the legends of her ancestors. Her explanation of the fullness and variety of her tale closes the main part of the novel and constitutes an eloquent protest against reductionism:

> I told such a lengthy tale because I did not want our battle with the pale men to become the only story our people would ever recite from now on. For we had other stories, too, happy as well as sad ones. Our encounter with the pale men was only a small piece of that story. Surely an important piece, but not the most important.
>
> Yes, I want our victory over the pale men to be a tale that will inspire us when we have other battles to fight, one that reminds us that, like Kalinas, we are a strong and powerful people. I do want it to be a story whose veracity the young ones will ask me to confirm when I am an old woman, a story that my Higuamota will

tell and retell to her own children. But I do not want it to become the only story we ever have to share with one another. It cannot be. It must not be. (155–56)

The final short phrases belie a sense of anxiety and lack of control, which are fully in line with what posterity had in store for Anacaona and her people. The indigenous populations of the land now known as Haiti have effectively been reduced to victims, and to some extent Danticat is herself guilty of this in the fleeting references to the Spanish invasion in both *Behind the Mountains* and the *Selavi* essay. In *Anacaona*, she seeks to redress the balance: giving the "victims" a voice, privileging their perspective, emphasizing their pride and dignity, and demonstrating, in short, that their identity far exceeds their victimhood.

Here, too, Danticat surely has an eye on the present. Anacaona's words are resonant and poignant in a contemporary context that all too frequently reduces Haiti to one or (at best) two propositions: the first black republic, and the poorest country of the Western Hemisphere. Haiti is commonly portrayed as a hell peopled by victims and villains. As we have seen, Danticat steers well clear of such simplification and atomization in both *Anacaona* and *Behind the Mountains*, in which Haiti is shown to be linked to the United States just as the past is linked to the present. Of course, the texts do not and cannot ever convey the full complexity of the situations portrayed, as the political and sexual aporias noted here suggest. Nevertheless, both texts emphasize complexity and the multiple rather than the monolithic. Danticat's use of language turns out to be perhaps the most important area in which multiplicity is maintained. Despite the use of English (and statements by Danticat and others) neither of her works privileges the non-Haitian reader over the Haitian. The text that serves as a window does so with respect to the entire readership, while *Behind the Mountains* can be both window and mirror because it constantly adopts the "both/and" rather than "either/or" approach. Danticat's writing for young readers can, in short, be many things to many people, and it is as a result of her stress on diversity and complexity that multiple functions are enabled, and a multiple readership served.

NOTES

1. Danticat also provides a short essay at the end of Youme's *Selavie* (2004), a picture book for young readers about Haiti. A further, French-language text, *Céli-*

mène: Conte de fée pour fille d'immigrante, trans. Stanley Péan (Montréal: Mémoire d'encrier, 2009) appeared in November 2009 as part of Mémoire d'encrier's new children's literature collection, "L'arbre du voyageur."

2. Katherine Capshaw Smith, "Splintered Families, Enduring Connections: An Interview with Edwidge Danticat," *Children's Literature Association Quarterly* 30, no. 2 (Summer 2005): 194–205 (197). Subsequent references are to this interview and are given after quotations in the main body of the text.

3. Terry Hong, "The First Person Fiction Series for Young Adults: A Conversation with the Authors," *Bloomsbury Review* 24, no. 1 (January/February 2004): 7, http://www.bloomsburyreview.com/Archives/2004/First%20Person%20Fiction.pdf (accessed February 12, 2009).

4. Smith, "Splintered Families," 203.

5. Danticat's desire for the widest possible audience for her work is further indicated in the following quotations from the interview with Smith: "no matter who the reader is" (198); "the readers, both Haitians and American kids of other backgrounds" (203).

6. Other titles in the series are Ana Veciana-Suarez, *Flight to Freedom* (2002); John Son, *Finding My Hat* (2004); Judith Ortiz Cofer, *Call Me Maria* (2006).

7. Marya Jansen-Gruber, "First Person Fiction," http://www.kidsreads.com/series/series-first-person-titles.asp (accessed February 12, 2009).

8. Edwidge Danticat, *Behind the Mountains* (New York: Orchard Books, 2002), 26. Subsequent references are to this edition and are given after quotations in the main body of the text.

9. Smith, "Splintered Families," 203.

10. Maya Jaggi, "Island Memories," *Guardian* (London), November 20, 2004, http://www.guardian.co.uk/books/2004/nov/20/featuresreviews.guardianreview9 (accessed February 9, 2009).

11. The maintenance of a wider Haitian audience via the publication of her latest book for young readers in French should be noted in this context.

12. Other titles in the series include Kathryn Lasky, *Marie Antoinette, Princess of Versailles* (2000); Patricia C. Kissack, *Nzingha, Warrior Queen of Matamba* (2000); and Patricia Clark Smith, *Weetamoo, Heart of Pocassetts* (2003).

13. Edwidge Danticat, *Anacaona, Golden Flower* (New York: Scholastic, 2005), 5. Subsequent references are to this edition and are given after quotations in the main body of the text.

14. "She was raped and killed and her village pillaged in a tradition of ongoing cruelty and atrocity." See Edwidge Danticat, "We Are Ugly, but We Are Here," *Caribbean Writer* 10 (1996), http://www.webster.edu/~corbetre/haiti/literature/danticat-ugly.htm (accessed February 11, 2009).

TRAVELING, WRITING

Danticat's
After the Dance

CHARLES FORSDICK

After the Dance, an account of a 2001 journey to the carnival at Jacmel in southern Haiti, is Edwidge Danticat's only current contribution to the genre of travel writing.[1] Commissioned as part of the "Crown Journeys" series, the text represents a departure from the author's previous and subsequent works of fiction, although, as I argue below, it nevertheless belongs to the more general and sustained reflection, which characterizes the rest of her writings, on what James Clifford dubs "travelling" and "dwelling."[2] Haitian authors have rarely written texts that might explicitly be identified as travelogues, and Danticat's venturing into the field of travel writing thus raises questions about the status, nature, and future potential of this genre. At the same time, what Angeletta K. M. Gourdine calls this "travelogue of native (re)discovery" nuances the author's own explorations of the complex itineraries and entangled memories—her own and those of others—that connect Haiti with North America and elsewhere.[3] The aim of this essay is to suggest the ways in which Danticat's text engages with, draws upon, and in many ways challenges the traditions of travel writing, while simultaneously producing a work that is in dialogue with her own fictional writing.

Genre, Gender, Location

Although authors and readers may not always be conscious of this process, the boundaries of most literary genres are carefully controlled.

Writers and their audience in certain cultures and traditions favor a range of literary forms, but there remain other genres to which access would appear to be more closely policed. Travel literature is a particularly striking example of these strategies of inclusion and exclusion. The form has traditionally been produced by a certain category of writer, often Western, white, well educated, and male, defined according to strict parameters of culture, class, gender, and ethnicity. The result is that travel writing as a genre tends to privilege certain types of journey to the detriment of others, leading inevitably to a progressive shrinking of the semantic field of what we understand by "travel." The emergence of postcolonial literatures has permitted a challenge to such restriction, and the pioneering work of a disparate and often loosely defined tradition of early black travel writers—such as Richard Wright and Bernard Dadié, as well as their precursors such as Olaudah Equiano, Mary Seacole, and Nancy Prince—has been complemented by the more recent narratives of authors such as Tété-Michel Kpomassie, Maureen Stone, and Gary Younge.[4] At the same time, publishers and scholars have become increasingly sensitive to the gendering of travel narratives, on the one hand unearthing a largely forgotten corpus of Victorian women's travel writing (particularly through the activity of Virago in the 1980s) and on the other bringing to readers' attention the existence of a contemporary tradition of female-authored travelogues.[5]

Despite these developments, encompassing both retrospective recovery and present recognition, the channeling of travel writing along lines of gender and ethnicity persists, and travel writers continue to be associated with what one critic has dubbed a guild identity.[6] (It is striking that of the fourteen authors published in or announced for the "Crown Journeys" series in which *After the Dance* appears, Danticat and Myla Goldberg remain the only women.) As Maureen Stone asks in *Black Woman Walking:* "But what of those travellers who never write? How far have gender, class, race and sexual orientation circumscribed the art of travel?"[7] Underpinning the question is an acute awareness of the cleavage between travel and the means of its textualization. As the recent anthologies referenced above have revealed, the apparent absence of black writers from the travel writing genre does not necessarily imply that an archive of black travel literature does not exist. James Clifford makes clear in *Routes,* however, that the literary privileging of certain journeys to the detriment of others muffles many travel accounts and restricts the experiential range that travel writing tends to articulate. Clifford's response is a radical prizing open of the genre, supplementing the exclusively literary with other textual and narrative forms describing journeys undertaken by "a long list of actors [currently] relegated to the margins," in order to transform an exclusive enclave into a diverse site at which a multiplicity of competing, contradictory, but often simultaneous journeys may be analyzed: "If contemporary migrant populations are not to appear as mute, passive straws in the political-economic winds, we need to listen to a wide range of 'travel stories' (not 'travel literature' in the bourgeois sense)."[8] Clifford's rethinking of the parameters of travel writing impacts on understandings of "travel" itself, which is expanded to encompass a range of different experiences of mobility and displacement. This extension of a semantic field, whose risks Clifford himself acknowledges, has been subjected to close and critical scrutiny. For instance, bell hooks has claimed that "holding on to the concept of 'travel' as we know it is also a way to hold on to imperialism."[9] In Clifford's understanding, however, "travel" becomes a federating concept in relation to which various types of journeying may be compared and contrasted, and it is in this sense that *After the Dance* may be seen to supplement and in many ways complement the many journeys—exilic or migrant—that underpin Danticat's fictional work.

Haiti, Travel, and Writing

Haiti, as J. Michael Dash amply illustrates, serves as a recurrent destination in European and North American travel writing.[10] What is more, through this repeated representation, it has acquired a tropological status, exemplifying and accentuating certain pejorative assumptions about postcolonial cultures that are perhaps summed up in the subtitle of Philippe Girard's *Paradise Lost:* that is, *Haiti's Tumultuous Journey from Pearl of the Caribbean to Third World Hotspot.*[11] This narrative of colonial prosperity transformed into postcolonial chaos is a common one, reflected in what Antony Maingot has described as a "terrified consciousness" of Haiti, and what Dash has dubbed a "repulsive otherness" or "predetermined strangeness."[12] In the development of such a national image, the role of travel writers from elsewhere, indulging in seemingly obligatory references to an exoticized Vodou, to zombification, and even (especially in earlier texts) to cannibalism, is not insignificant. Indeed, in the accounts of their journeys, many travelers to Haiti exemplify in a Caribbean context the same archival and textual sedimentation—dependent more on accumulated stereotypes than on any direct observation—that Edward Said describes in *Orientalism*. Graham Greene's *The Comedians*, a fictionalized account of his own stay in Duvalier's Haiti (to which "Papa Doc" famously replied in a retaliatory publication), is often cited as a key example of this tendency.[13] It belongs, however, to a substantial tradition of twentieth-century accounts of journeys to Haiti, some of the earliest of which—as the very titles of John Houston Craige's *Black Bagdad* (1933) and *Cannibal Cousins* (1934) clearly suggest—served as a justification of the "civilizing mission" underpinning the U.S. occupation of Haiti in 1915–34. Even in more recent works, such as Ian Thomson's popular *Bonjour Blanc: A Journey through Haiti* (which, like *After the Dance*, also describes an arrival in Jacmel during Mardi Gras, and to which Danticat refers in her account), Haiti becomes the site for cultivating self-consciously extreme journeys in which the quest for a zombie and attendance at a Vodou ceremony are seemingly obligatory.[14]

Dash's *Haiti and the United States* is an innovative contribution to studies in travel writing. It presents the discursive construction and domestication of Haiti, primarily through U.S. mythmaking, as a counterpoint to an emergent reaction to external travelers to be found among Haitian writers. Edwidge Danticat's contribution to travel writing, *After the Dance*, is thus part of the reconfiguration of the genre's boundaries described above. There are nevertheless few formal travelogues by Haitian authors, and even fewer by Haitian women: travel writers have traditionally written about Haiti, and Haitians have rarely produced travelogues describing their own journeys. That is not to say, however, that travel in its various forms has not played a key role in Haitian literature. One of the early texts in a national literary canon, Flignau's drama *L'Haïtien expatrié* (1804), is as its title suggests an account of exile, and it was similarly an enforced exile that triggered the writing of a key Haitian text, Toussaint Louverture's memoir, produced while its author was in prison at Joux and published by Joseph Saint-Rémy in 1850.[15] This tendency became particularly apparent, however, in the twentieth century, when authors began not only to describe foreign travelers to Haiti in their often fictional writings but also to privilege in their writing the Haitian experience of displacement, exile, and diasporization.

An early short story by Edmond Laforest ("Le crâne de l'Indian

Ciguäyo" [1902]), for instance, mocks an English anthropologist, whereas later works by Jacques-Stephen Alexis and J. B. Cinéas represent visiting North American scholars. Such texts reflect the tendency in much postcolonial writing for authors to respond to a long history of being represented by others; given the sensationalism of many external accounts of Haiti, this response among Haitian authors is arguably more marked and more vehement than elsewhere. At the same time, the tendency for Haitian "travelees" (traditionally exoticized, silenced, and "traveled over" in journey narratives) to write back may be seen as part of a shift toward focusing more on the mobility of Haitian culture itself. Jean Jonassaint has identified the exile experienced by a generation of authors under the Duvaliers as instrumental in this evolution, with the increased traffic of people to elsewhere in the Caribbean and in particular to the United States leading to a re-situation of Haiti in relation to a variety of transnational axes.[16] The errancy that characterizes the work of an author such as René Depestre, for instance, triggers questions—albeit with very different emphases—similar to those often essential to travel writing, regarding the nature of "home" and the possibility of return; and a text such as Emile Ollivier's *Passages,* centered on Miami, focuses on the implications for a national culture of increasing diasporization.[17]

There is a risk that a privileging of a "diasporic" Haitian literature, emphasizing the complexity of intercultural connections, downplays the characteristics of the work of authors, such as Frankétienne, who have stayed. Yet many texts focused specifically on Haiti's island space—such as Danticat's *Farming of Bones* (1998), inspired by Jacques-Stephen Alexis's *Compère Général Soleil* (1955)—pay equal attention to the intracultural flows, especially relating to rural exodus, that have shaped the country's recent history.[18] It is to such a tradition—"ethnographic" in diverse ways, inscribing the experiences of Haitians leaving, and returning to, Haiti, as well as those of foreign visitors (such as the female sex tourists in Dany Laferrière's *Vers le Sud*)—that Danticat's work belongs.[19]

Danticat as Travel(ing) Writer

Danticat's first novel, *Breath, Eyes, Memory* (1994), is an account of Sophie Caco's experience of rootedness, dislocation, and alienation as she travels to join her mother in New York and returns to Haiti on a complex journey that lasts for the whole of the text.[20] The narrative begins with a journey to Port-au-Prince, emphasizing the double displacement that Sophie's journey to Brooklyn implies. Whereas *Breath, Eyes, Memory* focuses on a traveling protagonist, tracking her journeys between Haiti and the United States, the interlinked short stories of *Krik? Krak!* present a variety of characters in motion: refugees on a sinking boat, a man seeking to flee Haiti in a hot-air balloon, a mother and daughter negotiating the alienating spaces of New York. In the final story, "Caroline's Wedding," a priest addresses his Haitian congregation as "Transients. Nomads."[21] Indeed, these are designations that might apply to the characters of Danticat's subsequent works: Amabelle, the heroine of *The Farming of Bones* (1998), forced out of the Dominican Republic and across the Haitian border as a result of the massacres of migrant cane workers in 1937, but returning in old age to the site of these earlier traumas; the various migrants and exiles constituting the cast of *The Dew Breaker* (2005), whose interconnected, disconnected journeys form the book's fragmented narrative; Celiane Espérance, the young narrator of *Behind the Mountains* (2002), whose diary recounts her departure from Haiti during the upheavals leading to Jean-Bertrand Aristide's re-election to power in 2000, and her slow adjustment to a new life with her family in New York. In Danticat's novels and short narratives, the relationship between journeys and stories is made tangible in repeated attention to the trappings of travel and separation: suitcases, photographs, letters, cassette tapes freighting voices of the absent, personal memories (significantly, in *The Dew Breaker,* memories of a first meeting between Michel and his wife at the Jacmel carnival). These are the objects that signal distance, while at the same time suggesting the possibility of its bridging through memory or indirect contact; they are the props whereby connections are maintained and the mobility of a diasporized culture signaled. Already in *Breath, Eyes, Memory,* however, the significance of return to Haiti as a place recovered and reconceptualized as "home" becomes clear. The tensions between the deterritorialization implicit in migration and the reterritorialization inherent in settlement elsewhere persist in the constant presence of Haiti as a site of possible, even necessary, return.

The generic conventions that *After the Dance* adopts permit the association of Danticat with a small group of Caribbean authors—such as Edouard Glissant, the Naipauls (both V. S. and Shiva), and Andrew Salkey—all of whom have written texts that are commonly and critically accepted as "travel writing." The text inscribes itself, however, into the questioning of the nature and location of "home" described above, as well as into an exploration of the identity of the diasporic subject—as tourist, traveler, or "revenant"—as she returns to a culture to which she was once native, in which she was once a "travelee." As such, it belongs at the same time to a wider corpus of "travel literature," understood according to James Clifford's definition of the term discussed above. The interest of *After the Dance* lies precisely in its location at an intersection of these competing, even contradictory, traditions. On the one hand, through its paratextual markers, intertextual references, and adoption of discursive conventions, it is part of an instantly recognizable tradition of travel writing. On the other, given its author's relationship to and knowledge of the place to which she travels, her sensitivity to the inhabitants she meets, and the access that her cultural and linguistic competence grants,[22] the text is to be integrated into the wider archive—both of Haitian literature and of travel literature—concerned with questions of exile, migrancy, and mobility.

The production of a formal travelogue, a genre whose links to autobiography or the memoir are manifest, permits Danticat an engagement with her personal journeys that remains only implicit in her fictional output. Although in interviews, prefaces, and various other short texts she describes the itineraries that have defined her own life, it is only in *After the Dance* that these are granted prominence. There is little actual travel in the text, given its detailed focus on a specific site, but the 2001 journey described is itself underpinned by memories of a series of other travels, not least of which are Danticat's childhood migration to the United States and subsequent return visits to Haiti arranged under the auspices of the Ministry of Haitians Living Abroad.

The journey to Jacmel is presented as the completion of a rite denied to the narrator as a child, when her pastor uncle removed the family from Port-au-Prince during the carnival season. Experiencing carnival vicariously in New York, through Wyclef Jean's 1997 *Carnival* album (13) or VHS tapes sold in Haitian music stores (15), Danticat styles herself as a slightly awkward "distant observer" (16), set apart from this key event in Haitian—and wider Caribbean—society not only by residence abroad but also by the nature of her local upbringing. Carnival accordingly acquires the status of a re-entry point into Haitian culture, a moment at which an everyday mask slips, and the reader is granted (some sort of) access to the sense of place that the traveler seeks. It is in the light of these observations about contact and re-acquaintance that the final three sections of this essay explore issues central to *After the Dance*—and to travel writing more generally: intertextuality; travel methodology; and the persistence of other, competing journeys.

After the Dance: Text and Intertext

A common critique of travel writing, articulated—as discussed above—by scholars such as Edward Said, is that the genre's practitioners rely so much on intertextual reference, replicating tropes and stereotypes bequeathed by earlier travelers, that they often become insensitive to the intricacies of the places through which they travel. This is not so much evidence of a largely redundant argument about the "authenticity" of the representations of elsewhere (which can never be more than representations) as a serious questioning of the nature of the travelogue's referent: geographical or textual, experiential or archival? Danticat, like many travel writers, avoids the extremes that such binaries imply, freighting her account of Jacmel through apparently direct and close engagement with the place, as well as through the reading of a variety of sources in which the city plays a role. The intertexts, explicit and implicit, of *After the Dance* are many and varied, drawing on novels and poetry, travel narratives (both literary and journalistic) and conventional guidebooks, and these are supplemented with references from a number of academic studies, ranging, across a series of disciplines, from cultural studies to history of art. This reliance on such a range of textual material might, in part, be read as evidence of Danticat's uneasiness with the genre in which she is operating: certain references seem largely redundant or undigested, and some reference to accounts of previous journeys to Jacmel (such as the novelist Tracy Chevalier's 1997 article in *The Independent* [67]) appear to add little to the author's own account. There is, however, a refreshing if reckless honesty to the inclusion of references to the guidebooks Danticat consulted—such as the *Lonely Planet Guide* (27) and the *Petit Futé* (67)—as if she eschews the majority of travel writers' residual desire for anti-touristic individuality in order to make clear her ambiguous status as what Gourdine dubs a "native touring her homeland."[23]

Such open acknowledgment of the supplementation of local knowledge with its prepackaged tourist equivalent is linked to the text's practical, even pedagogic, imperatives. The "Crown Journeys" series invites authors to describe a journey through a place in which they have a particular interest, the only apparent stipulation being that this should be on foot. The series' publisher Steve Ross, while alluding to the armchair tourist market at which titles are targeted, nevertheless stresses the portability of the volumes, seeing their potential transformation into audiobooks as an enhancement of their practicality for travelers in the field.[24] As such, the series contributes to the wider phenomenon according to which certain travel books dictate trends and open new tourist destinations.[25] Danticat presents, as a result, practical information—details of accommodation, for instance, such as the Pension Kraft (17), the Cyvadier Plage hotel (34), and the Auberge de la Visite (104)—and introduces the carnival through reference to a range of scholarly studies.[26] Such open evidence of the wide research on which preparation for and subsequent processing of the journey depended is unusual in contemporary travel writing, whose journalistic emphases often tend to erase, in an effort to persuade the reader of originality and to avoid any academic overtones, the multiple sources of the text.

These clear traces of preparatory reading, absent from a historical novel such as *The Farming of Bones*, reveal Danticat's self-conscious adjustment to an unfamiliar form as she negotiates the travelogue. At the same time, they are a deliberate reflection of her understanding of the travel described in the text as a multilayered activity: the physical passage through space is accompanied by the creation of wider connections, triggered by reading as well as by the remembering discussed above. Central to this process is an engagement with other texts that specifically "write" Jacmel. This aspect of the account illustrates Christine Montalbetti's claims that such intertextuality is a formal, generic marker of the travelogue, and Danticat makes clear that her own account supplements a number of recent works of travel writing that represent the city.[27] At the same time, however, she engages with the writing of place to be found, in both poetry and fiction, in works such as Rodney Saint-Eloi's *Pierres anonymes*.[28] Central to the account remains René Depestre's *Hadriana dans tous mes rêves*, a novel that features equally in the work of other travelers who, as Danticat says in *After the Dance*, are "looking for Hadriana" (67), such as Ian Thomson and Eric Sarner, in the second of whose accounts the novel achieves the status of a "relique."[29] Depestre is present from the text's opening epigraph, and a short chapter, "Hadriana in Jacmel's Dreams," is devoted to him. *After the Dance* acknowledges the importance of *Hadriana's* author in perceptions of Haiti—"Depestre's novel has such influence that pieces of it seem to appear everywhere" (66)—noting even the use of an adapted version of its title in the section of a national tourist guide devoted to Jacmel.

However, instead of using the novel, as tends to be the case in other travelogues, as a literary guidebook or inevitable reference, Danticat engages with it in a dialogue that might be read in similar terms to that which she initiates with Jacques-Stephen Alexis in *The Farming of Bones*.[30] It is this aspect of *After the Dance* that reveals its anglophone author's self-positioning in relation to a francophone Haitian canon. Danticat's allusions to Depestre signal not so much an anxiety of influence as an affiliation with a diasporic Haitian literature of which he was one of the first prominent exponents. At the same time, however, whereas *Hadriana* represents an imagined return through the evocation of the past, with the protagonists being reunited not in Haiti but in Jamaica, *After the Dance* signals a direct and contemporary reengagement with, and reaffirmation of, place. Developing Depestre's theme, Danticat claims: "A case can be made that the Jacmel I am visiting now cannot help but be a slightly zombified version of its former self" (69). The cautious, impersonal language makes it clear that this is not a case that she will herself be making. The clear attachment to the city—a key feature of all the volumes in the "Crown Journeys" series—distinguishes Danticat's account from Depestre's, which has been represented by Joan Dayan as a novel "disconnected from historical contexts" in which the narrator "abandons the inhabitants of Haiti to their fate, apparently forgetting their continued struggles against dictatorship, repression, and poverty."[31] Danticat's text is, by contrast, the account of an accommodation with change, a rejection of nostalgia in favor of an acknowledgment of modernization and diasporization. It seeks to situate historical traces of the past in the mobility of the present: "Simon Bolívar's house is a dress shop. Ogé's fort is a soccer field. Anacaona is living in Providence, Rhode Island. History is moving on" (49). Such a departure from Depestre becomes particularly apparent in the two final sections of the chapter, which discuss the modes of travel Danticat adopts and the implications for interrogations of identity these entail.

Walking through Carnival: Travel and the Attention to Place

After the Dance is primarily an account of dwelling or, in James Clifford's terms, of "traveling in dwelling."[32] Exploiting the methodology inherent in the "Crown Journeys" series, made clear in the emphasis in the work's subtitle, "A Walk through Carnival," Danticat engages in what Michael Cronin has called "vertical travel" and adopts a peripatetic mode of journeying to offer a microscopic account of a single site, much like the painted "microlandscapes" of Ronald Mews to which Danticat refers in her account (92–93).[33] Although the travelogue permits reflection on phenomena such as deforestation affecting the whole of the country (32, 86, 100), the macroscopic pretensions of an all-encompassing gaze remain, therefore, absent. Instead, Danticat's narrator uses the deceleration implicit in walking in order to pay attention to the entangled detail—both historical and contemporary, lived and fictional—that characterizes the city of Jacmel and its surrounding area.

The choice of Jacmel is a complex one, challenging many previous representations of Haiti, yet risking, it might be argued, a nostalgic exceptionalism. On the one hand, Danticat's representation of the city counters the (for a Western traveler) dangerous urban exoticism of Port-au-Prince, regularly presented by writers such as Graham Greene and Ian Thomson as metonymic of the chaotic state of the rest of the country. Although there is a residual if largely exceptional sense of danger (Danticat describes the five American Airlines employees drowned on Ti Mouyaj beach [127], the two French tourists and their Haitian driver murdered in 2000 [81–82], and recent tropical storms), Jacmel is posited as a corrective to much travel writing of Haiti: a still-functioning and far from "zombified" enclave, in which tourism persists and in which the annual carnivals, local and national, appear to thrive. On the other hand, the focus on Jacmel nevertheless permits the projection of a certain vision of Haiti: its New Orleans–style architecture, relative inaccessibility, and traces of nineteenth-century grandeur grant the place an exceptionalism that might be seen to lend itself to a denial of the city's "co-evalness" with the rest of the island.[34] It is in this way that Jacmel functions in *The Dew Breaker*, where the mother of Gabrielle Fonteneau (TV star and art collector, who had intended to purchase Ka's sculpture "Father") describes the city as "a place where we can say the rain is sweeter, the dust is lighter, our beaches prettier," in stark contrast to memories of involvement in dystopian dictatorship that Ka's father seeks to repress.[35]

This double bind, in which the travel writer, in engaging with a single site, is torn between the pitfalls of forced representativity and the risks of localized, unrepresentative selectivity, becomes most evident in the choice of the text's key subject: carnival. Gourdine criticizes the traveler's choice of activity, seeing it as a "theme-park-like venture."[36] It is important to stress, however, that carnival is only part of the city that Danticat projects, for her journey begins with a reflection on the cemetery (visited also by Thomson and Sarner), presented as one of several "entryways . . . to any town or city, the best places to become acquainted with the tastes of the inhabitants, both present and gone" (25).[37] Other focal points in the text permit an essential reflection on the status of the past in the present and the possible futures whose imagination these traces of history might permit. The search for a Watt steam engine on the Habitation Price, details of which are included in the Petit Futé guide, epitomizes for Gourdine an invocation of the "trope of timelessness."[38] The evocation of this unlabeled object—Danticat says, "I like the blank slate, the silence, which allows for ambiguity. . . . There is neither forced celebration nor condemnation in the moment. It is simply a flash of an era frozen in time" (91)—is not so much to do with fantasies of tourist desire as with resistance of the processes of commodification and instrumentalization of the past, according to which tourist sites often function. Danticat avoids the prescriptive overtones of formal historical markers, granting this "traveling" object an opacity that encourages a different mode of participation in place while permitting the author to imagine the narratives it conceals: "two centuries' worth of tales about the changes, or lack of changes, in the natural and human landscapes" (61).

It is carnival, however, that remains the principal alibi for travel, and the means of Danticat's access to, and attempted reconnection with, the aspects of Haitian culture that she was denied in her childhood and from which her migration to the United States has further distanced her. Through her title (whose full version, according to the Haitian proverb, would be, "After the dance, the drum is heavy" [155]) and through knowing references to Bakhtin's analysis of the carnivalesque as a form of reversal acting as a social safety valve, Danticat is clear that her purpose is not a blind celebration or romanticization of Haitian culture. Indeed, her behind-the-scenes account of the vicissitudes of carnival's preparation makes the slippage between appearance and reality abundantly clear, and the text presents past carnivals as "necessary distractions to their [participants'] daily struggles" (117). The description of the event itself emphasizes the ways in which it represents a relief from, but persistent refraction of, daily life: in a telling account of the procession, Danticat focuses on characters and floats portraying aspects of Haitian life that are privileged and distorted in external stereotypes, such as AIDS or immigration. A "small wooden boat with refugees packed shoulder to shoulder on the decks" is intercepted by a U.S. Coast Guard cutter, "acting out," Danticat states, "a crisis that many Haitians know only too well" (145). In presenting this scene as "renewed political protest," "cautionary tale," and "tribute to those who have perished at sea while dreaming of a better life" (146), Danticat succeeds in incorporating within the text traces of other travelers whose journeys highlight and challenge the inherent privilege of the travel writer's own.

Other Journeys: Relativizing the Traveling Self

After the Dance, with its epigraph from René Depestre, begins with an invocation of polyvocality: "Here and there, under the trees, while eating and drinking, the Jacmelians began to tell stories" (9). Although a clear introduction to the multiple personal itineraries that inform Danticat's account, the quotation privileges at the same time the competing journey narratives that complement and relativize the narrator's own voice. Within the travelogue, Danticat records evidence of the traces of other journeys, as she describes, for instance, the names carved into the stone at Fort Ogé, "a guest book for the ages" (45), or the visitors' book at the Auberge de la Visite (105). Similarly, the "travelees" who people the account, far from being static, circumscribed, and essentialized, are themselves repositories of travel experiences or travel stories: Ovid, the local who directs Danticat to the Watt steam engine, describes the scattering of his own family (56); the jewelry maker Paula Hyppolite recounts an itinerary of departure to the United States and return to Haiti (85); the shopkeeper Papayo has returned to Jacmel after forty-one years in Colombia (90). And to these individuals are to be added the anonymous travelers—epitomized in the floats discussed above—who undertake the unofficial, clandestine journeys central to contemporary Haitian life and culture. Part of Danticat's purpose in her own travelogue is to collect these journeys, alternatives to those that customarily dominate the genre in which she is writing. In doing so, *After the Dance* continues a series of collective projects, in which its author has been involved, of recovering personal testimonies, many of which relate to travel and migration.[39]

How does Danticat integrate these different itineraries, which are often dependent on very different vectors, into her travel narrative? On the one hand, they are used to constitute a vision of Haitian culture that foregrounds the porosity of national boundaries, in order to present a journey within what Clifford has dubbed a "traveling" culture. Other journeys evoked are thus parallel experiences, part of the same complex, constitutive networks and flows as Danticat's own journey, but presented without conflation of their manifest differences. The result—still uncommon in travel writing—is a relativization of the mobile self, a deflation of the genre's solipsistic tendencies. As part of the carnival in which she participates, Danticat witnesses a "theatrical piece about a local man who is pretending to be a *dyaspora*, a Haitian living in the United States." "The phony American accent," notes Danticat, "sends the crowd reeling" (121). The butt of the humor would appear to be the local man's flawed attempt at dissimulation and the deflation of any would-be social advancement this might have implied. At the same time, however, the playlet stages the dilemma underpinning Danticat's status as returned migrant. It is not only the imitation that is sent up, but also the pretension to *dyaspora* status that has motivated it in the first place. Recounting an earlier journey to the Parc de la Visite, the pine forest in the mountains above Jacmel, Danticat describes an encounter with locals who question her and her traveling companion about their patently external identities: "Are we reporters? Public officials? We proudly say we are Haitians trying to see more of the country" (101).

This encounter crystallizes the questions of identity that *After the Dance* seems to raise, and signals the importance of perspective in determining the answers they solicit. Danticat seems conscious, in her text's concluding stages, that there is a slippage between, on the one hand, her own search for cultural re-integration, and the self-awareness this permits, and, on the other, a persistent awareness of her difference as a *dyaspora.* In acknowledging this slippage, one needs to understand the risks, in reading travel writing, of conflating author and narrator, without recognizing the ways in which the latter may be deployed by the former in processes of self-performance. Danticat's author-narrator interprets the experience of carnival as a restorative means of achieving "anonymity, jubilant community, and belonging" (147). After she presents her text-journey as a means of "exorciz[ing] old ghosts and fears" (70), travel appears to lead to a concluding sense of solidarity with a complex but unified diasporic culture: "I am one of those marchers and migrants, back from the purgatory of exile, expatiating sins of coldness and distance" (147).

Gourdine sees such a restorative maneuver as a part of an "acting out and upon fantasies of the Caribbean space," indulging in the imagined performative exchanges with local inhabitants that characterize certain modes of tourist activity.[40] I would suggest, however, that the end of the text problematizes any such reading, for the journey account concludes with an unresolved dialectic of belonging to, and detachment from, Haiti understood as a national space. The morning following the carnival, as she views scenes from the previous day's events, Danticat catches sight of herself on the screen and experiences "a strange feeling of detachment": "Was that really me?" (158). Participation in the carnival acquires an epiphanic status: "Even as others had been putting on their masks, just for one afternoon, I had allowed myself to remove my own" (158), but the mask's removal is, as a result, inevitably temporary. This implies not the enlightened self-discovery for which certain travel writers aim, but instead a less-conclusive, incomplete reflection: the text's final section presents the traveler as others see her (i.e., belonging, but not belonging), rather than as she might like to perceive herself.

The carnival itself serves, therefore, as a detour in a more general transformation of travel into a means of exploring identity, both individual and collective. Travel writing, as Danticat presents this inherently intergeneric form, plays the role of both history and autobiography, permitting the creation of connections between past and present selves; at the same time, however, it offers its author an essayistic mode of expression, allowing the fragments of the journey to be turned into a performative text in which the dilemmas of current identity are brought to the fore. Diasporic creativity, and its relationship to a site that persists as "home," form a central theme in Danticat's work, whether her focus is on Ka's sculpture in *The Dew Breaker* or Moy's paintings in *Behind the Mountains*. *After the Dance* is no exception to this process of mise en abyme, in which the author reflects on the meanings of migration and return through repeated reference to the work of other

Haitian artists she meets. Danticat draws on the potentials of travel writing in order to root, in an individual experience of a personal journey, the dilemmas of "traveling" and "dwelling" fictionalized elsewhere in her work.

NOTES

1. Edwidge Danticat, *After the Dance: A Walk through Carnival in Jacmel, Haiti* (New York: Crown, 2002). Subsequent references are to this edition and are given after quotations in the main body of the text.

2. James Clifford, *Routes: Travel and Translation in the Late Twentieth Century* (Cambridge, MA: Harvard University Press, 1997), 17–46.

3. Angeletta K. M. Gourdine, "Caribbean Tabula Rasa: Textual Touristing as Carnival in Contemporary Caribbean Women's Writing," *Small Axe* 20 (2006): 80–96 (90).

4. See Farah J. Griffin and Cheryl J. Fish, eds., *A Stranger in the Village: Two Centuries of African American Travel Writing* (Boston: Beacon Press, 1998), and Alasdair Pettinger, ed., *Always Elsewhere: Travels of the Black Atlantic*, (London: Cassell, 1998).

5. See Derek Hall and Vivian Kinnaird, *Tourism: A Gender Analysis* (Chichester, UK: Wiley, 1994); Sara Mills, *Discourses of Difference: An Analysis of Women's Travel Writing and Colonialism* (London: Routledge, 1991); and Sidonie Smith, *Moving Lives: Twentieth-Century Women's Travel Writing*, (Minneapolis: University of Minnesota Press, 2001).

6. Charles Sugnet, "Vile Bodies, Vile Places: Travelling with *Granta*," *Transition* 51 (1991): 70–85.

7. Maureen Stone, *Black Woman Walking: A Different Experience of World Travel* (Bournemouth, UK: BeaGay, 2002), ix.

8. Clifford, *Routes*, 25, 38.

9. bell hooks, "Representations of Whiteness in the Black Imagination," *Black Looks: Race and Representation* (Boston, MA: South End Press, 1992): 165–78.

10. J. Michael Dash, *Haiti and the United States: National Stereotypes and the Literary Imagination*, 2nd ed. (1988; London: Macmillan, 1997).

11. Philippe Girard, *Paradise Lost: Haiti's Tumultuous Journey from Pearl of the Caribbean to Third World Hotspot* (New York: Palgrave Macmillan, 2005).

12. Anthony Maingot, "Haiti and the Terrified Consciousness of the Caribbean," in *Ethnicity in the Caribbean: Essays in Honor of Harry Hoetink*, ed. Gert Oostindie (London: Macmillan, 1996), 53–80 (53); Dash, *Haiti and the United States*, 10.

13. Graham Greene, *The Comedians* (New York: Viking, 1966).

14. Ian Thomson, *Bonjour Blanc: A Journey through Haiti* (1992; London: Vintage, 2004).

15. P. Flignau, *L'Haïtien expatrié, comédie en 3 actes, en prose* (Les Cayes, 1804); Joseph Saint-Rémy, *Vie de Toussaint Louverture* (Paris: Moquet, Librairie-Editeur, 1850).

16. Jean Jonassaint, *Le Pouvoir des mots, les maux du pouvoir* (Montreal: Arcantere et Dérives, 1986).

17. Emile Ollivier, *Passages* (1991; Paris: Serpent à Plumes, 1994).

18. See Edwidge Danticat, *The Farming of Bones* (New York: Soho Press, 1994), and Jacques-Stephen Alexis, *Compère Général Soleil* (Paris: Gallimard, 1955). Describing her own "personal journey" in the postface to *Behind the Mountains* (New York: Orchard, 2002), Danticat refers to the "two kinds of migration" that characterize many experiences of travel from Haiti to the United States: "one from the rural areas to the Haitian capital, Port-au-Prince, then from Port-au-Prince to a major American city, in this case, New York" (165).

19. See Dany Laferrière, *Vers le sud* (Paris: Grasset, 2006).

20. Edwidge Danticat, *Breath, Eyes, Memory* (New York: Soho Press, 1994).

21. Edwidge Danticat, *Krik? Krak!* (London: Abacus, 1996), 167.

22. The "native informants" who feature in *After the Dance* are, for instance, very different from those in Sarner's *La Passe du Vent: Une histoire haïtienne* (Paris: Payot, 1994), who seem restricted to aid workers and expatriate French people.

23. Gourdine, "Caribbean Tabula Rasa," 83.

24. Shannon Maughan, "Crown Journeys Tours Authors' Favorite Places," *Publishers Weekly,* July 6, 2004, http://www.publishersweekly.com/article/CA423276 .html (accessed February 27, 2007).

25. Danticat claims in an interview that "the Carnival book is supposed to encourage readers to visit Haiti—it's a 'happy' Haiti book." Bonnie Lyons, "An Interview with Edwidge Danticat," *Contemporary Literature* 44, no. 2 (2003): 183–98 (197).

26. Danticat refers, for example, to Elizabeth McAlister, *Rara! Vodou, Power and Performance in Haiti and Its Diaspora* (Berkeley: University of California Press, 2002); Peter Mason, *Bacchanal! The Carnival Culture of Trinidad* (London: Latin America Bureau, 1998); Robert Farris Thompson, *Flash of the Spirit: African and Afro-American Art and Philosophy* (New York: Random House, 1983); and Silvio Torres-Saillant, *Caribbean Poetics: Toward an Aesthetic of West Indian Literature* (Cambridge: Cambridge University Press, 1997).

27. Christine Montalbetti, *Le Voyage, le monde et la bibliothèque* (Paris: P.U.F., 1997).

28. Rodney Saint-Eloi, *Pierres anonymes* (Port-au-Prince: Éditions Mémoire, 1994).

29. René Depestre, *Hadriana dans tous mes rêves* (Paris: Gallimard, 1988); Sarner, *La Passe du Vent,* 70, 81.

30. See Martin Munro, "Writing Disaster: Trauma, Memory, and History in Edwidge Danticat's *The Farming of Bones,*" *Ethnologies* 28, no. 1 (2006): 81–98.

31. Joan Dayan, "France Reads Haiti: René Depestre's *Hadriana dans tous mes rêves,*" *Yale French Studies* 83 (1993): 154–75 (162, 174).

32. Clifford, *Routes,* 36.

33. Michael Cronin, *Across the Lines: Travel, Language, Translation* (Cork, Ireland: Cork University Press, 2000), 19.

34. Eric Sarner foregrounds this Jacmelian exceptionalism, presenting the city as

shut off from Port-au-Prince and still reliant on memories of the connections with elsewhere permitted by regular shipping links to Southampton and Le Havre (*La Passe du Vent*, 209), an aspect also mentioned by Danticat (142–43).

35. Edwidge Danticat, *The Dew Breaker* (2004; New York: Vintage, 2005), 209. Danticat does not fail to signal that Jacmel's apparent seclusion is in part due to François Duvalier's punitive closing of the city's port (*After the Dance*, 75).

36. Gourdine, "Caribbean Tabula Rasa," 91.

37. See Sarner, *La Passe du Vent*, 82–85, and Thomson, *Bonjour Blanc*, 68. As such, Danticat illustrates the thesis of the anthropologist of travel, Jean-Didier Urbain, for whom the initial entry point to an understanding of a culture is its graveyards. Jean Didier-Urbain, *L'Archipel des morts: Cimetières et mémoire en Occident* (Paris: Payot, 2005).

38. Gourdine, "Caribbean Tabula Rasa," 92.

39. See Beverley Bell, ed., *Walking on Fire: Haitian Women's Stories of Survival and Resistance* (Ithaca: Cornell University Press, 2001); Edwidge Danticat, ed., *The Butterfly's Way: Voices from the Haitian Dyaspora in the United States* (New York: Soho Press, 2001); and Patricia Justine Tumang and Jenesha de Rivera, eds. *Homelands: Women's Journeys across Race, Place, and Time* (Emeryville, CA: Seal Press, 2006).

40. Gourdine, "Caribbean Tabula Rasa," 84.

MARASSA WITH A DIFFERENCE

Danticat's
Breath, Eyes, Memory

MIREILLE ROSELLO

This reading of *Breath, Eyes, Memory* is the result of a long and difficult process of selection between what a critic may, can, must, or will say or not say when he or she is confronted with the representation of rape.[1] A young Haitian woman is violated, possibly by a Tonton Macoute. She discovers that she is pregnant and flees to New York, leaving the baby girl behind. She then sends for her daughter and tries, in vain, to live with the traumatic series of events, abusing herself and her child for years, the long and painful process of nonrecovery finally culminating in her bloody suicide.

Is a literary or even cultural critic not bound to feel more than the usual amount of self-doubt and irrelevance in the face of such narratives? It was certainly no comfort to keep reminding myself that *Breath, Eyes, Memory* is a book and that the raped characters are made of words. Because *Breath, Eyes, Memory* relates an event so traumatic that it becomes a matter of life and death for the characters, the fact that the story is made of words hardly provides a convincing shield behind which the reader can hide. And yet, forgetting that the story is made of words also distracts from the unique way in which the novel represents a specific rape and succeeds in proposing a unique narrative response that allows the reader a certain amount of interpretive freedom, a choice that raped victims precisely do not have.[2]

The undeniable literary qualities of the novel may appear, at first, to compound the problem: allowing oneself to be captivated by the story to the point of forgetting that we are reading a novel is a form of professional naïveté that we have learned to avoid. But suggesting that the story of a rape has a specific form of power or seduction that risks exhausting the reader's interpretive energy by ravishing him or her sounds even more irresponsible. It would be a way of suggesting that the text functions as a rapist mirror, which I am emphatically not suggesting. I am not arguing that the novel forces us in any way to concentrate on the theme of rape and to deny other aspects, especially the more literary or formalist qualities of the tale. If I were, I would be accusing the story of having raped me, metaphorically. I would be saying that this story of a rape ends up doing to the reader exactly what the character is said to have suffered, ends up raping the reader, ends up abusing the recipient in the same way as the faceless man abuses the mother who abuses the daughter. The accusation would be cheap and inaccurate.

First of all, the idea of metaphorical rape is itself highly problematic.[3] I can't help thinking that it must sound like an insult to bodies who cannot find words to alleviate their pain and continually re-experience rather than mediate the initial trauma. Besides, as Jenny Sharpe has shown in *Allegories of Empire*, rape as a trope is often used to conveniently displace violence along a continuum of supposedly comparable situations where one rape victim is made to stand in for another (metaphorical) one, so that the figure of raping, through a "chain of substitutions," is gradually disconnected from the originally violated body.[4] Even that possibility is denied to Martine, the character who never manages to get rid of the burden along any line of signifiers.

The other possibility that seemed doomed to failure from the start was to rely on the familiarity of keywords that postcolonial studies have taught us to recognize. Even the briefest of summaries point in the direction of well-known theoretical starting points such as migrations and gender, colonial patterns and violence. I could have been tempted to concentrate on such issues, to link the novel to well-formed bodies of discourse on trauma and silence, home and homelessness, national and personal identities. Sophisticated and compelling essays have indeed been written about the possibility of inhabiting two places at once, on the delicate articulation between the specific form of sexual abuse endured by women and the construction of a collective Haitian history, on the distinction between a literature of exile and migrant literature, or on the way in which specific gendered cultural practices such as cooking may enable the female Haitian migrant to come to terms with alienation and estrangement.[5]

For this reader, however, the usually comforting quest for relevant metadiscourse did not work. It certainly did not provide a relatively safe or at least ethical position from which to talk about rape in general or about the predictably horrific consequences such a traumatic experience will have on the victim, or rather victims. Critical discourse did not, in this context, offer any satisfying point of intervention into the issues of violence and trauma but appeared as a comforting yet ultimately self-defeating textual trick that would provide a shield from the violence of the text. Juxtaposing a level of metadiscourse was a form of distraction, and the novel itself warns us against tales that are meant to make us forget something else. In *Breath, Eyes, Memory*, one of the numerous and painful scenes that focus on the different types of violence endured by a female body revolves around the (mis)use of storytelling by a mother who, unable to tell her own story, resorts to a folktale to distract her daughter from the pain and humiliation that she inflicts. Martine, who suspects her daughter of being involved with a man, "tests" her virginity by forcing her to lie on a bed before penetrating her with a finger to make sure that her hymen is still intact. "As she tested me, to distract me, she told me . . ." (84), says the first-person narrator, before proceeding to quote the tale. The novel thus structures the mother's storytelling practice as an activity that the daughter cannot distinguish from an act of sexual violence. This folktale is supposed to be a distraction, but, of course, it does not work. The daughter finds no consolation in the tale.

On the other hand, and this is where the critic may find some hope of not having lost all relevance, the fact that the story fails to distract the daughter does not prevent us from reading it from within another frame. As a trick, it did not work, but now, it is also another textual performance embedded into the narrative that the daughter controls: ultimately, she chooses to reinsert Martine's little parable into her own account of their life. Its function and meaning are both transformed in the process. Here is the tale told by the mother: "The Marassas were two inseparable lovers. They were the same person, duplicated in two. They looked the same, talked the same, walked the same. When they laughed, they even laughed the same, and when they cried, their tears were identical. When one went to the stream, the other rushed under the water to get a better look. When one looked in the mirror, the other walked behind the glass to mimic her. What vain lovers they were, those Marassas. Admiring one another for being so much alike, for being copies" (84–85). Because the daughter pays as much attention to the point of the story as to the story itself, the reader is able to draw different conclusions about the supposedly ideal picture that the mother paints of the Marassas. First of all, this is not her story. It is a folktale whose hero is the Haitian equivalent of the Greek symbolon: "one" is "two." Here, sameness and love are one and the same thing: the Marassas are inseparable and identical. They love each other because they are alike and always together. In a different context, we may not be able to decide if the parable is supposed to be a warning or a model, but the mother soon indicates how her interlocutor is supposed to interpret the reference to the twins. She supplies the equivalent of the lesson at the end of the fable when she tells her daughter: "You and I could be like Marassas" (85).

Both the pronoun and the "could be" are crucial: the mother's "I" does not emerge as a self-contained and independent subject. The "I" is not only hypothetical (it "could" be), but it is dependent on the willingness of the "you" to be the other side of the Marassa coin. In a strange rewriting of the psychoanalytical formula that lets the "I" appear where the "id" had been, here the "I" could only "be" if "we" wished to become Marassas. The story can hardly be transposed onto a daughter-mother relationship without raising problematic questions. The mother is proposing a clearly incestuous relationship. At that very moment, she is "loving" her daughter incestuously and violently, without her consent. The tale of the Marassas is embedded into an episode of sexual violence, which forecloses any euphoric reading of an incestuous daughter-mother relationship. The mother's yearning for a Marassa lover is presented as the replication of the violence that she continues to both endure and inflict: the mother's story and her testing are inseparable. According to the story, if the little girl remains a virgin, she can be her mother's Marassa instead of abandoning her for an older man. Her daughter will be her, not *like* her but indistinguishable from her.

Breath, Eyes, Memory, the novel as a whole, argues against this trend by framing Martine's desire for or inability to renounce overall undifferentiation as the pathological consequence of her rape. As Ross Chambers lucidly argued in *Story and Situation,* stories do contain models of readership that function like mirroring effects of their own power of seduction, but it is the reader's prerogative to differentiate between different types of narrative reflection.[6] Danticat's novel can therefore be described as the story of two women that present the reader with two mirrors of a narrative of rape. As narrator, Sophie disqualifies the mirror handed out by the mother to another potential Marassa. For Martine, the story is an infinite series of mirrors, made of endless repetitions, of nightmares, of words and images that she experiences as imposing themselves upon her or emanating from her powerless body. The character is depicted as a subject controlled by the story, a subject as synonym of topic rather than as a narrator. This type of (de)subjectivation forecloses the possibility of her ever becoming an author (endowed with auctoritas) or a witness (capable of a testimony). In time, the body-story that is her kills itself/her, as Martine is driven to suicide by the violence of her dreams and hallucinations. The novel frames her as a powerless vessel possessed by the endless repetition of the rape rather than as a speaking subject capable of mediating the real and the traumatic through fiction, any kind of fiction. Her story is the impossibility to construct her post-rape self as a life-affirming narrative.

For a novelist, the portrayal of such a character is thus a paradoxical enterprise, and if Martine were the only protagonist, the story would remain literally unheard. How, then, does the novel both depict and resist the specific type of traumatized tale that acts as the author of destructive fiction and prevents any "I" from emerging as an even minimally empowered storyteller who believes in her ability to use discourse to organize the real as an effect of her words rather than the other way around?

The most deleterious manifestation of the trauma is that it has rendered Martine unable to articulate a certain number of oppositions that any coherent narrator or narratee takes for granted. For example, Martine has lost the ability to make a distinction between past and present. This is in synch with theories that have explained how "trauma is not simply a horrific event, but [that] it is also an event that misaligns our perception of time," but Danticat's intervention as a novelist is to recognize that the symptom has immediate consequence on the ability to produce fiction.[10] Not being able to separate her self from the moment of the rape, the mother will never distinguish between nightmares and reality, between herself and her daughter, between violence and life.

This is not to say that Danticat treats trauma as unrepresentable at all. Rather, her novel manages not simply to restore the seemingly natural order of binaries but to highlight our need for them. By writing the daughter in the position of the first-person narrator, *Breath, Eyes, Memory* redeploys a system of binary oppositions that, as readers, we need to at least provisionally recognize and accept as prerequisites. In other words, the novel does not simply suggest that the rape victim loses the ability to tell her story but suggests that as readers we become incapable of listening to her because the parameters that we look for in a story are precisely those that have been destroyed, not so much by the rape but by the consequences of the rape on both the subject and the story. By portraying a character who is incapable of organizing a story and who dies of that syndrome, *Breath, Eyes, Memory* makes a specifically literary contribution to the representation of rape because the novel invites us to reconsider the distinction not between facts and fiction but between the narrator who can choose to make rape the subject of a story and the body defined by an event that usurps the place that the storyteller should normally occupy.

As listeners, we can only respond to a subject who has access to what we could call here narrative rights or prerogatives: the ability to make those distinctions that Martine no longer controls. She cannot even say "I" to express the feelings of the (socially sanctioned) guilt that the rape triggers in her. When she becomes pregnant again, the fetus that she carries is perceived as a man who does and says things to her. Martine hears him talking to her and calling her name: "You tintin, malpróp. He calls me a filthy whore" (217). That "man" could also be the reader, incapable of deciphering her (body) language, and putting words in her body because somebody once haphazardly "put" a life in her (61).

Her failure to organize her self and therefore her tale is framed by the novel as evidence of what would have remained a silence had the daughter not been able to find a new poetics of representation. For the novel to even exist, Martine must be written into existence from a perspective that is not hers.

She is not a witness, nor is she the author of her tale. Her place as a storyteller is occupied by a type of activity that leaves her powerless and helpless: nightmares. What expresses itself in, through, and in lieu of Martine are horrific dreams: a sort of mental and bodily energy that has something to do with stories but cannot be used to testify, to accuse, or to process memories. The rape is not in the past—it belongs to the immediate present since it is re-enacted, re-presented every night, in Martine's dreams: "It's like getting raped every night" (190). At several intervals in the novel, other characters recognize that her nightmares are violent and self-destructive, potentially fatal. The first-person narrator explains: "I knew the intensity of her nightmares. I had seen her curled up in a ball in the middle of the night, sweating and shaking as she hollered for the images of the past to leave her alone. Sometimes the fright woke her up, but most of the time, I had to shake her awake before she bit her finger off, ripped off her nightgown, or threw herself out of a window" (193).

Martine's mouth does not form words. She "hollers" and then cannibalizes her own body: "At night, she tore her sheets and bit off pieces of her own flesh when she had nightmares" (139). Nightmares, in this novel, are the opposite of storytelling, not because they are the opposite of the real,[11] but because, structurally, they are a form of expression that abolishes all differences. The body inflicts on itself the violence that it endured without being able to fight back. Like the young girl who was "too stunned to make a sound" (138), the woman is left in a state of perpetual aphasia while her body takes over, becoming her own torturer. Nightmares are a dimension where the distinction between Martine's body and her self disappears, which reduces her to an ambiguous human state where present and past are fused, destructively. For the daughter, this principle of undifferentiation is represented as the potentially contagious force of Martine's nightmares: "Her nightmares had somehow become my own so much so that I would wake up some mornings wondering if we hadn't both spent the night dreaming about the same thing: a man with no face, pounding a life into a helpless young girl" (193). Nightmares, unlike novels, cannot be read. We would only have access to that tale if we, like the daughter, had similar dreams. But as readers, we need to receive the story from a different place, from someone who can turn the pain into words and perhaps even, as we are about to see, to transform the hurt into a love letter.

The novel presents us with two scenes that suggest the possibility of moving from nightmares to love letters. It is a decision that involves the conscious privileging between equally problematic uses of violence. In order to give up on memory as nightmare and to treat witnessing as the careful re-introduction of distinctions, the narrator does not choose between reality and fiction but between two potentially dangerous representations of herself that both involve metaphorizing her body and objectifying it. In the first scene, she remembers one of her own nightmares. The second passage, however, has to do with letters, with writing and with love, which announces the medium that Sophie will eventually choose: storytelling in general and writing in particular.

Both scenes have to do with how a child relates to a mother figure. The first one corresponds to the figure of the Marassas. In that passage, the biological mother, who has left Haiti and is about to send for the child, appears in the little girl's dreams as a force of containment and undifferentation that terrorizes her and that she is powerless to resist. The mother wants to immobilize and objectify her: "I sometimes saw my mother in my dreams. She would chase me through a field of wildflowers as tall as the sky. When she caught me, she would try to squeeze me into the small frame so I could be in the picture with her. I would scream and scream until my voice gave out, then Tante Atie would come and save me from her grasp" (8).

The body of the little girl who runs through a field of flowers risks being immobilized by the mother's will. Martine, when she was raped, was also stopped in her tracks in the middle of the field: the man "pinned her down" like a poster or a dead insect ("He dragged her into the cane fields and pinned her down on the ground" [139]). This is not to say that the mother rapes her child, of course, but that the fear expressed in the nightmare manages to express what it means to be violated and turned into a helpless thing. In another distorting mirror, the text suggests that the daughter's only possible relationship with the mother is to become what she is, an image. The only thinkable protocol of being "with" the mother is imagined here as coercion. The little girl passionately resists a grown-up's desire to reduce her to the status of inanimate object on Tante Atie's bed table. Only Tante Atie's intervention is capable of putting an end to the nightmare. The scream and the aunt's presence succeed in reinstating a clear distinction between the body of the little girl and that of the biological mother. As long as the dream is not interrupted, she cannot be a separate self, a separate space (here and there), nor even a separate time (the past of the rape and the now of new possibilities).

The mother has become a picture with power. The narration does not make any difference between the representation of the mother (the photograph) and the mother (the character), so the reader is forced to accept a supposedly realistic universe that mixes the mother as object and the mother as powerful agent. In the passage, the portrait itself has power over the little girl. It is a "she" and not an object, her photographed eyes can "see": "I only knew my mother from the picture on the night table by Tante Atie's pillow. She waved from inside the frame with a wide grin on her face and a large flower in her hair. She witnessed everything that went on in the bougainvillea each step each stumble each hug and kiss. She saw us when we got up when we went to sleep, when we laughed, when we got upset at each other. Her expression never changed. Her grin never went away" (8).

In this description, the mother's absence is read not as powerlessness but as quasi omnipotence. Once more, it is tempting to notice that she is represented as having acquired the characteristic of the man who raped her. Just as a vampire contaminates the victim, the mother becomes the man that remains present even though he no longer is there. The inert photograph is not a static object but functions as a surveillance device. The narration deliberately engages in what could be called willful paranoia. Of course, a photograph does not have eyes, cannot gaze, and yet not only is the framed mother capable of "seeing" what the daughter does, but the visual control that she exerts is almost infinite judging by the list of activities that the narrator takes the trouble to enumerate. Besides, not only does the portrait "see" things, but it "witnesses," a verb that implicitly gives her/it the authority to report on what has been going on, possibly to some higher and scary hierarchy or in a court of law. Martine is miles away, she is not present—what "witnesses" is a picture. But the object is subjectified by the story that endows her not only with agency but also with power. The free indirect style prevents the reader from clearly identifying the origin of such an interpretation. It is impossible to discern whether the vision is the product of the child's imagination or the adult first-person narrator's voice. The mother and the child have bad dreams in which someone overpowers them. At this point, Sophie is not able to spell it out in her own voice. At the place where a distinct "I" will eventually appear, the narrator inserts a vision that is contaminated by Martine's perpetual nightmarish vision of the world—no matter what she sees, nothing changes, she is literally stuck: "Her expression never changed" (8). The narration describes her as an image, incapable of words, incapable of evolving, but capable of instilling, in the onlooker, the fear of being contaminated by her traumatic consciousness. The child might be, if the mother catches her, turned into a picture too.

If I call this paranoid vision a "tactic," is it because it makes a specific point of whom and what to fear? The story suggests that Sophie's fear is to be denied the possibility of separation and not, for example, the possibility of being abandoned by the mother. It also recognizes the fact that the mother's lack of subjectivity, her being an image, does not make her harmless. But it also leaves the little girl helpless, dependent on the presence of Tante Atie, who can free her from the dream.

To this desperate construction of the relationship between Sophie and Martine responds another passage that is structurally very similar to the little girl's first nightmare of being immobilized, although it reverses all of its negative connotations. Once again, the narration describes the relationship between the little girl and a mother figure as a moment of physical transformation. This time, however, the body is squeezed not behind a glass plate but into an envelope, and no one is coercing Sophie into an inextricable situation of mutual dependency. The scene takes place in a post office, after Martine and her daughter have been reunited. They are at a counter, handing to the clerk a package that they want to send to Haiti, to Tante Atie, Sophie's first mother. The narrator says about herself:

> I kept feeling like there was more I wanted to send to Tante Atie. If I had the power then to shrink myself and slip into the envelope, I would have done it.
>
> I watched as the lady stamped our package and dropped it on top of a larger pile. Around us there were dozens of other people trying to squeeze all their love into small packets to send back home. (51)

This time, the "shrinking" of the body is not life-threatening, even if some self-inflicted violence is still discernible here. The body becomes the equivalent of a letter that can be slipped into an envelope and sent to a loving surrogate mother. Both here and in the first nightmare, the body's three-dimensionality and Sophie's physicality are ignored. But the two metamorphoses have radically different functions and consequences. A certain amount of dispossession occurs as a narrator accepts turning her life and her mother's into a story. But that self-objectification is willed and preferred to the violence of other options.

The first transformation would fit within an overall narrative that represents the mother's desire to make her daughter undistinguishable from her, a pathological drive for sameness. The two passages function like two distinct and incompatible myths of origin between which the young girl will have to choose before achieving the status of an independent subject, that is, a first-person narrator whose only existence, paradoxically it seems, is to be made of words.

Violence is not so much to be eliminated as to be distinguished from life, a separation that the mother cannot make because her child's existence is the result of the rape. What Sophie knows is that, when controlled and narrativized, violence is at times the only way out of the traumatic reiteration of nightmarish abuse, but that even this choice has to be articulated as a coherent and life-affirming narrative. For example, when she decides to put an end to the ordeal of the "testing" by deflowering herself with a pestle, two levels of resisting are described by the text. On the one hand, as Donette Francis argues, the character is not freed from the abuse since her own sexual desire will later be contaminated by the memory of that event. According to the critic, Sophie's taking the matter of testing into her own hands leads to a Pyrrhic victory because the character still has to learn "that the battle is to be fought on a cultural terrain rather than on the landscape of her own body" (85). On the other hand, the character's fate is to be differentiated from the textual representation of what was gained and what was lost in the process. This is a verbal as well as cultural terrain.

For the mother, the end of the testing period had involved no such limited success since it had corresponded with the rape. She had no control over the moment when the ordeal ended. When she tells her daughter about that episode, of the sexual violence that the characters both endure and inflict, the rape and the testing are fused together in a string of sentences that leave Martine passive and helpless: "My mother stopped testing me early" (61). Here, the marker of time, "early," is not an allusion to a mercifully short period. Rather, the abusive normative exercise was interrupted by an even worse form of violence. One form of helplessness was replaced by a ruthless experience of dispossession. Before the rape, the active subject is Martine's mother doing something to "me." Then, in order to describe the attack, the mother systematically avoids using the pronoun "I," accumulating passive constructions or statements that reduce her to a helpless body: "Did Atie tell you how you were born? . . . It happened like this. A man grabbed me from the side of the road, pulled me into a cane field, and put you in my body" (61). Martine, therefore, never fails the test. In her eyes, she is not even worth testing.

Sophie's deliberate intervention radically changes that narrative.

Once the pestle has broken through the "veil that had always held my mother's finger back every time she tested me" (88), Sophie patiently waits for her mother to test her once more (instead, for example, of letting her know that the exercise is now useless). And, she writes: "*Finally* I failed the test" (88, my emphasis). The "finally" is unexpected in the sentence and is the kind of ammunition that only words can add to a struggle: the adverb is what makes Sophie's story unique in spite of the reiteration of sexual violence that could be interpreted (and perhaps excused) as the traces of cultural tradition or the result of the mother's traumatized consciousness. Like her female ancestors, Sophie must suffer the incestuous indignity of being penetrated by her own mother. But unlike them, she chooses to put an end to the experience.

If this episode may be said to be representative of the novel as a whole, it is because of the way in which the first-person narrator manages to use language to operate a textual re-appropriation of the violence done to her. Saying "Finally I failed the test" suggests, counterintuitively, that the goal *was* to fail, and that in order to reach that unimagined objective, it took perseverance, preparation, patience, and determination. In short, it took the kind of qualities that we normally expect of those who pass rather than fail tests. Just as one says "I finally passed the test" (implicitly after several unsuccessful attempts, which connotes the difficulty of the enterprise), the narrator triumphantly claims failure and thus makes us read the failure as the goal (and therefore paradoxical "success") toward which she had been working all along. While Martine only uses "I" to describe the little girl that she was then and who could never change—"I was still only a young girl then, just barely older than you" (61)—Sophie says "I" to describe the result of her rebellion: that is, the fact that she can emerge as a separate self who has understood the story of the Marassas, refused that model, and refused, as well, to let the tale distract her.

NOTES

1. Edwidge Danticat, *Breath, Eyes, Memory* (New York: Soho Press, 1994). Subsequent references are to this edition and are given after quotations in the main body of the text.

2. In the chapter of his dissertation that he devotes to *Breath, Eyes, Memory,* Jeffrey Allan Jaeckle suggests that the place of language in Danticat's work has been so underestimated by critics that the author herself has wished to warn her readers against a tendency to read her fictions as documents on Haiti: "Danticat has repeatedly urged readers (be they students or scholars) to pay greater attention to the com-

plex texture of her prose. In a 2003 interview, Danticat insists, 'what I write are novels, not anthropology or social research'; she then reiterates her claim: 'Readers have to remember that we're writing fiction, telling stories' (Lyons 187, 190)." Jeffrey Allan Jaeckle, "Reading the Reiterative: Concordance Mapping and the American Novel," (PhD diss., University of Texas at Austin, 2005), http://www.lib.utexas.edu/etd/d/2005/jaecklejo6260/jaecklejo6260.pdf (accessed December 30, 2006), 32.

3. There is no reason to assume that the raped victim is not *also* raped metaphorically or that the metaphorical system of references that the rapist uses to construct his or her object as a prey, a temptation, or a culprit to be punished is not part and parcel of the rape. See George Lakoff and Mark Johnson, "The Metaphorical Logic of Rape," *Metaphor and Symbolic Activity* 21, no. 1 (1987): 73–79.

4. Jenny Sharpe, *Allegories of Empire: The Figure of Woman in the Colonial Text* (Minneapolis: University of Minnesota Press, 1993), 1.

5. Respectively, the works described are: Patrick Samway, "A Homeward Journey: Edwidge Danticat's Fictional Landscapes, Mindscapes, Genescapes, and Signscapes in *Breath, Eyes, Memory*," *Mississippi Quarterly: The Journal of Southern Cultures* 57, no. 1 (2003): 75–83; Donette Francis, " 'Silences Too Horrific to Disturb': Writing Sexual Histories in Edwidge Danticat's *Breath, Eyes, Memory*," *Research in African Literatures* 35, no. 2 (Summer 2004): 75–90; Carine Mardorossian, *Reclaiming Difference: Caribbean Women Rewrite Postcolonialism* (Charlottesville: University of Virginia Press, 2005); and Valérie Loichot, "Edwidge Danticat's Kitchen History," *Meridians: Feminism, Race, Transnationalism* 5, no. 1 (2004): 92–116.

6. Ross Chambers, *Story and Situation: Narrative Seduction and the Power of Fiction* (Minneapolis: University of Minnesota Press, 1984), 25.

7. Aimee Pozorski, "Trauma's Time," *Connecticut Review* 28, no. 1 (Spring 2006): 71–114 (71).

8. The theme of the dreamer who has access to a reality that science and rationality cannot tap is a radically different topos that recent television series such as *Medium* have been exploring in a rather conventional way. No link is ever made in the novel between dreams and prophetic powers or heightened perception.

VIOLENCE, NATION, & MEMORY

Danticat's
The Farming of Bones

MYRIAM J. A. CHANCY

The Farming of Bones, Edwidge Danticat's award-winning second novel, focuses on a stark period in Haitian-Dominican history, what is known in Haiti as "the cane-field massacres" and as *el corte* in the Dominican Republic.[1] It attempts to encapsulate the experience of both communal and personal terror during the 1937 massacre of countless Haitians living in the borderlands between the two countries by the armed forces of the Dominican dictator Raphael Trujillo. Trujillo's aim to "Dominicanize" the Dominican Republic (or to de-Haitianize it) made the borderlands between the two countries a battleground in which Dominicans and Haitians who had peacefully co-existed together, in trade and in conjugal unions, intermarrying, and so on, were rendered enemies. Haitians, by virtue of their Vodou-related "Africanness" and their poverty, which had grown ever more grave from the 1800s to the early 1900s, were seen as undesirables in the Dominican Republic. Though many historians contend that only ethnic difference separated the two populations, it is also clear that the de-Haitianization process hinged on the racialization of Haitians as a subspecies.[2] Women's bodies, in particular, associated with the market place and prostitution in exchanges of goods between the two countries, became abject entities. What these shifts in perceptions of border trade, wherein both goods sold by women and the prostitution of women operated with impunity, could not predict was the degree to which border zone women would reformulate the notion of the nation as a Europeanized male state (as imperial dictates always manifested in the discourses surrounding new nations as shown in the work of Jose Rabasa and Paul Carter, among others).[3] In focusing primarily on the exchanges between women, both Haitian and Dominican, in her novel, Danticat gives voice to the impact of these shifts upon "real" women while at the same time attempting to lift the veil of amnesia that obscures this painful period in both Haitian and Dominican history. In this, she continues in the trajectory of her previous work, situating her female characters within community and yet demonstrating that women are not lost in those communities but actors within them, poised to articulate a new imaginary for themselves, their loved ones, and their nation.

During the course of the island's tenuous history, what would first appear to be unimportant differences in race, class, and currency have eventually grown, with quite unforeseen results. What are the forces that conspired to produce such a cataclysmic event? Why is it that memory has been falsified with concern for the Haitian/Dominican conflict while race and gender issues pertaining to its maintenance have been dismissed as overly facile explanations? These are some of the questions this essay attempts to address through a historicized contextualization of Edwidge Danticat's *The Farming of Bones*. By focusing on current ideas on how cultural memory is built and sustained, I hope that this essay will serve to underscore the potential usefulness of a woman writer's perspective on historical issues as she attempts to overcome the erasure of women's lives reflected in a neutered history that forms the basis for her narrative reconstruction.

Memory

I am compelled here to distinguish the trope of memory I seek to expose in Danticat's text in particular from current theoretical explorations of memory that have become academically ubiquitous. Currently, the most prominent of these is that of French historian Pierre Nora, whose tomes on French history, entitled *Lieux de Mémoire* (*Realms of History*, 1996), have revolutionized turn-of-the-century approaches to historiography. In his general introduction, "Between Memory and History," Nora states: "Our consciousness is shaped by a sense that everything is over and done with, that something long since begun is now complete. Memory is constantly on our lips because it no longer exists."[4] It is not clear if here "our" refers to all of humanity or only to the French; the use of the collective pronoun already denotes an exclusivity of categorization that assumes that the audience concerned shares a like experience of history and consciousness. Nora's theorizations are thus deceptively inclusive, remarkable only to those who know themselves not to be included in this "our" because their reading of history or living in memory fails to coincide with Nora's claims. Pointedly, for many Third World subjects, history is not over as it is "History" that conspires to keep them in their subordinate position. The history that First World inhabitants fail to remember is the history that might give credence to Third World claims: for example, the destructive effects of enslavement and colonization on African nations gives rise to claims against European nations for adjustments to trade tariffs in an attempt to enable African merchants to recover from the devastation inflicted on their nations through imperialism; without a consideration of past harms, such adjustments cannot be made, and nations already impoverished by European colonial expansion become all the more impoverished and unable to compete on the world market. Thus, the inhabitants of the former colonized nations are often forced to live in conditions that duplicate or mimic those of earlier centuries; for them, history is not over but is frozen in constant replay. For such peoples, memory serves as a stay against despair; it exists because the past remains an undeniable element of the present, even if others have deliberately forgotten this past.

Although Nora concedes that formerly colonized nations have a role to play in this tandem between memory and history, he does so only to underline that their liberation has simply provided the passage into a previously organized understanding of history and memory; for Nora, whatever forms of memorializing these new nations might now engage in are severed from their own understanding of history and subsumed to the natural order of things centralized, of course, in Europe. He writes:

> Among the new nations, independence has swept into history societies only recently roused from their ethnological slumbers by the rape of colonization. At the same time a sort of internal decolonization has had a similar effect on ethnic minorities, families, and subcultures that until recently had amassed abundant reserves of memory but little in the way of history. Societies

based on memory are no more: the institutions that once transmitted values from generation to generation—churches, schools, families, governments—have ceased to function as they once did. And ideologies based on memory have ceased to function as well, ideologies that once smoothed the transition from past to future or indicated what the future should retain from the past, whether in the name of reaction, progress, or even revolution. (1–2)

In this way, the violence of colonization becomes merely the price of being awakened, suggesting that colonized nations had no real life of their own, no catalyst by which to energize growth prior to this cataclysmic historical moment. Already, it seems, Nora's explanations subsume the memories qua histories of nations considered "other" in order to legitimize the history, specifically, of France, whose processes of memory-making, Nora suggests, are replicated by most other nations.

Subsequently, decolonization from the imperial powers has destroyed, claims Nora, the memories of the formerly colonized who have had no true history to speak of (Nora does not allow that these "memories" construct history, hence the term "oral history," which describes the transmission of information from one generation to the next); thus, decolonization becomes a decolonization from cultural memory to assume one's place in linear history, a linear order, rather than decolonization from the violence of colonization. From this, Nora moves on to explain how "we" no longer organize "our" societies around rituals meant to preserve historical memory; in so doing, he sweeps away all those nations and cultures for whom ritual remains an important facet of the preservation of national identity. For a great number of Haitians and Cubans, for example, the rituals of Vodou and Santería secure the preservation of memory and consequently of unscripted history. For Nora, "a world that once contained our ancestors has become a world in which our relation to what made us is merely contingent" (7). For many "minority" cultures, ancestors are anchoring points that validate and guide the existence of their descendants. It becomes crucial, then, to give voice to theories articulated by Caribbean and feminist theorists who have already provided us with blueprints by which to better redraw the parameters of official history and create a space for what has been called the Other's "non-history."[5]

The Martinican theorist Edouard Glissant has written in an essay entitled "The Quarrel with History" that the French Caribbean "is the site of a history characterized by ruptures and that began with a brutal dislocation, the slave trade." He continues: "Our historical conscious-ness could not be deposited gradually and continuously like sediment, as it were, as happened with those peoples who have frequently produced a totalitarian philosophy of history, for instance European peoples, but came together in the context of shock, contradiction, painful negation, and explosive forms." For Glissant, this process of negation and rupture has erased collective memory and distorted received history through a process that is purely ideological. Hence, he asserts that "the ideo-logical blockade functioned just like the economic blockades against Haiti in the past, and against Cuba in the present" and that "in order to repossess their historical space, the French Caribbean countries needed to break through the dead tissue that colonial ideology had deposited along their borders." According to Glissant, this repossession was made impossible due to its oppositional character as well as the hybrid char-acter of Caribbean societies, which, unlike African nations, could not sustain linguistic, religious, and traditional characteristics as a mode of continuous resistance (62–63). However, remnants of that wiped-out collective memory remain, and it is, ironically, the conqueror's history that makes its recollection possible, as "history is a highly functional fantasy of the West" (64); its very construction points to the possibility of alternatives that, for Glissant, are most accessible to the Caribbean writer whose imaginary forms a bridge to the nexus of collective mem-ory searching for a port of entry. Examining this port through women's eyes, however, provides added layers to the collective memory to be resurrected since women are, within Caribbean societies, as marginal to men in the political order as the Caribbean is to Europe or North America. Hence, my investigations here seek to interact with a history that enacts what bell hooks has termed a "politicization of memory," one that brings to light the particular collective and individual legacies of the dispossessed in broad relief.[6]

In *Yearning,* hooks defines the "politicization of memory" as an act "which distinguishes nostalgia, that longing for something to be as once it was, a kind of useless act, from that remembering that serves to illuminate and transform the present" (147). Implicit in this process is an identification of the process of official history (of the type Nora has redefined as constituted through cultural practices) as an act of nostal-gia emptied of political import. The purpose of politicizing memory is to provide a space within which those deemed "without a history" within official discourses of history may create a new history created from their own internal collective/individual resources. This is why hooks then turns to speak of the "margins" as a "site of resistance" from which change can be enacted (149–51). Further, hooks writes eloquently and forcefully of a need for a paradigmatic shift followed by effective action: "I am waiting for them to stop talking about the 'Other,' to stop even describing how important it is to be able to speak about difference. It is not just important what we speak about, but how and why we speak. Often this speech about the 'Other' is also a mask, an oppressive talk hiding gaps, absences, that space where our words would be if we were speaking, if there were silence, if we were there. This 'we' is that 'us' in the margins, that 'we' who inhabit marginal spaces that is not a site of domination but a space of resistance. Enter that space" (151).

To enter that space, this space, is to understand, as Adrienne Rich has written in her essay on feminist history "Resisting Amnesia," that "without our own history we are unable to imagine a future because we are deprived of the precious resource of knowing where we come from."[7] Implied here is the understanding that official history (History), has been written by the conquerors (imperial or patriarchal) and that by shifting the ground of the politics of historicization, another version or other versions of history will emerge. Rich comments: "To draw strength: Memory is nutriment, and seeds stored for centuries can still germinate" (146). Or, as postcolonial theorist Trinh T. Minh-ha has written, a necessary "nourricriture"—a nourishing, nurturing writing—which contains ancestral women's voices as well as contemporary ones and by virtue of giving voice to the feminine elements of societies,[8] necessarily, according to Rich, "looks afresh at what men have done and how they have behaved, not only toward women but toward each other and the natural world" (146–47).

Memory-Making in *The Farming of Bones*

Named for the brutal work of Haitian *braceros* in the Dominican cane fields in which the repetitious nature of unrewarded harsh menial labor followed by death marks the Haitian life cycle, Edwidge Danticat's novel links the Haitian experience of the Trujillo massacre to national identity by describing how Dominican land becomes a Haitian burial ground. The novel reflects both the nature of Haitians' harsh existence and the nature of their hope through a systemic twinning of individuals to land, Dominicans to Haitians, and kindred spirits. Danticat brings a face to the slain masses, gendering the experiences of the *braceros* and ultimately reconfiguring the possibility of reconciliation between Haitians and Dominicans in the border crossings of her female protagonist, Amabelle Zéphir. The novel points to the idea that Haitians and Dominicans are one people, that Hispaniola is one land, even though history and border zones have obscured these truisms. Thus, there are peaceful twinnings in this novel though, ironically, the only twins who would seem to find a measure of peace are those who find it after death. Through the ingenious use of the *marassa* trope, or cult of twins in Vodou, that she has used elsewhere (most notably in *Breath, Eyes, Memory*) Danticat signals the necessity of achieving balance between bipolarized racial identities, the unification of male/female and of the spirits of the dead with those of the living.[9]

Danticat thus makes use of *marassas*, or twinnings, in the novel as a way to invert the usual paradigms associated with twins (ideas of oneness, for example) so that the twin characters—those associated with birth, as in the case of the Ignacio twins (the children of Amabelle's mistress), and those associated with pain, as in the case of two Dominican women, Dolores and Doloritas, escaping the massacre to Haiti—come to signify differing aspects of the relationship between Haitians and Dominicans. The twinnings associated with women suggest not only the transcendence of earthly pain but also reconciliation through the transmutation of the border zones that they inhabit into a zone that will lead to freedom.

As the *braceros* and other Haitians flee the land and Trujillo's violence, one character, Tibon, says: "The ruin of the poor is their poverty. . . . The poor man, no matter who he is, is always despised by his neighbors. When you stay too long at a neighbor's house, it's only natural that he become weary of you and hate you" (178). His comment is spurred by the presence of the two Dominican sisters seeking safety, as afraid of the Dominican soldiers as they are of the Haitians. All this would appear, on surface, to suggest that the differences between Haiti and the Dominican Republic are irreconcilable, but one needs to look "under the bone" to see that this is not actually the case. The Dominican sisters Dolores and Dolorita have been so named by their mother because she "suffered much when each one of [them] was born so gave [them] these grave names" (176). Their names are grave indeed, suggesting a life-long tethering to pain and suffering, which sees its external manifestation figured in the chaos of Trujillo's killing frenzy. The sisters' appearance in the text highlights that Dominicans were not spared Trujillo's terror. One sister, Doloritas, has lost her Haitian betrothed, Ilestbien (literally, "he is good"), and both are now on their way to the border to look for him and then go on to Haiti. Their joining with the Haitian group marks a solidarity across cultural and national boundaries. Even language barriers do not stop them from communicating with the Haitians, who take them in only to ultimately abandon them as the danger for the Haitians grows. Presumably, the text suggests, the sisters will survive because of language, because they will not mispronounce the Spanish word for "parsley," an act for which countless Haitians were slain; and although it is not stated in the novel, one also presumes that they will survive through prostitution as a result of their light skin, for Dominican women made up (and still make up) a large part of the prostitution networks in Haiti. The novel stops short of imagining what these women's lives might be in the foreign land of Haiti, which they will come to claim as their own in their moment of sheer panic. Still, their presence in the Haitian group bespeaks a common pain to be remembered and actualized in the present.

In fact, the novel strongly conveys the necessity of facing the suffering and the pain of the past, acknowledging that the harms caused by man's inhumanity to man harms the conquering as much as the vanquished, if not more, for having deluded themselves as to the value of their convictions to such an extent that harming other human lives finds its ideological justification. One of the characters in the novel comments that there is usefulness in facing the past and in recognizing the commonalities between Haitians in Haiti and the Dominican Republic. Connected to Amabelle through their common birthplace, Cap Haïtien, Father Romain comes to symbolize the forces of conciliation as well as of self-affirmation. "In his sermons to the Haitian congregants of the valley," comments Amabelle, "he often reminded everyone of common ties: language, foods, history, carnival, songs, tales, and prayers. His creed was one of memory, how remembering—though sometimes painful—can make you strong" (73). Amabelle learns from him the importance of holding on to the past through language and custom rather than through blood or material possessions; in part, he teaches her the value of her own soul's belonging wherever her body might travel.

In a manner of speaking, Amabelle's body is the conduit through which readers are made to enter the space of history in which the genocidal attack on Haitian workers in the Dominican Republic is all but denied. As Amabelle enters the nightmarish dreamscape of the massacres and re-encounters there her love Sebastien, survives her pilgrimage to Haiti and then another to the Dominican Republic, she apprehends the fragility and tension between life and death, a fragility that only the work of memory can sustain. She says: "The slaughter showed me that life can be a strange gift. . . . Breath, like glass is always in danger. I chose a living death because I am not brave. It takes patience, you used to say, to raise a setting sun. Two mountains can never meet, but perhaps you and I can meet again. I am coming to your waterfall" (283). Amabelle has yet to comprehend that her "living death" is a state of grace, of courage, and that, unlike Sebastien, she has been able to bridge the mountains in *failing* to harbor rancor in her heart for Sebastien's loss or against Dominicans for their complicity with the Trujillo order to "whiten" the nation.

It is no coincidence that Amabelle is associated with water from the beginning to the end of the tale she has to tell. At the end of the novel, when Amabelle returns years later to the site of the massacres and to the household where she was once a maid, the mistress of the house, Valencia, tells her: "I understand why you would come this very long distance to see it. When we were children, you were always drawn to water, Amabelle, streams, lakes, rivers, waterfalls in all their power; do you remember?" She continues: "When I didn't see you, I always knew where to find you, peeking into some current, looking for your face. Since then I can't tell you how many streams and rivers and waterfalls I have been to, looking for you" (302–3). Valencia's observations are revelatory of Amabelle's association not only with water but also with the powers that it symbolizes and, most especially, Amabelle's protectress Metrès Dlo.[10] Ultimately, in her ability to cross borders, both physical and spiritual, Amabelle comes to assume her function as an opener of doors, as a god in the flesh, a female Legba.

In my estimation, Amabelle represents in her own being an interstice. She is neither entirely human nor entirely divine. She becomes a goddess in the flesh or a crossroad of the flesh. When one considers the symbolism of possession (through dance) in Vodou rituals, as Joan Dayan notes in her *Haiti, History, and the Gods*,[11] it becomes easier to interpret Amabelle in this light: "In the horrors of the New World, the ability to know the god in oneself meant survival, which is nothing other than the ability to keep expressing the self, and acceding, if only temporarily, to a form of power that defies compromise" (74). The ambivalence Amabelle displays throughout her recounted story, with regard to her own identity, can thus be recast as a coming to terms with her function as translator between the gods and the earthly. Her distanced voice or narrative of witness can thus be read as that of one who occupies both inside and outside positions simultaneously, who is possessed by both. It is significant, then, that she invokes the realm of shadows in the opening of her narrative. She recounts: "When I was a child, I used to spend hours playing with my shadow, something that my father warned could give me nightmares, nightmares like seeing voices twirl in a hurricane of rainbow colors and hearing the odd shapes of things rise up and speak to define themselves. Playing with my shadow made me, an only child, feel less alone" (4). In this, Amabelle is her own *marassa*, her own twin.

Amabelle twins with her soul-self, a self from which she gains a second sight and ability to transcend the earth-bound even as she expresses her desire to cling to her companion, Sebastien. She admits that when she did have playmates, "they were never quite real or present for me," yet that "Sebastien . . . guarded me from the shadows. At other times he was one of them" (4). The novel thus opens at its end; Sebastien is already counted among the missing since the text is a remembrance, a memoir of a horrific past; the many passages in which Amabelle tells of their great love are all in the past tense. Sebastien is a shadow, a ghost, and Amabelle joins him in this alter-space as she clings to their love and refuses to let it go, or to take another. She gains strength from the "other" she meets in the shadow contained within herself; with or without Sebastien, she remains an only child who is never quite alone, who embraces her negative double, unlike the twins born to Valencia.

When the twins are born to the Dominican woman, Doctor Javier contends: "It's as if one [Rafael] tried to strangle her" (89). But it is Rafael who dies. Javier explains: "It seems he simply lost his breath. . . . He stopped breathing. I thought Rosalinda was the one in danger, but he was the one whose strength failed" (90). The symbolism at work is impossible to ignore: Rafael, the light-skinned boy child, appears to have attempted to stop the dark-skinned girl child's breath; in the end, however, it is he who fails to breathe—in effect, he has harmed his own shadow, his own self, his twin, and suffers the consequence. The child who, as Valencia notes, favors Amabelle is the one who survives. Amabelle, as midwife, thus functions as a healing agent amid the upheaval in this particular household, and she is able to fulfill this function because she consistently embraces the "other" in her midst, whether that other is defined as her shadow, her lover, her mistress, or as her Dominican charges.

At the novel's end, having made the courageous journey back to the Dominican Republic, to the home she had fled during the *corte*, Amabelle faces the waters of the Massacre River again. She is forced to remember the drowning deaths of her parents, partings she has yet to fully understand. She muses: "I thought that if I relived the moment often enough, the answer would become clear, that they had wanted either for us all to die together or for me to go on living, even if by myself. I also thought that if I came to the river on the right day, at the right hour, the surface of the water might provide the answer: a clearer sense of the moment, a stronger memory. But nature has no memory. And soon, perhaps, neither will I" (309). In this passage, Amabelle reveals that she is already a part of nature since her memory has grown no stronger since the moment of the drowning; she also reveals that she is returning to nature, to the land. This return, however, is performed in a border zone, at the literal crossroads or convergence of Haitian and Dominican destinies. Amabelle is greeted there by a shadow, the "crazy" professor, a man who has already blessed her and acted as her opener of doors, another incarnation of Legba. Amabelle tells us: "I wanted to ask him, please, to gently raise my body and carry me into the river, into Sebastien's cave, my father's laughter, my mother's eternity" (310). But the professor disappears before she can make her request, before she can find out his name, and she follows her own way into the river, removing her clothing, lying in the current of the river, which is shallow beneath the falls, unable to do her harm. She lies there, "half-submerged," half in the past and half in the present, healing the rift of past violence and future hope: "I looked to my dreams for softness, for a gentler embrace, for relief from the fear of mudslides and blood bubbling out of the riverbed, where it is said the dead add their tears to the river flow." Letting the tears of the river flow over her, looking out into the sky, Amabelle heals and is reborn, "paddling like a newborn in a washbasin," "looking for the dawn" (310).

In connecting the cane fields to the massacres of the late 1930s, Danticat reveals that the relationship of the Haitians to the land is an antagonistic one. They are tied, as with umbilical cords, to killing grounds.

The novel is, in part, an exercise in reclaiming the ground that is imbued with death, with images of corpses thrown into water (200), and mass graves, as in the case of the burial of Odette, one of the female Haitians attempting to flee the Dominican Republic for Haiti in the latter part of the text. Comments Amabelle, "We did not ask where Odette would be buried, for we knew she would likely have to share her grave with all the others there" (205). Fleeing for their survival, already migrants, the Haitians are forced to leave the bones of their beloveds and kin behind, in unfamiliar and hostile territory, thereby underscoring the depth of their alienation from that land. Still, as Danticat herself notes, the burial of the dead in foreign ground transforms the relationship of individuals to that land; it makes them part of the alienating landscape, creates a history, a lineage. Commenting on the father of the slain *bracero*, ironically named Kongo,[12] Danticat says: "He can't let himself be comforted because of this idea that he's putting his son in the ground, there, in this hostile land. Marquez, in *One Hundred Years of Solitude*, said that you don't really belong to a place until you've buried your dead there. And the idea of still belonging after that. You have the sense that for Joel's father, he's not going to leave ever because his son is now part of this place. So, I think the relationship to the land is transformed."[13] The burying of the dead in a new landscape transforms that landscape into a home ground even as un-belonging persists. It is for this reason, this alienation, that the bones become more important than their burial place; their spirituality transcends both land and physical matter. Thus we can understand when Anabelle comments of Odette: "I must have been standing over the body for several hours. Wherever I go, I will always be standing over her body" (205). The bones of the slain, commemorated and buried, travel with the living to their new destination: no one is forgotten nor truly left behind.

Haitian Suppression in the Dominican Republic

In re-examining the trauma of the Haitian massacre from the vantage point of the present, *The Farming of Bones* presents us with a unique challenge, that is, to understand the place of nationalistic unrest between the two countries in the present. The novel does not operate simply as a fictionalized recounting of what once was, bringing the past to the fore of present-day memory; it excavates the past in order to reveal the vestiges of that history in the present. Despite blood ties, antipathy for Haitians is a long-standing facet of Dominican national politics.

As James Ferguson writes, "A myth of racial superiority has grown which paints the Dominican Republic as European, modern and democratic and Haiti as African, archaic and dictatorial."[14] This myth paradoxically fuels the inhumane treatment of Haitians contemporaneously. The constant flow of Haitian workers into the Dominican Republic appears to be the major stumbling block for a reassessment through Dominican eyes of the weight of history upon the present. Thus, a number of writers have sought to clarify the reasons for present-day Haitian migration as well as the effect it has had on the Dominican psyche, but none have done so as effectively as Danticat, perhaps due to their location within the psyche of the dominant rather than dominated culture. Latin American writer Mario Vargos Llosa, for one, writes against the common view in the Dominican press that Haitians are a blight upon Dominican soil, as one journalist wrote, "a sanitary problem for the Dominican Republic" and a drain on national resources. Vargos Llosa points out that Dominican views against Haitians parallel closely that of U.S. legislators against Dominican migrants. He surmises: "Above all, (Haitians) reflect an ancestral panic over contamination by the other (the other race, the other language, the other religion), a fear of being dissolved in a promiscuous mix as a result of the collapsing of traditional borders that for a long time kept everything—countries, men, cultures, beliefs—walled in their own places."[15] The fear of racial and cultural contamination is deeply embedded in the Dominican psyche.[16] This fear has, however, become anachronistic. What propels Haitians to overflow Haitian borders are factors directly related to economic and political deprivation.

Haitians are seen as interlopers within a body politic that resists contamination without regard for the fact that the body politic that has become synonymous with the Dominican nation is already a body "morcelé"—in pieces. Literally, the western arm of Hispaniola sits disembodied from the rest of the island; occupying the eastern portion of Hispaniola, the Dominican Republic is tethered to Haiti. It is, at best, an uncomfortable union exacerbated by the distortions of history. Dominican national identity assumes a bipolarization from Haiti and Haitians: the Dominican Republic celebrates its national independence as independence from Haitian rule even though that rule came as a result of efforts to free enslaved Africans in the French and Spanish colonies and, subsequently, to unify the two sides of the island. In the present day, this has led to the denigration of forms of employment formerly associated with slavocracy. What historians have failed to note is the triangular relationship Dominicans occupy with regard to the period of enslavement. Slavery continues to be connected in the popular imagination solely to Haiti; by displacing such humiliation onto Haitians, Dominicans release themselves from the shame associated with their own slave past. Another issue that divides the two nations is that of land ownership; and the link here to slavery is an interesting one connected to the U.S. interventions of the early twentieth century.

In Haiti, since the land reforms of the revolutionary era, peasants had been awarded tracts of land that were then passed down within family units; this has resulted in a larger percentage of land-owning peasants in Haiti than in the Dominican Republic. In his discussion of the rural population, David Nicholls notes that it is possible to break down the superstructure of these areas into that of the *"gros habitants,"* the 2 percent of the rural population who own land, often as absentee landlords, and who employ others to work their land; the landless-earners who account for 10 percent of the population; a "rural sub-proletariat" who make up 35 percent of the population working on land owned by family; and the "habitants" who make up over 50 percent of the population.[17] What these approximate statistics reveal is that land ownership is not non-existent among the peasant classes and that it mediates between mass migration and necessary movements from the rural classes into other lands for work. In contradistinction, in the Dominican Republic, the U.S. presence of the late nineteenth century and early twentieth century that focused largely on the cane trade (as the Dominican Republic and Cuba provided the majority of the sugar crop for North America), took away the livelihoods of many peasant land workers. Before the early 1900s, Dominican peasants had subsisted on cattle raising rather than on cane cultivation; the U.S. factories bought the land of the common land workers in order to capitalize on the land's potential for sugar cultivation. Farmers, according to Bruce Calder, thus "had to leave the area, probably migrating to a town or northward into hillier country, or they had to accept jobs with the sugar companies which had taken over their lands."[18] The rest, for a short time, became cane workers but, unhabituated to the demanding labor of the cane fields and unrewarding wages (as well as short cultivation period), most went into other lines of work while the cane industries relied on Haitian and other migrant labor in their stead. The irony here is that Haitian workers were lured to the Dominican cane fields out of economic need in spite of their land ownership on the other side of the border divide; while Dominicans lost their right to their land, Haitians sought the wages to keep theirs. Not coincidentally, I believe, the dwelling places of the newer *arrivants* to the cane fields, called "*barracones*," "often date from the colonial era, when they served as quarters for slaves."[19]

Transnational Healing

In the end, the continued division between Haitians and Dominicans impoverishes both nations: it prevents the healing of historical wounds and the possibility of regaining a common, familial past. But are Haitians prepared to forgive? Are Dominicans prepared to bring down economic barriers? Our objectives for unification are still unclear, and yet this is a discussion *The Farming of Bones* suggests that we must have. Within the context of such reparation, *The Farming of Bones,* then, is Danticat's healing text. It is situated in her own corpus as a text of transnational and international reconciliation at the most basic components of both Haitian and Dominican populations: the workers in the fields and in the homes of the most privileged. It imagines healing in the form of sharing lived memory of a time that both nations would rather forget. In a certain manner, though her characters within it are highly personalized and individual, it is a text poised to take its place in the canon building of national literature(s) for the region. It is less about the personal migrant experience figured in *Breath, Eyes, Memory,* or the particularized haunting of terror under the Duvaliers for Haitians alone as figured in *The Dew Breaker,* or the more mythic nature of her children's books and travel tomes. *The Farming of Bones* is of Haiti and the Dominican Republic as well as of the United States; it demands a breaking down of national borders and boundaries to actualize a cross-national healing; it encourages a discussion across nationalities so that we might begin to halt forgetting in favor of building a more conscious future in which the hauntings of the past, mired in the hatred of the "other" through racial and gendered grounds, can be altered and replaced by a common love that is rooted in facing the pain of the past and recognizing in that pain a potent and healing balm for a better future.

NOTES

Portions of this analysis previously appeared in "Facing the Mountains: Dominican Suppression and the Haitian Imagination," *Journal of Haitian Studies* 9, no. 1 (Spring 2003): 4–22. Reprinting of excerpts from the *JHS* article here is by permission of the editors of *JHS*.

1. Edwidge Danticat, *The Farming of Bones* (1998; New York: Penguin Books, 1999). Subsequent references are to this edition and are given after quotations in the main body of the text.

2. Such historians include Mayo Pons, James Ferguson, and Bruce Calder, among others.

3. For a complete discussion of these issues, see Lauren Derby, "Haitians, Magic, and Money: Raza and Society in the Haitian-Dominican Borderlands, 1900 to 1937," *Comparative Studies in Society and History* 36, no. 3 (1994): 488–526.

4. Pierre Nora, *Realms of Memory: Rethinking the French Past*, vol. 1, trans. Arthur Goldhammer (New York: Columbia University Press, 1996), 1. Subsequent citations to this work are given in the main body of the text.

5. Edouard Glissant, "The Quarrel with History," *Caribbean Discourse: Selected Essays*, trans. J. Michael Dash (Charlottesville: University Press of Virginia, 1989), 62–63. Subsequent citations to this work are given in the main body of the text.

6. bell hooks, *Yearning* (Boston: South End Press, 1990), 147. Subsequent citations to this work are given in the main body of the text.

7. Adrienne Rich, "Resisting Amnesia," *Blood, Bread, and Poetry: Selected Prose, 1979–1985* (New York: Norton, 1986), 148. Subsequent citations to this work are given in the main body of the text.

8. See Trinh T. Minh-ha, *Woman, Native, Other: Writing Postcoloniality and Feminism* (Bloomington: Indiana University Press, 1991).

9. For my further discussion of the concept of the *marassa* in Haitian women's literature, see Myriam J. A. Chancy, *Framing Silence: Revolutionary Novels by Haitian Women* (Piscataway, NJ: Rutgers University Press, 1997); also see Florence Bellande-Robertson, *The Marassa Concept in Lilas Desquiron's Reflections of Loko Miwa* (Dubuque, IA: Kendall/Hunt, 1999); for discussions of the *marassa* or cult of twins in Haitian Vodou, see Maya Deren, *Divine Horsemen: The Living Gods of Haiti* (1953; New Paltz, NY: McPherson, 1985), in particular.

10. Literally, "mistress of the water"; a folk figure equivalent to the sea goddesses such as Ochun and Yemaya usually imaged in Haitian Vodou as a variation of the goddess Erzulie; Metres Dlo appears to be differentiated from the latter in that her domain is the rivers and lakes rather than the sea.

11. Joan Dayan, *Haiti, History, and the Gods* (Berkeley: University of California Press, 1995).

12. The term "Kongo" is usually used as a pejorative in the Dominican context; it is meant to highlight the Africanness of Haitians and to undermine that lineage; here, reclaimed by Danticat to name a character, the word is given significance and valorized.

13. Edwidge Danticat, telephone interview with author, fall 2001.

14. James Ferguson, *Dominican Republic: Beyond the Lighthouse* (Washington, DC: Latin American Bureau, 1992), 20.

15. Mario Vargos Llosa, online article, no longer traceable.

16. For a complete discussion of these issues, see Lauren Derby, "Haitians, Magic, and Money: Raza and Society in the Haitian-Dominican Borderlands, 1900 to 1937" *Comparative Studies in Society and History* 36, no. 3 (1994): 488–526.

17. David Nicholls, *Haiti in Caribbean Context: Ethnicity, Economy and Revolt* (Oxford: Macmillan, 1985), 25–30.

18. Bruce Calder, *The Impact of Intervention: The Dominican Republic during the U.S. Occupation of 1916–1924* (Austin: University of Texas Press, 1984), 94.

19. *Haitian Cane Cutters in the Dominican Republic* (New York: Americas Watch Committee, November 1989), 33.

CONCEALMENT, DISPLACEMENT, & DISCONNECTION

Danticat's *The Dew Breaker*

MARY GALLAGHER

While the principal distinctiveness of Edwidge Danticat's third novel lies undoubtedly in its poetics of fragmentation, and while Danticat does pursue in *The Dew Breaker* many of the thematic preoccupations that have propelled her writing from the outset, it would be a distortion to suggest that this book is innovative on a formal level only. In fact, Haitian displacement and alienation again form the backdrop of this work, where they are associated, again, with a broken sense of the past, of connection, and indeed of personal identity. These thematic threads are woven, as in *Breath, Eyes, Memory* and in *The Farming of Bones*, into deftly drawn interpersonal relationships, and once again Danticat's writing communicates a powerful sense of a general axis of loss, as trauma is passed on from one Haitian generation to the next and from one locus to another. However, while it reworks these thematic veins, the third novel expands them to include, most notably, the paternal relationship. This emphasis on the figure of the father, resulting in the intensified triangulation of the representation of family relations, is highlighted by the father who is the central eponymous character of the book. Not only does this emphasis allow Danticat to renew her matrifocal repertoire, but it also leads her to explore a whole new set of ethical dilemmas linked not just to the moral issues of silence, concealment, guilt, complicity, witness, and redemption, but also to the more political question of justice and the matter of responsibility toward the "third party," a question already to the fore in *The*

Farming of Bones. In addition, the figure of the father connects with the Duvalier (father and son) dictatorship, a connection that resonates with particular force when the word "papa" appears in the text (François Duvalier was, after all, known as Papa Doc).

The publisher's presentation of *The Dew Breaker* reveals a certain generic confusion. The list of previous outings (as short stories) of various parts of the book, the terms of the quoted book reviews—some critics referring to short stories and others to a novel—and the reference to its shortlisting for various literary prizes (none rewarding novels specifically) do more to highlight than to answer the question as to whether Danticat's book is a collection of stories or a novel. Because only a minority of short-story collections present characters whose lives or dilemmas are enmeshed across the various stories, the best answer to that question is that *The Dew Breaker* is a hybrid form and that an essential part of its meaning derives from its subversion of the boundary between the two genres.

The Dew Breaker spans nine chapters, each shaped as an individual story, most of which were published as separate short stories and subsequently rewritten slightly for inclusion in the book. Three concentrate directly on the central figure of the "Dew Breaker" (from a Kreyòl circumlocution meaning "torturer"), depicting this character's trajectory in reverse chronology: they are the first story, "The Book of the Dead," set in Florida; the fourth, "The Book of Miracles," set in his Brooklyn exile where he works as a barber; and the final story, "The Dew Breaker," set in his Haitian past. The three pivotal stories are separated (more than linked) by six others. This structure raises many questions, but rather than asking how successful the book is as a novel, and to what extent it remains a collection of stand-alone units that create a sense more of discontinuity than of consequential development of character or plot, readers may find themselves searching for secret passages connecting the eponymous plot and the individual stories, even if the author might not seem to have provided enough keys to identify the links. This hermeneutic shortfall opens up the meaning of the individual stories, the suspicion of a hidden continuity lending each story additional, if uncertain, depth. Moreover, the fragmentation of the book's structure itself enacts the brokenness of the lives portrayed and performs the concealment, displacement, and disconnection that the book also configures thematically.

Fault Line

The eponymous (yet anonymous) figure is presented from the outset as an enigma: the reader's introduction to him in the first chapter is as a missing person. In this reversal of the traditional "runaway" motif, where it is the child, not the parent, who goes missing, the father has disappeared from the Florida hotel room that he has been sharing with his adult, sculptor daughter, Ka, the story's first-person narrator. Ka is on a mission to deliver a wood carving of her father to a celebrity Haitian actress who has commissioned it for her own father. The heroic stature that Ka implicitly confers on her father by making him the sole subject of her art is undercut by his anti-heroic appearance: he is short, rotund, and scarred. Although his "ecce homo" pose in the commissioned work lends him the messianic nobility of the sacrificial victim (kneeling, beholding his hands), the fact that he destroys his putative likeness by throwing it into a pond raises doubts about Ka's identity and legitimacy as an artist. His act also inaugurates the central theme of false identity and misplaced trust that runs through the whole book.

There is an obvious dissonance at the heart of this Haitian father-daughter pair: whereas the latter seems thoroughly Americanized and only sporadically nostalgic for the Haitian past that she does not share with her parents, the father seems in need of belief in the Other World. The reader thus learns early on that he named his daughter after the Ancient Egyptian notion of the "double of the body," the soul, or the Haitian "good angel."[1] Moreover, the mother's overreaction on the telephone to the news of the father's disappearance confirms that all is not as it seems in this family. The fulcrum of "The Book of the Dead" is the father's five-point "confession" to his daughter, which is triggered by his hurting Ka. Whereas the book opens with Ka's discussion of her missing father with a benign police officer who calms her by gently stroking her wrist, the anger of the eventually located father at his child's hysterical reaction to the destruction of her sculpture prompts him to grab her wrist and crush it in his painful grip. He apologizes immediately, saying that he never meant to hurt her, and adds that he never meant to hurt anyone, before admitting that, in his previous life, he had been the hunter, not the prey. The binary hunter-prey model is crucial to the father's representation of his past, although Ka questions this model, suspecting that there may have been other unnamed choices available. The "hunter" then admits that he had been working, not imprisoned, in the prison. Thus in the final story, the reader learns that when he ambiguously told his future wife that he was "free" and had "finally escaped," it was because he "had escaped from his life. He could no longer return to it, no longer wanted to" (237). His third admission is that it was "one of the prisoners inside the prison who cut my face in this way" (21)—and it emerges in the final story that the prisoner had done this with a piece of wood; and his fourth admission is that he killed that man "like I killed many people" (22). Finally, in response to his daughter's first question about his nightmares, he confesses that they were inspired by "what I, your father, did to others" (23).

Significantly, each time that the emphasis shifts from what Ka's father is confessing to Ka's reaction, she is focusing not on her father's guilt but on her mother's co-implication or complicity. Thus, after her father's first cryptic declaration, she dreads that he is going to explain her parents' reclusive life in Brooklyn and their lack of contact with Haiti, and wonders more specifically: "Is he about to tell me why *Manman* is so pious? *Why she goes to daily Mass*" (21). Again, after the subsequent stream of revelations, Ka contrasts her father's well-rehearsed delivery of his monologue with her lack of preparation, noting that "there is no time yet, no space in my brain to allow for *whatever my mother might have to confess. Was she huntress or prey? A thirty-year plus disciple of my father's coercive persuasion?*" (22). Following the admission of the real cause of the nightmares, *"another image of my mother now fills my head, of her as a young woman, a woman of my age, taking my father in her arms"* (23).[2] This repeated shift of focus from the father's guilt onto the mother's implication therein highlights the centrality of the issues of displacement and connection in the book, issues that explain, indeed, why the dramatic tension at the heart of the Dew Breaker's story derives not from the portrayal of the depravity of the aberrant individual but rather from the relations between that individual and the entourage that accepts and shelters him. Right up to the end of the book, the only name given to Ka's father in the narratives is "The Dew Breaker": he can only be identified by the reader either by this name or by reference to his connection to others—he is Ka's father, Anne's husband (although it is suggested that they are not legally married)—or by his role for others—barber, landlord, torturer, executioner. The impact of the graphic but economical description of the Dew Breaker's depravity in the final story of the book is undeniable. What is much more shocking, however, is the cohabitation or coexistence of this extreme potential for a barely speakable sadism, inflected by sexual and deeply misogynistic connotations, with the potential for an apparently normal family life. The plot forces this point to an extreme by giving the erstwhile torturer a daughter as his only legitimate child, the step-sister of his ultimate expiatory victim as a loving wife, and as a lodger the son— himself a tender, uxorious man—of more of his dead victims.

That the father is caught in a plot less of linear redemption and transformation than of sporadic cohabitation of the past and the present is made clear when he hurts his daughter's hand, an act that resurrects the past momentarily. And just as the Dew Breaker's present and past connect in this act, in the scar tissue on his face, and in his guilty nightmares, so too they connect in every interaction with his wife, the stepsister of his last victim. The Dew Breaker's cohabitation with an indirect victim of his violence seems to confirm the miracle of his transformation, but it also deepens the mystery of his story, in that— even in his former life—a spiritual impulse and a certain capacity for empathy with or concern for another person (his own father, destroyed by injustice, or the young boy outside the church in the final story) had cohabited with his appetite for power and cruelty. Moreover, when Ka wonders why, in her mother's miracle tales, the people to whom the miracles happened were all foreigners, it is her father who answers: "Because Americans don't have much faith" (73). However, neither a religious nor even a spiritual sensibility is shown to be any guarantee of a moral compass: after all, the Dew Breaker was "seeing" angels and souls long before his final conversion. A woman with whom he shared these hallucinations had indeed warned him that he couldn't "afford to be a spiritual man" (193).

Others' Stories

Just as the first story communicating Ka's perspective on her parents is moderated by "The Book of Miracles," which presents her mother Anne's world-view in her Brooklyn exile, and also by the final story, which illuminates the Dew Breaker's past and recounts his first encounter with Anne, so too the intervening stories offer different subjective perspectives on the same events (not just events involving the Dew Breaker). This plurality of perspectives both enriches and complicates the reader's interpretation of the various stories and also reflexively points toward the difficulty of establishing a univocal meaning for any particular character, situation, or text. The second story, entitled "Seven," dwells on the reunion after a seven-year separation between an unnamed man and his wife. The man is, it emerges, an unmarried Haitian sharing a basement apartment with two other Haitian exiles, Michel and Dany, in the Brooklyn house belonging to the eponymous Dew Breaker. The third story, "Water Child," is the story of Nadine, a Haitian nurse working in exile in the United States in *the* ear, nose, and throat department of a large hospital. She has aborted her baby, the Water Child of the title. It seems, however, as though the father of her dead baby is Eric, the unnamed third man of the barber's basement. Although both stories dwell on exile, impeded communication, and dislocated or broken relationships, the emphasis on the parent-child bond in "Water Child" echoes the focus on family relations in the opening tale, whereas this emphasis barely features in "Seven." "Night Talkers" tells the story of Dany, housemate of Michel and of Eric, who returns to Haiti to tell his aunt that he has located in New York the man responsible for the death of his parents and for his aunt's blindness. In Haiti he witnesses his aunt's death and meets Claude, the young patricidal "night talker" returned from New York. Issues of crime and guilt, secrets and conscience, pervade this story, then, as does the problematic (or absent) father-son relationship. The story of the eponymous "Bridal Seamstress," another New York survivor of a Haitian torture chamber, is told to a young journalist intern and thus reflexively raises questions of writing and memory, testimony or witness, artistry or creativity, linking them to the themes of torture, guilt, and appearance/disappearance. "Monkey Tails," set in Haiti and centered on a father's refusal to acknowledge his son, focuses not just on illegitimacy but also on the troubled political situation of the island. It is told from the retrospective (first-person) point of view of Michel, one of the characters in "Seven," now married and expecting a child. Continuing the Haitian exile topos, "Funeral Singer" is about a trio of young women, exiles from Haiti and political violence, and is narrated by Freda, the funeral singer. As each of their stories gradually unfolds against the backdrop of their effort to integrate into the new land, Freda recalls that her father, a fisherman, had fallen foul of the *Macoutes:* "I was asked to leave the country by my mother because I wouldn't accept an invitation to sing at the national palace. But I also left because long ago my father had disappeared" (172). This fidelity to the memory of her broken father provides a counterpoint to Ka's relationship with her father.

The How and the Why

The resonances between the six "other" stories and the three movements of the Dew Breaker tale seem to suggest that the source of the distress of the victims and the survivors is not just violence per se, but rather a violence that is absolutely arbitrary. Thus Dany, looking down at the sleeping "barber's face, which had shrunk so much over the years, . . . lost the desire to kill" because of "the dread of being wrong, of harming the wrong man, of making the wrong woman a widow and the wrong child an orphan. It was the realization that he would never know . . . why one single person had been given the power to destroy his entire life" (107). The Dew Breaker's violence is never explained. We know how but not why it began, how but not why it continued, and how but again not why it stopped. The lack of reason, let alone of sufficient reason, is echoed in the apparent triviality of the motive of Claude's patricide. "Claude wiped a shadow of a tear from his face with a quick swipe of the back of his hand. 'I'm the luckiest fucker alive. I've done something really bad that makes me want to live my life like a fucking angel now'" (119). The numerous references to angels in connection with the (never named) Dew Breaker, to Ka being his good angel and to her mother's faith in miracles, including the miracle of her husband's recovered humanity, suggests not just a particularly Manichean worldview, but also that something irrational, if not otherworldly, is involved both in the mystery of the Dew Breaker's past and in the putative miracle of his reformation.

It is not so much the Dew Breaker's direct victims, but rather their children, who are haunted by the "why," as though a cogent, rational answer might calm their distress. As far as Michel in "Monkey Tails" knew, "I had lost my father to something my mother would only vaguely describe as 'political,' making me part of a generation of mostly fatherless boys, though some of our fathers were still living, even if somewhere else—in the provinces, in another country, or across the alley not acknowledging us" (141). The irony is that Michel's mother is, in fact, lying to her son. His father is not politically active but is rather an opportunistic and greedy neighbor living literally "across the alley," who has refused to acknowledge Michel as his son. And it is Michel's best or only friend, Romain, whose father is in fact politically active, who eventually reveals the secret identity of Michel's father to the boy. Unable to admit the truth in public, Michel kept the lie of his fatherlessness alive. It was easier for the son (as it was also easier for Dany and for Ka) to live with the idea of his father being a victim of political violence than to live with the truth. Similarly, Dany's burning question to his aunt when he returns to Haiti is: "Were my parents in politics?" Estina's answer is evasive and echoes both Dany's concern with mistaken identity and Ka's mistaken view of her father: "'No more than any of us. . . . They didn't do anything bad, Da,' she said, 'or anything at all. I didn't know all my brother's secrets, but I think he was taken for somebody else'" (109).

Tales of Trauma and Loss

Trauma and loss loom large in the psychological landscape of *The Dew Breaker*. As in much of Danticat's writing, the characters' memory and identity are structured by loss, and the memory of trauma is often inscribed in the body: in mutilation or maiming (the Dew Breaker's ambiguous scar, Beatrice's scarred scalp, Dany's blinded aunt Estina). Yet, in *The Dew Breaker*, it is not simply—as is usually the case in Danticat's writing—a question of living with the memory of loss or trauma suffered, nor, as in *The Farming of Bones*, a question of living in the discomfort of moral ambivalence, but also of living with the tenacious and unambiguous memory of having (arbitrarily) inflicted trauma and loss on others. Like memory, the experience of loss is based on the counterpoint of absence and presence. From the Japanese-inspired water shrine to Nadine's aborted baby to Anne's cemetery phobia— what her daughter terms her "issues with cemeteries" (72)—and which is linked to the death of her baby brother by drowning, the absence of the dead or of the missing is omnipresent in the stories. The role of the memorial is a particularly important thematic thread in *The Farming of Bones*, where the impossible burial compounds loss. Similarly, the story of Freda's broken and innocent father who goes missing at sea provides in *The Dew Breaker* a painful counterpoint to Ka's only temporarily missing but guilty father. Dany in "Night Talkers," however, suffers not just the loss of his assassinated parents but also the dearth of memories linked with them: "He had so little information and so few memories to draw on that every once in a while he would substitute moments from his own life in trying to re-create theirs" (99).

Secrets and Lies

The Dew Breaker traces, both formally and thematically, the secrets and failures, the cracks and short circuits, that undermine authentic connection in relationships, not only parent-child relationships but also relationships between husbands and wives, lovers, and friends. Concealment is a form of deception and betrayal that often leads to such disconnection. We have already seen how the themes of hiding and secret inform the central plot: the Dew Breaker's Brooklyn life has imprisoned both himself and his wife in a web of concealment and denial. Thus, when Ka asks her mother to tell another miracle tale, Anne wants to tell the "simple miracle of her husband's transformation" (73): "Look how calm he is. Look how patient he is" (72), she wants to say. But as she couldn't share that secret with her daughter, "instead she told of another kind of miracle" (73), that of a "twenty-one-year-old Filipino man who'd seen an image of the Madonna in a white rose petal" (73). On the last page of the book, Anne faces Ka's consequential rejection as her daughter hangs up on her from Florida, disappearing into the "hum of the dial tone" (242).

Concealment is also a crucial theme in the other stories, where it is often, as in the central plot, intertwined with a dynamic of restricted, deficient, or failed communication. In "Water Child," Nadine's concealment from her parents of her abortion—and of her general loneliness and sorrow—is compounded by her unreasonable expectation that they somehow intuit her pain, despite her silence on the subject. Having to hide all negativity imposes a destructive strain on relationships. In "Seven," Eric's wife "wasn't to know that he'd ever done anything but work his two jobs . . . and she was never to find out about those women who'd occasionally come home with him in the early-morning hours" (38). She, however, had "wanted to tell her husband about that neighbor who had slept next to her those days after he'd left and in whose bed she had spent many nights after that. Only then would she feel like their future would be true. Someone had said that people lie only at the beginning of relationships. The middle is where the truth resides. But there had been no middle for her husband and herself, just a beginning and many dream-rehearsed endings" (48). Even if Eric realizes that his wife is hiding something from him, "he did not want to trespass on her secrets" (49), perhaps because he had secrets of his own that he wanted to keep. However, the ultimate consequence of the couple's concealment of their infidelities is the breakdown of all meaningful, present- or future-oriented connection between them. Although the Dew Breaker and his wife seem tightly connected by the secret that they share and together conceal from their daughter and the wider world, a pattern of shared or reciprocal secrecy and deception takes its toll, as the plot of "Seven" shows: just as this tale ends with the observation that the couple's seven-year separation had been "a temporary silence, unlike the one that had come over them now" (52), similarly, the final story ends with Ka hanging up on her mother.

Connection/Disconnection

Concealment is not the only cause of disconnection in *The Dew Breaker,* however. The normal twists and turns of life can militate against the desired contact. In "Night Talkers," for example, Dany only "dreamed that he was having the conversation he'd come to have with his aunt. . . . He began the conversation by recalling with his aunt the day his parents had died" (104). Earlier on the same day his (actual) conversation with his aunt had been interrupted by various intrusions; on the night of his dreamed connection with her, it is terminally interrupted by Estina's death.

Along with concealment, displacement is represented in this book as one of the chief triggers for disconnection. When Eric shows his wife the New York park "where he came to ponder seasons, lost time, and interminable distances" (51), he could be referring to the lost time and interminable distance that in so many contexts keeps the characters from making or maintaining meaningful connections. Not being able to speak directly and having to rely on the telephone, or letters, or photographs undermines direct communication. In "Water Child," the notes that Nadine's laryngectomy patient, a young teacher, must now use in order to communicate and Nadine's communication with her own parents by letter and telephone highlight the value of physical presence and contact in maintaining truthful connection. Although the patient is voiceless, she has the comfort of her parents' physical presence. Conversely, Nadine has stopped telephoning her parents because she fears that "her voice might betray all that she could not say" (57). She also failed, perhaps for the same reason, to return Eric's messages. The association of this disconnection with her shrine to the lost baby suggests the abortiveness of her relationship with Eric: "She had filled her favorite drinking glass with water and a pebble and had added that to her own shrine, along with a total of now seven microcassettes with messages from Eric, messages she had never returned" (57).

Danticat's writing illustrates performatively that attentive reading is required in order to make certain connections. Thus, the reader of "Seven" and "Water Child" is invited to make the connection retrospectively between Nadine and the unnamed husband of another woman in "Seven," Nadine's "former beau, suitor, lover, the near father of her nearly born child," Eric, who had called her "once a month since their breakup" (56). Eric had thus been telephoning Nadine for seven months, all the while planning to bring his wife to America once he had got his green card. In "Seven" the reader had learned that just before his reunion with his wife, and seven months into his separation from Nadine, he had cancelled his telephone connection: "Gone was the phone number he'd had for the last five years, ever since he'd had a telephone. (He didn't need other women calling him now)" (39). Eric's view that "those women, most of whom had husbands, boyfriends, fiancés, and lovers in other parts of the world, never meant much to him anyway" (38) retrospectively reduces Nadine to the status of one of many "other women" who had meant little to him and who had other significant others to take care of them. The harm done by Eric's misreading or misidentification of Nadine is underscored by the irony of the fact that it is Eric himself, not Nadine, who has a spouse in Haiti.

A Poetics of Resonance

The impact of *The Dew Breaker* derives in great part from Danticat's aesthetic of reverberation. This operates most overtly at a thematic and more broadly intertextual level between the different stories. Thus, Dany's concern not to harm "the wrong man" is echoed in an episode in "The Book of Miracles" where Ka and her mother come close in church to misidentifying a different man as a former *Tonton Macoute*. Similarly, various smaller motifs are interwoven, sometimes to opaque effect, from one story to another. For example, it is difficult to know what exactly to make of the fact that Eric's wife in "Seven" "smelled [of] a mixture of lavender and lime" (41), exactly the same scent as the Dew Breaker's as reported by his daughter in the previous story. In a more unproblematic textual echo, the toothless man whom Dany mistakes in the mountain village for a "grandfather" (91) recalls Freda's tortured father (all his teeth pulled out as torture) and Ka's father (whose teeth are broken when he falls from bed during one of his night terrors). Moreover, the fact that the man appears elderly to Dany recalls Freda's comment in "The Funeral Singer": "One day one Macoute came to take [my father's fish stall] over and another one took my father away. When my father returned, he didn't have a tooth left in his mouth. In one night, they'd turned him into an old, ugly man. The next night he took his boat out to sea and, with a mouth full of blood, vanished forever" (172). Another striking intertextual motif is that of the (wedding) dress. This is central to "The Bridal Seamstress," where it is interwoven with the maternal theme (Beatrice has her customers call her "Mother"), but it is also important in "Night Talkers" in that the childless midwife Estina, who had dreamed of being a baby seamstress and had sewn—in vain—her own bridal trousseau, is buried in the unworn blue dress that Dany had sent her from New York. The dress motif also interlocks with the theme of false identity in "Seven," in the reference to the Carnival bridal couple's cross-dressing, and in the pink satin robes that Eric's roommates don in honor of his wife.

However, the poetics of reverberation also operates at other levels in the book. For example, the notion of memory is given added cultural resonance by reference to Egyptian, Japanese, and Catholic mythology and religion. In foregrounding the Egyptian *Book of the Dead*, Danticat emphasizes the theme of the Other World and its relation to human destiny: according to Barry Kemp, "the Egyptians created a world of supernatural forces so vivid, powerful and inescapable, that controlling one's destiny within it was a constant preoccupation."[3] The motif also highlights writing itself, or the book as record, and thereby the notion of the historical record and its link to memory. This recalls the Dew Breaker's reluctance to have his likeness displayed and echoes the relation between Beatrice and the young journalist, Aline, who records her story in "The Bridal Seamstress." Moreover, the parallel titles given to the first two "Dew Breaker" stories ("The Book of the Dead" and "The Book of Miracles") draw attention to the fact that both Anne's miracle tales and her husband's Ancient Egyptian lore mediate messages that the couple cannot articulate directly to their daughter, to each other, or even to themselves.

Certainly, the predominance in *The Dew Breaker* of allusions to Christianity, both to Catholicism (Anne's mass going and miracles) and to Protestantism (her stepbrother is a preacher), makes reference to

Vodouism conspicuous by its absence. This is an absence that is paradoxically made even more present by the intertextual reference conveyed by the title "Dew Breaker" to Jacques Roumain's famous novel, *Gouverneurs de la rosée* (Masters of the Dew, 1978).[4] In this novel, a messianic figure manages to harness, not break, the dew by uniting a whole community around a common purpose against a strongly religious background in which Vodou plays an important role.

In its communication of a sense of place and in its language, Danticat's writing produces a strongly relational sense of cultural reality. "Seven," for example, contains two references to the racist persecution of Haitian immigrants in New York, and both "Seven" and "The Funeral Singer" focus on the process of immigration itself (the procuring of a green card and the effort to integrate linguistically and culturally into the United States). The problematic of intercultural relation is also central to the poetics of language in Danticat's text, where metalinguistic commentary, usually in relation to French Kreyòl, is designed to counteract the distorting effect created by the fact that whereas many of the characters would logically speak Kreyòl to one another, their words are nonetheless represented in English. One example of such commentary occurs in "Night Talkers" when the Haitian villagers seem to forget that Dany, unlike Claude, was brought up speaking Kreyòl: "They were speaking about him as though he couldn't understand, as if he were solely an English speaker, like Claude. . . . He wanted to close his eyes until he could wake up from this unusual dream where everyone was able to speak except the two of them" (112). Whereas the English of the narrative is, for the most part, (necessarily) limpid and rather uninflected, Ka's English and Claude's English sound quite different in that these two characters were brought up in New York and speak colloquial American, or "bad" English. Ka's language includes, to her mother's chagrin, a "meaningless litany" of American expletives such as "Ouch," "Cool," "Okay," "Whatever" (69).

The reverberation of the absent language, the shadowing of the language of the text (English) by the lost, unmarked native language of the characters (Kreyòl) is inscribed in the text, not just in metalinguistic commentary—as when the Dew Breaker tells his daughter, "I say rest in Kreyòl . . . because my tongue too heavy in English to say things like this, especially older things" (17). Perhaps in part in order to offset the unnatural effect of Haitian Kreyòl speakers apparently speaking in English to each other, some Kreyòl words are introduced into the text.

Sometimes they are translated: "'Non,' he replied. 'Mèsi.' Thank you" (90) and sometimes not: "Bonjou, cousins" (89) or "upset and sezi" (55). Moreover, the English text is sometimes haunted, perhaps involuntarily, less by Haitian Kreyòl specifically than by the French that itself underlies Kreyòl. Thus, the phrase "I was always appreciated and well compensated" (175)—to mean (presumably) that Freda's singing was well received and well paid—is based on gallicisms that are obvious as such to an ear attuned to French.

The Dew Breaker incites and rewards a reading open to the multiple, layered, if not concealed, relations that it establishes on the levels of genre, language, narrative, text, theme, and plot. This layering or reverberation complicates and even blurs—both hermeneutically and ethically—the contours of identity (who we are for ourselves and for others) and the lines between innocence, implication, complicity, and guilt. Moreover, in its self-reflexive dimension, Danticat's writing subtly but powerfully suggests the delicate, demanding, if not problematic nature not just of the act of reading, naming, or judging any given act, situation, character, story, and so on, but also the moral complexity involved in telling stories and, in particular, in making others the subject of art: Ka's sculpture, for example, but also Danticat's own writing.

NOTES

1. Edwidge Danticat, *The Dew Breaker* (New York: Vintage, 2004), 17. Subsequent references are to this edition and are given after quotations in the main body of the text.

2. Emphasis mine in these three quotations.

3. Barry Kemp, *How to Read the Egyptian Book of the Dead* (London: Granta, 2007).

4. Jacques Roumain, *Gouverneurs de la rosée* (1944; Paris: Éditeurs français réunis, 1964).

Danticat &
Her Peers

This section moves away from the scholarly analyses of the preceding section and presents essays written by Haitian, Caribbean, and African American fiction writers. These authors—Maryse Condé, Évelyne Trouillot, Madison Smartt Bell, and Lyonel Trouillot—offer their personal interpretations of and reactions to Danticat's writing. These essays shift the attention subtly onto more authorial concerns, such as the relationship between the writer and the nation, the constraints and dangers of literary nationalism, and the importance of language and style. Together, they complement the scholarly essays in their sensitivity to the challenges, obligations, and opportunities that Danticat has had to negotiate in her career to date.

FINALLY
EDWIDGE
ARRIVED

MARYSE CONDÉ

If I choose to paraphrase in my title Boileau's celebration of the poet François Malherbe's eruption on the French literary scene in his *Art Poétique* (1674), I do not do so lightly. It is a way for me to hoist myself onto his pulpit, thus lending more solemnity to my words. I intend to emphasize this young writer's invaluable contribution to Caribbean literature, and this from her first books.

We belong to countries where the literary terrain is so chartered, controlled, regulated that the neophyte must wade into it with extreme caution, bombarded as he is by virulent dictates. First, Aimé Césaire, the great Martinican poet, founding father of our literature, in his *Cahier d'un retour au pays natal* enjoins: "My mouth will be the mouth of voiceless misfortunes / Of those sinking into the dungeon of despair."[1] Which means that the writer, if he wants a work that endures, must forget his individuality and assume the collective voice. His "I" must mean "we." For his part, Edouard Glissant, one of the region's greatest theorists, recommends in the *Discours Antillais* that Caribbean people must be their own ethnologists.[2] He also demands that literature create myths and participate in the construction of a national identity. Finally, most recently, the writers of the Créolité movement exclaim in the opening of *Eloge de la Créolité:* "Neither European, nor African, nor Asian, we declare ourselves Creole."[3] They then emphasize the incomparable character of the Creole language, so-called mother tongue, born of the prison life of the plantation, which combines authenticity with the most perfect expressiveness. Also in the same book, they declare a few pages later: "Every time a mother, thinking she is favoring the learning of the French language, represses Creole in a child's throat, she is in fact bearing a blow to the latter's imagination, repressing his creativity" (104).

These orders and counter-orders should not surprise us. It's that Francophone Caribbean literature emerged after a long silence, a long time during which the *natif-natal,* the island native, considered to be subhuman, was dispossessed not only of his land but also of his most profound self and was forced to look upon his own realities with borrowed eyes. Negritude's heart-wrenching chant initiated the process of exploration, of re-appropriation and affirmation of a Caribbean identity. This process, which is not over, is still perceived as a factor capable of contributing to political liberation. The quest for political liberation has never ceased to irrigate the literary field. Clearly, these two quests are largely entwined. The great francophone writers, from Aimé Césaire to Patrick Chamoiseau, have never ceased to denounce in their writings the dependence in which their countries are maintained, even today, and to emphasize domination's perverse effects. In his essay *Ecrire en pays dominé,* Chamoiseau questions: "How can you write when your imaginary is swamped from morning until dreams with images, thoughts, values that are not your own? How can you write when what you are stagnates outside of the impulses that determine your life? How can you write, dominated?"[4]

The mission of the writer—renamed "marker of words" by the Creolists—remains the same. It remains forever and everywhere sacred like the demiurge whose Word gives birth to a harmonious world, freed from all wounds, including those of colonialism. In this scheme of things, Haiti holds a place that is both unique and ordinary. If its dysfunction is largely attributable to internal causes (violence, corruption, negligence, and selfishness on the part of the ruling classes) it no less falls prey to international capitalism as its victim of choice. Haiti, humiliated, depleted, invaded by U.S. Marines since its unseemly independence of 1804. Let us not forget, it was won by those "gilded Africans" who horrified Napoleon Bonaparte, who was impatient to return them to their shackles. One after the other, newspapers and literary groups from La Ronde to Les Griots, without forgetting the Spiralists, alleged to be working toward the nation's edification. It is revealing of this duality that Jacques Roumain, perhaps the most popular of Haitian writers, was at the same time the founder of the Bureau of Ethnology and of the Haitian Communist Party. Similarly, it is no coincidence that the great Jacques-Stephen Alexis was one of the dictator François Duvalier's first victims and that François Duvalier himself, before turning to politics, was a member of the Griots. During the dictatorship, with the exception of Frankétienne, who clung to his land, writers, fearful of the danger each of them were facing, took the road into exile.

I discovered Edwidge Danticat fairly recently. I hadn't ever read anything of hers, in spite of friends' enthusiastic recommendations. There are so many books to read, so many islands to explore. One day I happened across a copy of the journal *Meridians*. "I am an immigrant," she said in essence, "that is to say the least authentic of beings—both for the country I am from and for the one in which I live."[5] What confounded me was not the apparent modesty of her words. It was, on the contrary, her extreme audacity. Here was a Caribbean writer publicly renouncing of her own free will her authenticity, that is to say, her essential characteristic, that which allowed the people to identify with her and find themselves as proclaimed in the last pages of Césaire's *Cahier d'un retour au pays natal*: "Standing / and / Free/ . . . unexpectedly standing" (62). This meant that the myth of the writer as demiurge was crumbling. He was now an individual like any other. Edwidge Danticat, exiled in the United States, having suffered a fate the same as that of thousands of Haitians, did not claim any exceptional status for herself. On the contrary, she offered her vulnerability and naked hands to all.

Convinced of having missed out on something, I set out in her pursuit and devoured all of her books, from *Breath, Eyes, Memory* to *The Dew Breaker*. I already knew that she wrote in English. However, I hadn't fully taken the measure of this linguistic upheaval. Upon reading her novels, it immediately appeared to me that what could be thought of as a simple subversion or individual transgression of taboos was not that at all. It was rather the inscription into modernity of our new dependence. We were no longer just the "descendants of slaves" as some persist in calling us. We had become the *"disposable people,"* tossed from one continent to another, from one land, one language, to another. Second, third generation . . . Our history always stops at the first globalization, the one that during the seventeenth century tore us from the coasts of the African continent; the one that transported us in ship holds to a new habitat that we had to somehow make our own. The time has come to include the second globalization, which is taking place before our eyes. Is it forgotten because it is accompanied by neither slave ships nor brands nor chains, and finally, no imprisonment within the plantation system? Yet, it deprives us just as cruelly of our lands and our languages. It forces us to live beneath unknown skies; Edwidge Danticat, of Haitian origin, by the sole virtue of writing in English was updating History. Her novels restarted the stopped clock of time. They transformed the referent. The scenery and places of residence changed, were populated by scarcely used characters.

However, far be it from me to see in Edwidge's work a pure and simple update or a reworking of so-called committed literature. One has only to compare *The Farming of Bones* and Jacques-Stephen Alexis's *Compère Général Soleil* (*General Sun, My Brother,* 1999), both of which deal with the same historical event. If Tontons Macoutes, torturers, and boat people abound in her writing, it's that they exist in the reality from which fiction draws with both hands. Her texts are not at all anti-establishment, at least not in the traditional sense. She has completely forgotten the lessons of social realism.

This linguistic modification also brings about a revolution that Edwidge might not have considered nor even wished for. The act of writing in English for this child of Haiti, that is to say, originally stuck between two languages, French and Creole, is fraught with intense meaning for us Guadeloupean and Martinican writers. In fact, it announces, more than a liberation, a revolution. In our islands, as stated above, French was declared the language of colonization and as such was incapable of expressing our inner self. Only Creole, the so-called mother tongue, seemed capable of expressing it. In this regard, we can recall that Césaire himself did not escape criticism. For his having neglected the rhythms and sounds of Creole, certain critics do not hesitate to exclude him from the Martinican literary landscape. On the other hand, the native-white poet Saint-John Perse was able to relegate to memory his castor oil–scented *métisse* maid, his servants-with-faces-the-color-of-papayas-and-boredom, in short, his haughty vision of Guadeloupe because he knew how to praise the "kako seed." Well, this linguistic hierarchy is no longer valid, if indeed it ever was. Or, should we add a third element to it that we could call the language of exile? In any case, Edwidge Danticat proves to us that identity, the tributary of historical vicissitudes, can express itself in any idiom. Consequently, the creator is equipped with choices as to his mode of expression. French as well as English or German, all are equally valid to express one's self.

An important question results from all of this. Identity has wrongly been considered a garment that is sewn once and for all. What identity do Edwidge Danticat's novels express? Neither European, nor African, nor Asian in the terms of the *Eloge,* can she still be proclaimed Creole? If so, what is the nature of her Creoleness? Is it the one defined by a now obsolete discourse? Or rather, isn't it the outcome of a History that has been restarted and that has taken into account the trials of our present? If so, isn't this a new phenomenon? And shouldn't we try to grasp it in its new form and study it? I will not answer such an arduous question. I will limit myself to praising Edwidge Danticat's writing as beautiful as nascent oxygen, to paraphrase Andre Breton discovering Aimé Césaire.

NOTES

1. Aimé Césaire, *Cahier d'un retour au pays natal* (Paris: Présence Africaine, 1983 [1939]), 22. Translation mine.

2. Edouard Glissant, *Le Discours antillais* (1981; Paris: Gallimard, 1992).

3. Jean Bernabé, Patrick Chamoiseau, and Raphaël Confiant, *Eloge de la créolité,* trans. M. B. Taleb-Khyar (1989; Paris: Gallimard, 1993), 75.

4. Patrick Chamoiseau, *Ecrire en pays dominé* (Paris: Gallimard, 1997), 17.

5. "Voices from Hispaniola: A *Meridians* Roundtable with Edwidge Danticat, Loida Maritza Pérez, Myriam J. A. Chancy, and Nelly Rosario," *Meridians: Feminism, Race, Transnationalism* 5, no. 1 (2004): 68–91. I am paraphrasing Danticat's words.

THE RIGHT SIDE
OF HISTORY

ÉVELYNE TROUILLOT

I first met Edwidge Danticat through her texts—from sketch to character, sentence to paragraph. Then, more significantly, through her questions for a *Bomb Magazine* interview in which—she in the United States, and I in Haiti—we talked writing, family, memory, childhood, literature. We spun tales of our country, exchanging sorrows and humanity.[1]

There's something strange about confiding that way, through a virtual space, when you can't see the other and can't hear her voice. When you can't gauge the sharpness of a gaze, nor weigh the silence that accompanies a question. When thoughts come to us as words that appear with a click of the finger, a hand gesture.

Oddly enough, I felt neither particular concern nor the apprehension that can sometimes seize the Haitian writer, or any writer from a country outside the economic and political norms fixed by the dominant nations when he or she speaks before a foreign audience. The weight of the other's eyes on a country in distress, on a population constantly stumbling over its own delusions and obstacles imported from elsewhere. A smug look that without necessarily trying to destroy becomes condescending despite itself. Due to the superiority of those who find themselves on the right side of history, the side held up as example without reserve, the side that makes it possible to forget the particulars of their encounter with others, having long ago convinced themselves they were in the right. Oddly enough, I felt neither hesitation nor reserve, for from the start, I had understood that Edwidge Danticat placed herself on the side of history that is not always comfortable, but where the truth springs forcefully forth when cornered.

This obvious bias, the concern for historical and social truth, the open-mindedness toward the other that makes it possible to overcome clichés—for me, all constitute Danticat's strength. In Danticat's work, I recognized, as did many others, the contribution of Haitian cultural elements. The unavoidable presence of childhood drew me in right from the start. Haitian childhood, as one cannot help but encounter it in this country where 45 percent of the population is under fifty years old; childhood of the countryside, of the city, holding the ambiguous status of a being both adored and denied its rights. Gift of God, social investment, security for better days. A being that is loved, obsessed over, stifled, adored. Who is called upon to live up to family expectations, with no regard for his or her own orientations, tastes, or individual fancy. That child, I see her in *Breath, Eyes, Memory.* I hear her and I see her, small against adult demands, confused, but determined, anxious to please as are all children, but independent and capable of finding her place at the end of the journey. A journey that is painful, but not without moments of tenderness, even when that tenderness is hidden beneath a thorny hubbub. This image of a complex childhood, beyond clichés, that we can also find in some of the short stories in *Krik? Krak!* leaves behind all stereotypes to touch upon something fundamental in our society.

In *Breath, Eyes, Memory,* growing up, the little girl knows she is loved, but she also understands in her very flesh that her dreams, her private wounds, can hold no weight against adult choices. Most likely, all societies, in one way or another, shape childhood to fit their molds, with more or less severity, more or less flexibility, but Danticat was able to render these specificities of Haitian childhood with know-how and sensitivity.

In fact, Edwidge Danticat's gaze rests upon Haitian society with no indulgence. A society that refuses to contemplate its wounds, that hangs onto its prejudices, its taboos, in spite of the symptoms of a never-ending crisis. Edwidge Danticat touches upon the taboos, sometimes commenting on them with a sentence, an image, a paragraph. A short story. The malaise of two parents anxious for the future and their grim determination to spare their son their hopelessness. The tragic life of a fifteen-year-old girl whose baby dies. *Krik? Krak!* takes us back to many different aspects of Haitian life, of Haitian lives.

This ability to explode Haitian reality in thousands of pieces, to alter the lighting and to adjust the point of view, counts among the strongest traits of Edwidge Danticat's literary work. Danticat's characters reflect a social reality in constant evolution. True and complex, they cross through the reader's life with their load of pain, of hopelessness, of resilience and dignity, taking him or her to a complex and intense universe, where there is not just one truth. The universe depicted in Danticat's texts allows us to see the convulsiveness of a situation of continual political crises and economic slumps on the family and on the individual, on society in general.

During my interview for *Bomb Magazine,* the exchanges with Edwidge naturally drifted toward the role of memory in the literary text. Individual and collective memory, the images that remain of a dictatorship, for example, of which one only speaks in terms often tinged with dry generalities. The memory of wounds that cannot heal in indifference and silence. Edwidge Danticat's texts also refer to the past, and sometimes to history. Family memory, from one generation to the next, the thread that passes on legends, taboos, values plagued by clashes with reality. Memories of crimes, hidden memory, the weight of silence and mysteries. Memory that is necessary to drive the present toward change. Danticat reveals with great skill an atmosphere that is both dream-like and real, which can seem almost muddled at times. It is then up to the reader to dive into this entanglement to find the strings and climb out, or to stay—a willing prisoner! Some writers challenge themselves by creating twists and turns and interlacing ideas, facts, sentences and words in which the reader cannot help but invest himself or herself as well—the easy road is not an option.

I respond to Edwidge Danticat's texts as a woman, a writer, and a Haitian. I notice that certain themes are akin to my own imaginary: the role of childhood; women's place in society; community ties; social, linguistic, religious, and color prejudices; taboos; Vodou; the influence of economic problems on value systems; irresistible and sometimes unexpected humor; the resilience of family ties. These traits run through Edwidge Danticat's writing not in a folklorist or voyeuristic manner, but with sensitivity. Danticat invokes them, not to praise or condemn, but to show their impact on the individual and to reflect upon society.

The same goes for the violence that constitutes an important part of the total oeuvre. Always present, but as a pretext for something else, not an all-purpose garment used to dress up scenes and satisfy the expectations and tendencies of societies hungry for exoticism—for cruelty that is appeasing, because it is so far from their own experiences—but rather, painted in depth, with attention paid to the context, to the underlying reasons and truths. I return here to the concern for the plural, for different voices, carried by a common heritage of diverse yet recognizable cultural elements. Without privileging one over the other.

A truth-seeking eye—that is how I interpret Danticat. An eye free of arrogance, with a social intelligence that makes it possible to see the other. This absence of judgment, in spite of a few moralizing touches, is refreshing. It is a gaze from within. Born not of a physical presence that does not necessarily correspond to a real need to understand, but from the gut, from the upheavals, the bursts of joy and of revolt in an often disparaged country. The fact that her principal place of residence is outside of Haiti or that her writings are in a language other than Kreyòl or French only becomes significant when one looks to assign nationality or origin to texts! I think that one of Edwidge Danticat's characteristics is precisely the ability to explode certain stereotypes: is she an African American author, a short story writer from the Anglophone Caribbean of Kreyòl-speaking origin? A novelist speaking of Haiti, writing in neither Kreyòl nor French, a well-integrated immigrant (what a dubious expression when each successful integration implies a certain distance or rejection of his or her experience, each failure supposes a suspicious allegiance to the past!) or simply a woman writer who unites several of these elements?

The rise of Edwidge Danticat, *American novelist of Haitian origin, who writes in English,* also opens the way for another type of discourse. Some see Danticat as the symbol of a new trend in Haitian literature, finally liberated from the French language. The choice of English would almost symbolize the rupture with the culture and language of the former metropole. A number of Haitian writers have already questioned and continue to question the role of the French language as an instrument of domination, as a way to maintain privileges and a tool of exclusion. On a number of occasions, they have also questioned the notion of *francophonie* in its double excess: the marginalization of texts coming from places that inherited the French language historically (and violently!), and the hegemony of a literature that would position itself as the central point in light of these same historical criteria and its economic superiority. However, considering Edwidge Danticat's work as a symbol of rupture with the French language entails ignoring the reasons adjacent to the migration of so many Haitian families, the difficulties encountered by these immigrants in an increasingly savage world context and the relations of dependence as well as the struggles of societies of the so-called South against world powers. It is to forget the pain that accompanies the migration of families pushed out of their homes by poverty, by economic and political oppression; daily cultural frictions and the fortunate or unfortunate adjustments. Above all, it is to enclose Edwidge Danticat in a logic of futile conflicts when the use of the language of the *destination* country (I prefer to use this term, as it is more objective than that of *host* country) is inscribed in a complex, painful, and fertile movement of appropriation that comes from survival, self-affirmation, and creativity. As Edwidge Danticat says herself in an interview: "My writing in English is a consequence of my migration, in the same way that immigrant children speaking to each other in English is a consequence of their migration."[2] Just as Haitian writers appropriate the French language that came to them through colonization, through its history of domination, of struggles, and of resistance. Just as they appropriate Kreyòl, born of this history of struggles to bestow upon it the status of literary language in its own right.

Edwidge Danticat is not the only writer of her generation displaced from Haiti by family choice, thus as a child who found herself in a foreign land (North America, Europe, the Caribbean . . .) with a need within her to write, a need to tell that pays no regard to language or place. The crisis situation that has prevailed in Haiti for the past few decades has provoked many departures, scattered many energies, and given rise to creativities that explode elsewhere. Haiti is everywhere. In poetry, fiction, essays. The artist, the writer emerging from Haiti or from any other country of the "periphery" (another one of those terms that needs to be redefined and that I use with caution since to speak of a periphery is to automatically refer to a center that needs to be called into question) finds himself or herself in many cases transformed if not into a spokesperson, then at least into a specialist of his or her country of origin. He or she to whom the public of the host country gives carte blanche because he or she is judged the most apt to present the situation from his or her point of view, having happily integrated (there's that word again) into the host country. Edwidge Danticat is not the only one in this situation, moreover. Any writer who enjoys a certain success beyond the spheres of his or her own country is invested with this role. On the one hand judged capable of understanding and explaining the country from which he or she hails, and on the other hand sufficiently familiar with the ways of the normative countries to take their position into consideration. At least, that's often the implicit challenge issued when he or she is given the floor. Independently of the person's opinion, willingness, or ideology. It is up to each individual to handle this carte blanche in his or her own way. Edwidge Danticat wields the authority conferred upon her with little fanfare. Her attitude of humility and respect as expressed in the previously cited Random House interview goes along with her refusal to assign the role of spokesperson to the writer. Edwidge claims only the need to write and to tell.

As I was writing this text, there came to me via the traveling technology that is the Internet, and that can bring to us as much refuse as ferment, an article by Edwidge Danticat on the use of torture to crack terrorists.[3] This new evil that spreads terror and that would have us forget the inequitable distribution of world riches; just like at home, urban violence tends to relegate to the backburner the issues of exclusion and inequalities that are constants in our history. Addressing this matter of torture, with apparent simplicity, Edwidge Danticat has, once again, dived into the Haitian universe to reveal the human. The Haiti that she knew as a child, and that later came to her through intermediaries, parents, friends, readings, and testimonies, she intentionally claimed as hers, with neither apology nor vocation, as we claim all that is human. Without dressing it in pathetic intentions.

In my view, choosing to write is to signify one's refusal of silence. When interviewing me for *Bomb Magazine,* Edwidge brought up the question of the weight of silence in our trauma as a people, whether from slavery, or from more recent tragedies like dictatorship, oppression, embargo, or war. The silence around social injustice, sexual or religious taboos, all kinds of discrimination, all that hinders breathing and becomes a source of malaise and unhappiness. When silence threatens our humanity, it deserves to be destroyed. To do so, Edwidge Danticat deliberately chose to place herself on that side of history that frightens some people. The side where production capacity and that of consumption do not correspond to the norms established by the economic and political powers. The side through which history passed with its load of pillaging, exploitation, oversights, and silences. We are in a world that, under guise of being more and more interconnected, feeds and reproduces inequalities between peoples more than ever, reinforces borders, and strengthens laws to divide humans and return them to their origins, be they in the Maghreb, Africa, or the Caribbean. On our side of history, we cannot afford to cover our eyes for very long. Light blazes in with pain and beauty. Knowing that the stakes are high, Edwidge Danticat chose, without fanfare, to position herself on that side of history to write and to tell.

NOTES

1. Edwidge Danticat, "Evelyne Trouillot," *Bomb Magazine* 90 (Winter 2005), http://www.bombsite.com/issues/90/articles/2708 (accessed September 2, 2009).

2. Edwidge Danticat, "Author interview," Reading Group Guides, http://www.readinggroupguides.com/guides_B/breath_eyes_memory2.asp (accessed 2 September 2009).

3. Edwidge Danticat, "Does It Work?" *Washington Post*, September 24, 2006.

BALANCING
THE JAR

MADISON SMARTT BELL

I met Edwidge Danticat for the first time in the fall of 1995 at the National Book Award ceremony in New York City. She and I were both finalists for the fiction prize that year: I for *All Souls' Rising,* the first volume of a trilogy about the Haitian Revolution at the end of the eighteenth century; and she for *Krik? Krak!* a book of stories about Haiti and Haitians at the end of the twentieth century. I read the list of finalists with a prick of disappointment soon followed by a surge of relief, for it seemed obvious to me that Danticat and I would cancel each other out. My book outweighed hers, in a certain respect, but it was impossible that a 1995 prize committee would prefer a book about Haiti by a white male from Tennessee to a book about Haiti by a Haitian *native-natale.* Moreover *Krik? Krak!* ounce for ounce, was and remains strong enough to hold its own with any work of literary fiction of the period. So the prize would certainly go to one of the other three finalists, I figured (and it did).

The element of relief in that insight was substantial, for the National Book Award evening can be stressful for finalists and their publishers. No one learns the result till it is announced from the podium, and that uncertainty has been known to tell on some people. To be a finalist for the award was a large (and most unexpected) boon to me—it more or less guaranteed that I would be able to publish the next two installments of the trilogy, a prospect that otherwise would have been far less certain. I had won as much as I needed to win, and (oddly) it was thanks to Edwidge Danticat's presence in the group that I could kick back and enjoy the evening without fretting about whether or not I was going to win more.

I wondered, though, if it would all be quite so easy for her. I was thirty-eight years old that year and had had, presumably, more opportunity than she to exploit the consolations of philosophy (at least, within the narrow confines of the "literary life"). *All Souls' Rising* was my tenth book. *Krik? Krak!* was her second, and she was twenty-six. Old enough, certainly, not to be called a child prodigy . . . but she had published her first work at the age of fourteen. American culture is not particularly kind to its *wunderkinder.* I took some interest in the literary side of that situation. In the late 1980s, as the entry-level age for American novelists went down, down, down, one saw a lot of very young writers get severely shaken by extraordinary early success. They didn't call them "the Brat Pack" for no reason.

Edwidge was awfully young to be where she was, and I was curious to see how she would handle it. At the event she seemed to feel none of the pressure. "Seemed," I suppose, may be the operative word. She spent the evening in the midst of her large and close-knit family, which may well have helped to assure her. Yet I felt that she would have displayed the same grace and poise and natural ease if she had been walking all by herself on a bed of hot coals. She sailed through the situation with an almost eerie calm. In that first meeting and the several we have had since she has always struck me as one of the most well-centered people I have ever met—young or old; white or black; American, Haitian, or Martian.

This remarkable equilibrium is also a salient quality of her work:

The young toughs waved parsley sprigs in front of our faces.

"Tell us what this is," one said. "Que diga perejil."

At that moment I did believe that had I wanted to, I could have said the word properly, calmly, slowly, the way I often asked "Perejil?" of the old Dominican women and their faithful attending granddaughters at the roadside gardens and markets, even though the trill of the *r* and the precision of the *j* was sometimes too burdensome a joining for my tongue. It was the kind of thing that if you were startled in the night, you might forget, but with all my senses calm, I could have said it. But I didn't get my chance. Yves and I were shoved down onto our knees. Our jaws were pried open and parsley stuffed into our mouths. My eyes watering, I chewed and swallowed as fast as I could, but not nearly as fast as they were forcing the handfuls into my mouth.

Yves chewed with all the strength in his bulging jaws.

At least they were not beating us, I thought.

I tried to stop listening to the voices ordering the young men to feed us more. I told myself that eating the parsley would keep me alive.[1]

The viciousness of the action portrayed is tempered, without being diluted, by the precisely balanced calm with which it is described. Ernest Hemingway was the first to pioneer this sort of purity in the representation of action in English, and he never did it better than Danticat does here. But Danticat's writing also has a frankness of feeling that Hemingway could seldom achieve without great conflict:

As we sat there with Odette under a canopy of trees in the middle of a grassy field, she spat up the chest full of water she had collected in the river. With her parting breath, she mouthed in Kreyòl "pèsi," not calmly and slowly as if she were asking for it at a roadside garden or open market, not questioning as if demanding of the face of Heaven the greater meaning of senseless acts, no effort to say "perejil" as if pleading for her life. Que diga amor? Love? Hate? Speak to me of things the world has yet to truly understand, of the instant meaning of each bird's call, of a child's secret thoughts in her mother's womb, of the measured rhythmical time of every man, of the color of the inside of the moon, of the larger miracles in small things, the deeper mysteries. But parsley? Was it because it was so used, so commonplace, so abundantly at hand that everyone who desired a sprig could find one? We used parsley for our food, our teas, our baths, to cleanse our insides as well as our outsides. Perhaps the Generalissimo in some larger order was trying to do the same for his country.

The Generalissimo's mind was surely dark as death, but if he had heard Odette's "pèsi," it might have startled him, not the tears and supplications he would have expected, no shriek from unbound fear, but a provocation, a challenge, a dare. To the devil with your world, your grass, your wind, your water, your air, your words. You ask for perejil, I give you more. (203)

One of the things I find almost intimidating about Danticat's talent is that she executes it in her third language. I can't think of many other cases of that. Second language, yes; third language, no. But her explanation is marvelously simple. In the Haitian educational system of the 1970s, she learned to speak Kreyòl in the world outside of school and to write French in the classroom . . . so English was the first language she spoke and wrote at the same time. It's obvious when you think about it that way.

But I think Danticat's mastery of English has something to do with her having come to it from a different place. In my twenty-odd years of teaching novice fiction writers I have stopped being surprised by the fact that so many of the best of them turn out to be dyslexic. Because text is alien to them, at first they are apt to wield it more originally than those to whom it comes naturally and easily, without effort and struggle . . . just as successful immigrants may become extraordinarily fluent in the terms of a culture not originally their own.

In that sense among others Danticat may represent the archetype of twenty-first-century _____ American writer (you fill in the blank), at the beginning of the period when the majority of people living in this country do speak some other language before English. These are people who bring language and experience and culture from their many different versions of elsewhere into an American situation that resembles less a melting pot than a loom where strands remain distinctly visible even as they are being interwoven. Edwidge Danticat's work features the weaving of a Haitian experience into the American world (especially in *Breath, Eyes, Memory*) and sometimes the weaving of American experience into the Haitian world (especially in *The Dew Breaker*). But the unusual *authority* of her writing seems to come out of some connection to more universal truth.

Danticat's prose style is radically simple and wonderfully expressive—so graceful, poised, and apparently effortless that, lulled by the pleasure of reading, one may forget what terrible stories she has to tell—what terrible stories she is, in fact, telling. There are the horrors of the inner life, where, for example, a young woman may find it reasonable to rape herself with a pestle. And there are endless examples of human beings' capacity to violate and mortify each other: the state terror of the Duvalierist regime, or the massacre of Haitians on the Dominican border by Trujillo's government, or the atrocities of the defacto regime of the 1990s, or . . . And all of it is presented with a lucid simplicity that lends the most awful scenes a mysterious beauty, a preternatural, surreal air of calm.

How to explain it? A part of the answer may lie in Danticat's other-than-American side; she is American like the rest of us, but Haitian like herself. Haitian culture was born, in the 1790s, out of one of the most violently cathartic episodes in all human history. Since then, the best and worst of human capability have been very close at hand in Haiti, and very close to one another. Haitian culture is given to sudden, cathartic eruption, and catharsis is commonly followed by deep calm.

The branches of Danticat's fictional tree put forth their leaves in the American atmosphere, but its roots are Haitian and reach all the way back to Africa, where the whole human genome originates. The centeredness of her work and this rootedness are the same. Her characters struggle in the fractured world of our century's turn, but they each have an inner portal that opens onto the primal origin of our species. That striking sense of equilibrium comes through there.

When I look at Danticat and her achievements I think I am seeing something very different than the usual picture First-Worlders have had, since the nineteenth century if not before, of the artistic ego gratifying itself through acts of sublimation. I don't meant to impute this next idea to Danticat (she may share it, she may not), but my own experience in and of Haiti taught me a different idea of inspiration, a more literal idea in which the egoistic self yields its place to some other spirit that enters into and inhabits one's being. In this model, the emptied self becomes a vessel for carrying messages that come from a long way off. It is a purifying experience, as a vessel may be purified by water or by fire. A deeper, stronger centeredness, too, comes from the passage of another spirit through one's being. I see a woman appear on the horizon, bearing a jar on the top of her head, moving toward us with such perfect balance, such an easy natural grace that we may forget that her poised equilibrium is accomplished with great effort, extraordinary strength, and at a price of pain.

NOTE

1. Edwidge Danticat, *The Farming of Bones* (New York: Soho Press, 1998), 193. The subsequent reference is also to this edition.

TO THE TEXT

LYONEL TROUILLOT

When I first heard of Edwidge Danticat, I suspected some kind of ruse. I know the market is capable of inventing anything and everything. "Of Haitian origin," "writing in English," "folk art"; it's the kind of thing that sells easily. And when the market is accompanied by a critical discourse that seeks to "dislodge," or "delocalize" authors, to drown the loss of cultural practices and referents in the great melting pot of "hybridity," while all over the place they are expelling refugees, one might wonder behind what dwarf tree they are trying to hide the forest. I knew the legend of Danticat before her work, and I do not trust legends.

Then I encountered the work and the person. It may sound like a statement of the obvious, but for me, Edwidge Danticat is first and foremost a person. A person in the sense that, contrary to the way that the American literary establishment has sought to recuperate her, she is not typical of the journey of a whole category of people. She is an individual voice. There is no norm for individuality. All of the little girls who have grown up in a familial world of mystery and flux, rediscovered other parents at the age of twelve, switched countries, switched worlds at that age, moving almost from the rural to the hyper-urban, passing from one language to the other, do not produce something uniform. And in my view the struggle to find for her a "literary nationality" that might conform to the idea that people have of the state of the world is extremely vulgar and is born of parasitism. Edwidge Danticat, Haitian writer, American writer of Haitian origin, African American writer of Haitian origin, or quite simply American writer, a woman writer adding on all the preceding qualifiers. Edwidge Danticat is the person that she is, that she must construct secretly, lose from time to time, find again and lose again, lose again and find again, like all of us. That is her life—her human and civil bonds and engagements. Her writing is her territory. I am happy to say that I do not find in her novels any posture or plea in favor of the fashionable clichés: idealization of hybridity, exacerbated individualism . . . It happens that certain writers from formerly colonized countries who have emigrated to the center of the West turn into ideologues, their work becoming written proof by means of interposed metaphors of their own journey, and their journey being presented as an example that devalorizes the country of origin (troubled country: repression, exacerbated nationalism . . .) and that valorizes the new country (freedom of expression, multiculturalism . . .). The moment that ideology triumphs, becomes sufficiently *real* to believe in its death, I adopt on the question of Edwidge Danticat's status a variable, political position. When people suggest that Haiti is not enough for her imagination and that the journey is in itself a necessity, I claim her as Haitian. When the authenticity of her imagination is questioned because she has traveled and speaks of several places, I make a case for the authenticity of individualities, thus for liberty. Not to take her anchoring from her, nor to chain her to a rock. This is a work and a person that have become objects to be coveted.

The work, because that is what is finally most important, is not, however, a pretext. It is built up without an excess of identity and without misrepresentation. Edwidge Danticat does not plead for her condition; she tells stories. Her first novel—but is this not typical of many first novels?—*Breath, Eyes, Memory,* has autobiographical touches, and one might read in her work a metaphor not of exile, but of return. Return to childhood: *Breath, Eyes, Memory.* Return to history: *The Farming of Bones.* Return to the home country: *After the Dance.* This kind of reading is a reconstruction, no more or less pertinent than any other, that would have the merit of privileging *the act,* that of the character or narrator who returns, believing they are "displaced people." This expression favored by Emile Ollivier seems to me applicable to Edwidge Danticat and to the characters that she brings to life.

There is also another thing that I read in Danticat's work; that is, the way she favors goodness. I know the word has a naive, innocent connotation, but I can think of no other. There is in much modern and postmodern literature a sense of indifference, of losing faith in the human. Human beings become beasts following routines or drifting in existences with no meaning. The quest for positive, modest, personal action is for me one of the distinguishing features of Danticat's work. It gives to her work a kind of youthfulness, indeed a freshness that you do not really find much these days. The Kreyòl saying *"kenbe la"* (hold on to it) that she likes to add when signing her books for friends is present in her writing.

And then there is the person. I think once again of this idea of return. Return to the language too. The Kreyòl that is hidden behind and inside her texts. Her consideration of Haitian literature, of Haiti. She is not the "great absent one." One feels the need for dialogue with Haitian literature. And the English language is not a barrier that prevents her from relating to the vast corpus of Haitian literature in Kreyòl and French.

And, finally, what attracts me, and what connects her with the Haitian novel since indigenism: the poetic rhythm of her phrasing, her visual metaphors and the rhythm that gives the prose a beat, a cadence. Since *Gouverneurs de la rosée* (*Masters of the Dew*, 1978), and without this being an obligation, a master text, or a model, everyone being free to construct their own grammar, the phrasing of certain Haitian novelists has had hips, an almost carnal swinging quality. Even when the phrasing is quite dry and very visual, as in *Gouverneurs de la rosée:* "And the old Délira Délivrance plunged her hand into the dust."[1] I find in certain Danticat phrases this rhythm and this capacity to make things visible.

I have not spoken of Danticat's place in "women's writing." I am wary of this concept. It seems to hide an essentialism. And it allows for the amalgamation of things that are completely different. There are women writers who vaunt amorous slavery and affective dependence and those who ask of their own bodies the question of its liberty. I cannot read Edwidge Danticat's work as an ideological proposal in this domain either.

I am not sure that what I have said is very clear. The essential thing for me is to read her. For that, readers do not need my commentaries. All they have to do is to give themselves over to the pleasure of the text, to the emotions and reflections that it provokes. The rest is perhaps only discourse that is more or less pretentious or scholarly, out of step and parasitic.

To the text, quick, to the text.

NOTE

1. Jacques Roumain, *Gouverneurs de la rosée* (1944; Paris: Editeurs Français Réunis, 1961), 13. Translation mine.

Interview & Bibliography

This section presents a new interview with Edwidge Danticat by Renee H. Shea. The interview focuses on Danticat's 2007 work, *Brother, I'm Dying*, and her motivations for writing this compelling and moving memoir. Finally, there is a bibliography of work by and on Danticat and on classic and contemporary Haitian literature. The bibliography aims in particular to encourage readers to explore further the great tradition of Haitian writing and to engage with the works of such authors as Jacques Roumain, Jacques-Stephen Alexis, Marie Chauvet, Dany Laferrière, Gary Victor, Louis-Philippe Dalembert, Lyonel Trouillot, Joël Des Rosiers, Stanley Péan, Frankétienne, and Evelyne Trouillot. Danticat's readers will find in these other Haitian authors echoes of her work, and further demonstrations of the remarkable creativity that is the hallmark of Haitian literature.

A FAMILY STORY

Danticat Talks about
Her Newest—and Most
Personal—Work

RENEE H. SHEA

In her 2007 work *Brother, I'm Dying*, Edwidge Danticat writes about the deaths of her father André, or Mira, and his older brother Joseph and the birth of her daughter Mira. As in so much of her writing, the personal becomes political in this story about the beloved uncle who cared for her in Haiti after her parents immigrated to the United States. Although filled with scenes of the loving extended family during Danticat's first twelve years growing up in Haiti, the immediate context is 2004 when Joseph, a minister, fled the increasingly chaotic situation in Haiti to seek safety in Miami. Detained by customs agents and the Department of Homeland Security, he died in prison within a few days. Soon after, his brother, Danticat's father, died of a lung disease, though not before he held his granddaughter and namesake Mira when she was only a few weeks old.

RS: Before we get to the new book, I'd like to ask you a few questions about *Breath, Eyes, Memory*. I recently taught the novel and realized there is an afterword. Why did you decide to write that?

ED: I wrote it around 1998 when the book was selected for the Oprah Book Club. I had gotten a lot of criticism on the issue of testing from the Haitian American community, and I thought I should address it at the time that more people were going to be reading the book.

RS: I'm teaching the novel in a course on literature about mothers and daughters. I am wondering now that you have a daughter of your own if you would write this novel differently or if you see the conflicts it explores differently.

ED: I probably would write if differently now even if I didn't have Mira. Now that more than ten years have gone by since the publication of the book, I have grown a lot as a woman and as a writer, so I think I would delve deeper into a lot of the issues the book addresses if I were writing it now. I think the book has a lot of brush strokes, you know, generalities. There's some naive idealism in it, like the Joseph character. He's so good, too good. (Maybe I was basing him on my uncle.) I would change a lot of little things like that, add nuance to the story, to the people. I'd also add a lot more ambivalence to Sophie's choice of becoming a mother. Not just the usual ambivalence that a lot of us have, but also her own particular kind after being born as a result of a rape and having a mother who essentially did not want her. What can I say, it was a first novel and first novels teach us how to begin learning to write.

RS: Why did you decide to write a memoir/autobiography (do you prefer one term over the other?) and not fiction this time? You clearly could have fictionalized some of this—but is it that you want the work to stand as a tribute to your father and uncle?

ED: Of the two terms, I prefer memoir, as this book is not really an autobiography. It's not even really memoir as I am not the central subject, but my father and uncle are. I chose to write this as nonfiction because I wanted to pay tribute to my father's and uncle's lives. They were both extraordinary people whose lives could have gone under the radar, who no one but us, their loved ones, could have known about. They were so hardworking, so good, so loving. We all have those people in our families, in our lives, heroic people. The way my uncle died also made me want to tell their stories, particularly his. A great injustice was done to him, and part of my healing process was vowing to out this and tell the world about it, shame the people who basically condemned him to death both in Haiti and here. In the book there is a folktale that ends with the morale, "It is not our way to let our grief silence us." That's basically the reason I am telling this story in that way. I did not want to let my grief silence me. I wanted to speak for my uncle and my father, for my family, but also for the hundreds and thousands of families who lose loved ones in this way.

RS: You've written articles about your uncle that were published in newspapers and other periodicals. When did you realize this would be a book? Why?

ED: I realized it could be a book when I saw the actual files from his journey across the U.S. immigration nightmare. A group called the Florida Immigrant Advocacy Center helped us sue the U.S. government to get his files from the Department of Homeland Security. We filed Freedom of Information requests that went nowhere, so then we had to file a lawsuit to get his file as well as the Office of the Inspector General report. When I saw the maze that my uncle went through, the maze that led to his death, it felt to me like something you would read in a book, a book by someone like Kafka. So I decided to write a book about not just his death, but also his life, my own file on him if you will. At the same time that my uncle was dying, my father was also dying of a very painful lung disease, and I was pregnant with my daughter, so I decided to put all that in. And it became a book.

RS: To my mind, all of your work is activism of one sort or another, but this one is more so than most. Are you concerned—in terms of the safety and security of you and your family—about the accusations you make and the graphic descriptions of what can only be described as abuse?

ED: I am not making any unwarranted accusations. The government files speak for themselves. One immigration official told the press that my uncle was carrying "voodoo" potions, which is why they took away his crucial medications. Another said maybe it was his time to die, that we all have our time and maybe this was his. The records from Krome, the prison where he was held, the report from the Office of the Inspector General show that a medic did say to the inspector, just as he did to my uncle's lawyer, that he thought my uncle was faking his illness when he became sick in prison. I rely heavily on these documents so that the facts may speak for themselves.

RS: Who do you envision as your audience? Do you think those who are unaware of the detainees' situation will be moved to take some kind of action?

ED: I envision as my audience anyone who's ever read me before and everyone who is interested in these issues of justice and immigration and human rights and parity in immigration policy. In the book, too, there is an intriguing story, I think, of two brothers separated for so long and finally reunited in death.

RS: If this is a disrespectful question, forgive me—but as I've heard you talk over the years and now reading this, it seems that this is the story of your two fathers, not only your father and uncle. Is that how you feel?

ED: Indeed, I have always thought of my uncle as my second father. My dad used to say when my uncle was coming to visit that "your father is coming." That was always how I felt. My uncle *was* like a father to me. He was my second father, and I loved him very much.

RS: Has the process of writing about this time of such terrible loss (though renewal with your Mira) helped you to cope or heal? Won't it be unusually difficult for you to do readings from this work?

ED: All my tears are on the page. I don't imagine myself crying at public readings—as I did, for example, for *The Farming of Bones*. Writing this was extremely healing. It was like visiting with my uncle and father. They're not dead to me because they are so alive in this book, through both good and bad times. Being with my daughter is also healing, though I am so scared sometimes of the kind of world she's come into.

RS: Has your immediate family read this yet (your brothers)? They must have at least read the parts that have been reprinted, such as the one in Oprah's magazine. What is their response?

ED: My brothers have not read the whole book. They've only seen parts. They were happy to revisit certain moments, I think. I am not sure yet how they'll respond to the whole thing. Sometimes what bothers loved ones is some detail you never think is important and not what you fear will upset them. We'll have to see.

RS: Did you keep journals or diaries about this time period when you were pregnant, your father ill, and your uncle in distress? You write with so much detail and dialogue and bring such immediacy to every moment you describe that I wonder how you can recall.

ED: I kept some journals of my father's hospital visits and a pregnancy journal, but with general notes, not with details as I have it in the book. Sometimes I find that to remember something all you need is a word or detail that takes you all the way back.

RS: Much of this is about your childhood and your father's illness—all times you remember or at least bring to us through some process of memory. But there is so much that recounts fighting and struggles in Haiti when you were not there, events you did not experience. How did you gain such intimate knowledge of things like the skirmishes between gangs and your uncle's journey to elude those who blamed him?

ED: I know the places that I'm writing about intimately, so that helped. When I was told that this happened in a certain location either in the house or neighborhood, I could see it and describe it adequately. I have also seen the gang guys during my visits. I knew who they were and what they looked like. Knowing the people and the places I could describe the things I was told by my cousin and aunt who were there or had been told what took place. Also there were a lot of press reports on the day my uncle's church was used in the operation in Bel Air. I put all that together to place myself there.

RS: You bring such a cast of "characters" to poignant and powerful life here—Tante Denise, Granmè Melina, Granpè Nozial, and my favorite Marie Micheline. Do you see yourself as the family historian, the one who not only tells the stories but also records them?

ED: Even before this book, that was my role in the family. I was always asking questions, especially of my uncle, who wanted to write a book about his life and wanted me to help him with it. He never had time to settle down for us to do it, and unlike most eighty-one-year-olds thought he still had a long life ahead, so we never got around to it. But he confided a lot of things in me as did my father because I was always curious and always asked questions. I also had the largest collection of family photographs until I sent some to a *New York Daily News* reporter named Nick Chiles, who was writing a story about me in 1995; he promised to messenger them back and lost them, so until then I was considered a family archive. When I became a writer it was even more so, people would tell me stories, my uncle and father included, that they wanted to guard for prosperity.

RS: I'm fascinated by the chronology, or lack of it. The backbone is the death of your uncle and father and the birth of Mira, yet the memoir includes so much history, both political and personal. How did you figure out the way you'd tell it? When did you realize the form the "story" would take, interweaving past and present, personal and political? Some of the convergences seem quite natural, such as the story of your birth recounted as we read about Mira's. But others that are less obvious also have such natural grace: e.g., "The day Aristide returned, Tante Denise suffered a mild stroke."

ED: It was tough to decide how to tell it all in an interesting way. But I settled on the back and forth between the present and the past because that's how I experienced it, the past merging with the present in the midst of all this tragedy and joy. There were so many ways that political events affected the personal that it was natural to have that link. Tante Denise, for example, we think had that stroke because she was so worried about what would happen after Aristide returned. She thought there might be a civil war, so this was very stressful for her. The past interwoven with the present and the personal merging with the political is so normal for us in life that I wanted the book to reflect that.

RS: With the publication of this, you will have written novels, short stories, a children's book, a travel memoir, and a full-fledged memoir. What can possibly be next?

ED: I think I'm going to ease back into fiction slowly again. I am working on short stories right now, one of which will soon be published in an anthology edited by Zadie Smith called *The Book of Other People.* The story is called "Lele."

RS: Have you been back to Haiti with your Mira?

ED: We went back to Jacmel, which I wrote my book *After the Dance* about. It was so wonderful to see Mira in Haiti before she was even two. She just blended in the atmosphere like she would everywhere else. It was just great. I loved seeing her there, being with her there. I love that she can say she was there before she was two.

RS: Are you doing any teaching right now? I remember a few years ago you were involved in a project in Haiti.

ED: I visit a lot of schools in Miami and elsewhere, hoping to link some of them with independent schools in Haiti. One such school is the Little Flower School, a rural school started by a great Haitian linguist named Yves DeJean. Recently, a private school in Broward County in Florida adopted them after I visited there. I'd love to do more visits like this that lead to something long term. I'm not actually teaching now, but next year I'll be at the University of Miami for a semester.

RS: How has the move from New York to Miami affected you?

ED: It is very hard to be away from my family, but I see them quite often and they visit, so we have a migrating relationship. We talk all the time, so I still feel like I'm with them but in a different way. Living in Little Haiti is great. I have wonderful neighbors, some of whom have no idea who I am but still treat me nicely. It's a vibrant neighborhood with lots of young people coming back to live here—altogether a wonderful experience.

EDWIDGE DANTICAT

A Selected Bibliography

NADÈVE MÉNARD

The following selected bibliography is not exhaustive. Rather, it is an attempt to help the reader navigate Danticat's writings and also to situate them within a Haitian context. Indeed, most of Edwidge Danticat's texts reference Haiti, whether directly or indirectly. The bibliography first lists Danticat's own works: her novels, short stories, travel writing, and memoir as well as children's literature and a number of essays and articles originally published in magazines, newspapers, and online. Also included among texts authored by Danticat are the translation of Jacques-Stephen Alexis on which she worked and films for which she was associate producer. The bibliography then progresses to the important body of critical works pertaining to Edwidge Danticat and her work. It includes books, chapters, and articles, as well as both MA and PhD theses and interviews conducted with the author. The next section of the bibliography is devoted to classic and contemporary texts of Haitian literature. Translations into English have been indicated when they exist. There then follows a list of texts on Haitian literature, history, culture, and society. The works listed are both contemporary and classic and refer to both historical and contemporary Haiti.

Works Authored by Edwidge Danticat

NOVELS

"My Turn in the Fire: An Abridged Novel." MFA thesis, Brown University, 1993.

Breath, Eyes, Memory. New York: Soho Press, 1994; New York: Vintage Books, 1995.

The Farming of Bones. New York: Soho Press, 1998; Penguin, 1999.

The Dew Breaker. New York: Knopf, 2004.

SHORT STORY COLLECTIONS

Krik? Krak! New York: Soho Press, 1995; New York: Vintage Books, 1996.

SHORT STORIES

"Dream of the Butterflies." *Caribbean Writer* 5 (1991): 98–99.

"Graduation." *Caribbean Writer* 5 (1991): 100–103.

"Lost Shadows and Stick Figures." *Caribbean Writer* 6 (1992): 104–6.

"Between the Pool and the Gardenias." *Caribbean Writer* 7 (1993): 66–70.

"The Missing Peace." *Caribbean Writer* 8 (1994): 104–12.

"A Rain of Daffodils." *Literary Cavalcade* 52, no. 6 (March 2000): 4–9.

"The Dew Breaker." In *Gumbo: A Celebration of African American Writers,* ed. Marita Golden and E. Lynn Harris. New York: Harlem Moon, 2002.

"Freda." In *Brown Sugar 4: Secret Desires: A Collection of Erotic Black Fiction,* ed. Carol Taylor. New York: Washington Square Press, 2005.

MEMOIR

Brother, I'm Dying. New York: Knopf, 2007.

ESSAYS/TRAVEL WRITING

After the Dance: A Walk through Carnival in Jacmel, Haiti. New York: Crown, 2002.

EDITED ANTHOLOGIES

The Beacon Best of 2000: Great Writing by Women and Men of All Colors and Cultures. Boston: Beacon Press, 2000.

The Butterfly's Way: Voices from the Haitian Dyaspora in the United States. New York: Soho Press, 2001.

CHILDREN/YOUNG ADULT LITERATURE

Behind the Mountains: The Diary of Celiane Espérance. New York: Orchard Books, 2002.

Anacaona, Golden Flower. New York: Scholastic, 2005.

Brisquette et les serpents—Conte de fée pour fille d'immigrants. Montréal: Mémoire d'Encrier, 2009.

TRANSLATION

In the Flicker of an Eyelid. Trans., *L'espace d'un cillement* by Jacques-Stephen Alexis. Trans. with Carrol F. Coates. Charlottesville: University of Virginia Press, 2002.

FILMS (ASSOCIATE PRODUCER)
Courage and Pain, 1996. Dir. Patricia Benoit.
The Agronomist, 2003. Dir. Jonathan Demme.

NONFICTION

Women: A Celebration of Strength. Ed. with Louise A. Gikow, Kathy Rodgers, Lynn Hecht Schafran, and Anna Quindlen. New York: Legal Momentum, 2007.

ARTICLES

"My Father Once Chased Rainbows." *Essence,* November 1993, 48.

"Let My People Stay." *Essence,* July 1994, 124.

"A Fountain of Peace." In *On the Wings of Peace,* ed. Sheila Hamanaka. New York: Clarion, 1995.

"From the Ocean Floor." In *Rhythm and Revolt: Tales of the Antilles,* ed. Marcela Breton. New York: Plume, 1995.

"We Are Ugly, But We Are Here." *Caribbean Writer* 10 (1996): 137–41.

"Hanging with the Fugees." *Essence,* August 1996, 85–86.

Foreword to *The Magic Orange Tree and Other Haitian Folktales,* ed. Diane Wolkstein, vii–viii. New York: Random, 1997.

Foreword to *Starting with "I": Personal Essays by Teenagers by Youth Communication,* ed. Andrea Estepa and Philip Kay. New York: Persea, 1997.

Foreword to *A Community of Equals: The Constitutional Protection of New Americans,* ed. Owen M. Fiss, Joshua Cohen, and Joel Rogers. Boston: Beacon, 1999.

Foreword to *Like the Dew That Waters the Grass: Words from Haitian Women,* ed. Marie M. Racine and Kathy Ogle. Washington, DC: EPICA, 1999.

"A Brief Reflection on the Massacre River." *Kreyòl* 5, no. 2, issue 17 (May 19, 1999), http://www.ahadonline.org/eLibrary/creoleconnection/cc_Header.asp?ccID=500.

"Aha!" In *Becoming American: Personal Essays by First Generation Immigrant Women,* ed. Meri Nana-Ama Danquah. New York: Hyperion, 2000.

"Westbury Court." In *The Best American Essays, 2000,* ed. Alan P. Lightman. Boston: Houghton Mifflin, 2000.

Foreword to *Their Eyes Were Watching God,* by Zora Neale Hurston. New York: HarperCollins, 2000.

"Epilogue: Women Like Us." In *Step into a World: A Global Anthology of the New Black Literature,* ed. Kevin Powell. New York: Wiley, 2000.

"My New York." *New York* 33.49 (2000): 96.

"Papi." In *Family: American Writers Remember Their Own,* ed. Sharon Sloan Fiffer and Steve Fiffer. Collingdale, PA: Diane, 2000.

"Bonjour Jean." *Nation,* February 19, 2001, 20–22.

Foreword to *Walking on Fire: Haitian Women's Stories of Survival and Resistance,* ed. Beverly Bell. Ithaca, NY: Cornell University Press, 2001.

"Brave New Worlds: The Future in My Arms." *Essence,* May 2001, 169–70.

"I Pass On." *Essence,* May 2001, 160.

"Voices from Hispaniola: A Meridians Roundtable with Edwidge Danticat, Loida Maritza Pérez, Myriam J. A. Chancy, and Nelly Rosario." *Meridians: Feminism, Race, Transnationalism* 5, no. 1 (2004): 68–91.

"On Writing and Significant Others." *Journal of Haitian Studies* 10, no. 2 (Fall 2004): 4–8.

"Roundtable: Writing, History, and Revolution with Dany Laferrière, Louis-Philippe Dalembert, Edwidge Danticat, Evelyne Trouillot and J. Michael Dash as Moderator." *Small Axe* 18 (2005): 189–201.

"Ghosts of the 1915 U.S. Invasion Still Haunt Haiti's People." *Miami Herald,* July 25, 2005.

Preface to *Massacre River,* by René Philoctète. Trans. Linda Coverdale. New York: New Directions, 2005.

Foreword to *Vale of Tears: A Novel from Haiti,* by Paulette Poujol Oriol. Trans. Dolores A. Schaefer. Bethesda, MD: Ibex, 2005.

Foreword to *Brown Girl, Brownstones,* by Paule Marshall. New York: Feminist Press at CUNY, 2006. First published 1959 by Random House.

"Does It Work?" *Washington Post,* September 24, 2006.

Foreword to *Homelands: Women's Journeys across Race, Place, and Time,* ed. Patricia Justine Tumang and Jenesha de Rivera. Seattle: Seal Press, 2006.

Introduction to *The Kingdom of This World,* by Alejo Carpentier. Trans. Harriet de Onis. New York: Farrar, Straus and Giroux, 2006.

Introduction to *Love, Anger, Madness: A Haitian Trilogy, by* Marie Vieux-Chauvet. Trans. Rose-Myriam Réjouis and Val Vinokur. New York: Modern Library, 2009.

Critical Texts on Edwidge Danticat and
Interviews with the Author

BOOKS, CHAPTERS, AND ARTICLES

Anatol, Giselle Liza. "Caribbean Migration, Ex-Isles, and the New World Novel." In *The Cambridge Companion to the African American Novel*, ed. Maryemma Graham. Cambridge Companions to Literature. Cambridge: Cambridge University Press, 2004. 70–83.

Asim, Jabari. "Speaking Volumes: Young Literary Lions." *Emerge*, October 1998, 70–71.

Bloom, Harold, ed. *Caribbean Women Writers (Women Writers of English and Their Work)*. Philadelphia: Chelsea House, 1997.

Braziel, Jana Evans. "Daffodils, Rhizomes, Migrations: Narrative Coming of Age in the Diasporic Writings of Edwidge Danticat and Jamaica Kincaid." *Meridians: Feminism, Race, Transnationalism* 3, no. 2 (2003): 110–31.

———. "Defilee's Diasporic Daughters: Revolutionary Narratives of *Ayiti*, *Nanchon*, and *Dyaspora* in Edwidge Danticat's *Krik? Krak!*" *Studies in the Literary Imagination* 37, no. 2 (2004): 103–22.

Brice-Finch, Jacqueline. "Edwidge Danticat: Memories of a Maäfa." *Ma-Comère* 4 (2001): 146–54.

Burchell, Eileen. "As My Mother's Daughter: *Breath, Eyes, Memory* by Edwidge Danticat (1994)." In *Women in Literature: Reading through the Lens of Gender*, ed. Jerilyn Fisher and Ellen S. Silber, 60–62. Westport, CT: Greenwood Press, 2003.

Casey, Ethan. "Remembering Haiti: *Breath, Eyes, Memory*." *Callaloo* 18, no. 2 (Spring 1995): 524–26.

Chancy, Myriam. "Léspoua fè viv: Female Identity and the Politics of Textual Sexuality in Nadine Magloire's *Le mal de vivre* and Edwidge Danticat's *Breath, Eyes, Memory*." *Framing Silence: Revolutionary Novels by Haitian Women*, 104–33. New Brunswick, NJ: Rutgers University Press, 1997.

Charters, Mallay. "Edwidge Danticat: A Bitter Legacy Revisited." *Publishers Weekly*, August 17, 1998, 42–43.

Christophe, Marc A. "Truths, Half Truths, and Beautiful Lies: Edwidge Danticat and the Recuperation of Memory in *Breath, Eyes, Memory*." *Journal of Haitian Studies* 7, no. 2 (Fall 2001): 96–107.

Clitandre, Nadège. "Body and Voice as Sites of Oppression: The Psychological Condition of the Displaced Post-Colonial Haitian Subject in Edwidge Danticat's *The Farming of Bones*." *Journal of Haitian Studies* 7, no. 2 (Fall 2001): 28–49.

———. "Reformulating Haitian Literature Transnationally: Identifying New and Revised Tropes of Haitian Identity in Edwidge Danticat's *Breath, Eyes, Memory.*" *Journal of Haitian Studies* 9, no. 2 (Fall 2003): 90–110.

Cobham, Rhonda. "The Penance of Speech." *Women's Review of Books* 21, no. 8: 1–3.

Crouch, Cameron. "The Flow of History." *In These Times*, November 29, 1998): 24.

Davis, Rocio G. "Oral Narrative as Short Story Cycle: Forging Community in Edwidge Danticat's *Krik? Krak!*" *MELUS* Summer 2001: 65–81.

Francis, Donette A. "Silences Too Horrific to Disturb: Writing Sexual Histories in Edwidge Danticat's *Breath, Eyes, Memory.*" *Research in African Literatures* 35, no. 2 (Summer 2004): 75–90.

———. "Unsilencing the Past in Edwidge Danticat's *The Farming of Bones.*" *Small Axe* 5 (March 1999): 168–75.

Gerber, Nancy F. "Binding the Narrative Thread: Storytelling and the Mother-Daughter Relationship in Edwidge Danticat's *Breath, Eyes, Memory.*" *Journal of the Association for Research on Mothering* 2, no. 2 (2000): 188–99.

Goldblatt, Patricia. "Finding a Voice for the Victimized." *MultiCultural Review* 9, no. 3 (2000): 40–47.

Gregory, Deborah. "Word Star: Edwidge Danticat Dreaming of Haiti." *Essence*, April 1995, 56.

Griffiths, Emilie. "A Bookbag for Fall: A Roundup of the Season's New Offerings." *America*, November 6, 1999, 8.

Gyssels, Kathleen. "'Couper le cordon ombilical': Edwidge Danticat, Marie-Hélène Laforest et 'the French connexion.'" In *Le Monde Caraïbe: Défis et dynamiques*, vol. 1, *Visions identitaires, diasporas, configurations culturelles*, ed. Christian Lerat, 531–51. Pessac, France: Maison des sciences de l'Homme d'Aquitaine, 2005.

———. "Littérature doublement exilée: *Krik? Krak!* d'Edwidge Danticat." *Ruptures* 13 (October 1997–March 1998): 187–202.

Herndon, Gerise. "Returns to Native Lands, Reclaiming the Other's Language: Kincaid and Danticat." *Journal of International Women's Studies* 3, no. 1 (2001): 1–10.

Hower, Edward. "A New Voice from Haiti: *Krik? Krak!* by Edwidge Danticat." *World and I*, July 1995, 238–43.

Johnson, Kelli Lyon. "Both Sides of the Massacre: Collective Memory and Narrative on Hispaniola." *Mosaic: A Journal for the Interdisciplinary Study of Literature* 36, no. 2 (2003): 74–91.

Journal of Haitian Studies 7, no. 2 (Fall 2001): 5–137. Special issue on Edwidge Danticat.

Laforest, Marie-Hélène. *Diasporic Encounters: Remapping the Caribbean.* Naples: Liguore Editore, 2000.

Lahens, Yanick. "L'apport de quatre romancières au roman moderne haïtien." *Journal of Haitian Studies* 3/4 (1997–98): 87–95; *Notre Librairie* 133 (1998): 26–36.

Larrier, Renée. "'Girl by the Shore': Gender and Testimony in Edwidge Danticat's *The Farming of Bones.*" *Journal of Haitian Studies* 7, no. 2 (Fall 2001): 50–60.

Loichot, Valérie. "Edwidge Danticat's Kitchen History." *Meridians: Feminism, Race, Transnationalism* 5, no. 1 (2004): 92–116.

Marxen, Patti M. "The Map Within: Place, Displacement, and the Long Shadow of History in the Work of Edwidge Danticat." *Journal of Haitian Studies* 11, no. 1 (Spring 2005): 140–55.

Meacham, Cherie. "Traumatic Realism in the Fiction of Edwidge Danticat." *Journal of Haitian Studies* 11, no. 1 (Spring 2005): 122–39.

Mead, Rebecca. "Stepmother Tongue." *New Yorker,* November 20, 1995, 50–51.

Mortimer, Mildred. "Edwidge Danticat, *Breath, Eyes, Memory:* Rewriting Home." *Writing from the Hearth: Public, Domestic, and Imaginative Space in Francophone Women's Fiction of Africa and the Caribbean.* Lanham, MD: Lexington Books, 2007: 167–85.

Munro, Martin. *Exile and Post-1946 Haitian Literature: Alexis, Depestre, Ollivier, Laferrière, Danticat.* Liverpool: Liverpool University Press, 2007.

Nge, Carmen. "Rising in the Ashes: *Krik? Krak!* as a Response to 'Can the Subaltern Speak.'" In *Postcolonial Perspectives on Women Writers from Africa, the Caribbean, and the U.S.,* ed. Martin Japtok. Trenton, NJ: Africa World Press, 2003. 193–208.

N'Zengo-Tayo, Marie-José. "Children in Haitian Popular Migration as Seen by Maryse Condé and Edwidge Danticat." In *Winds of Change: The Transforming Voices of Caribbean Women Writers and Scholars,* ed. Adele S. Newson and Linda Strong-Leek, 93–100. New York: Peter Lang, 1998.

———. "Rewriting Folklore: Traditional Beliefs and Popular Culture in Edwidge Danticat's *Breath, Eyes, Memory* and *Krik? Krak!*" *MaComère* 3 (2000): 123–40.

Ortiz, Lisa M. "Re-membering the Past: Weaving Tales of Loss and Cultural Inheritance in Edwidge Danticat's *Krik! Krak!*" *Journal of Haitian Studies* 7, no. 2 (Fall 2001): 64–77.

Peepre, Mari. "Home, Hybridity, and the Caribbean Diasporas." In *Bridges across Chasms: Towards a Transcultural Future in Caribbean Literature,* ed. Bénédicte Ledent. Liège, Belgium: Liège Language and Literature, English Department, Université de Liège, 2004. 221–31.

Peters, Linda. "More Talk about Books: Of Mothers and Stories." *English Journal* 88, no. 6 (July 1999): 118.

Poon, Angelia. "Re-writing the Male Text: Mapping Cultural Spaces in Edwidge Danticat's *Krik? Krak!* and Jamaica Kincaid's *A Small Place.*" *Jouvert* 4, no. 2 (Winter 2000), http://english.chass.ncsu.edu/jouvert/v4i2/con42.htm.

Putnam, Amanda. "Braiding Memories: Resistant Storytelling within Mother-Daughter Communities in Edwidge Danticat's *Krik? Krak!*" *Journal of Haitian Studies* 9, no. 1 (Spring 2003): 52–65.

———. "Mothering the Motherless: Portrayals of Alternative Mothering Practices within the Caribbean Diaspora." *Canadian Woman Studies/Les Cahiers de la Femme* 23, no. 2 (2004): 118–23.

Pyne-Timothy, Helen. "Language, Theme & Tone in Edwidge Danticat's Work." *Journal of Haitian Studies* 7, no. 2 (Fall 2001): 128–37.

Ragbar, Nadia. "Imagining Post-colonialism as a Revolutionary Reality: Edwidge Danticat's Opus as a Testimony of Women's Survival through Narration." *Journal of Haitian Studies* 7, no. 2 (Fall 2001): 110–26.

Saint-Éloi, Rodney. "L'écriture Bizango: Edwidge Danticat, le go-between." *Notre Librairie* 143 (January–March 2001): 58–61; *Journal of Haitian Studies* 7, no. 2 (Fall 2001): 22–25.

Samway, Patrick. "A Homeward Journey: Edwidge Danticat's Fictional Landscapes, Mindscapes, Genescapes, Signscapes in *Breath, Eyes, Memory.*" *Mississippi Quarterly* 57, no. 1 (Winter 2003–4): 75–83.

Scott, Helen. "Ou libéré? History, Transformation and the Struggle for Freedom in Edwidge Danticat's *Breath, Eyes, Memory.*" In *Haïti: Ecrire en pays assiégé: Writing under Siege,* ed. Marie-Agnès Sourieau and Kathleen M. Balutansky. (Francopolyphonies: 1.) Amsterdam: Rodopi, 2004. 459–78.

———. "Replacing the 'Wall of Disinformation': *The Butterfly's Way, Krik? Krak!* and Representation of Haiti in the USA." *Journal of Haitian Studies* 7, no. 2 (Fall 2001): 78–93.

Shea, Renee H. *Edwidge Danticat Visits Her Haitian Roots.* DVD. Full Duck Productions, 2003.

———. "'The Hunger to Tell': Edwidge Danticat and *The Farming of Bones.*" *MaComere* 2 (1999): 12–22.

Shelton, Marie-Denise. "Identité créole et mémoire: Edwidge Danticat et Fabienne Pasquet." *Journal of Haitian Studies* 3/4 (1997–98): 103–8.

Shemak, April. "Re-Membering Hispaniola: Edwidge Danticat's *The Farming of Bones*." *Modern Fiction Studies* 48, no. 1 (Spring 2002): 83–112.

Suárez, Lucía M. "*Breath, Eyes, Memory:* Rape, Memory, and Denunciation." *Journal of Haitian Studies* 9, no. 2 (Fall 2003): 111–25.

Sturgis, Ingrid. "Young Author Reclaims Haiti's Stories as Birthright." *Emerge*, April 1995, 58–59.

Tabuteau, Eric. "American Dream, Urban Nightmare: Edwidge Danticat's *Breath, Eyes, Memory* and George Lamming's *In the Castle of My Skin*." *Alizés: Revue angliciste de la réunion* 22 (2002): 95–110.

Thomas, Katherine M. "Memories of Home: Edwidge Danticat's *Breath, Eyes, Memory*." *Kentucky Philological Review* 18 (2004): 35–40.

Valbrun, Marjorie. "Haiti's Eloquent Daughter: In the Bicentennial Year of the Conflict-Ridden Land of Her Birth, Edwidge Danticat Lives in Miami's 'Little Haiti' and Continues to Write about 'Those Things That Haunt Me.'" *Black Issues Book Review* 6, no. 4 (2004): 42–43.

Walcott-Hackshaw, Elizabeth. "Home Is Where the Heart Is: Danticat's Landscapes of Return." *Small Axe* no. 27 (vol. 12, no. 3) (October 2008): 71–82.

Wucker, Michele. "Edwidge Danticat: A Voice for the Voiceless." *Americas Magazine* 52, no. 3 (May/June 2000): 40–46.

THESES

Barnes, Missy R. "'The Tale Differs with the Teller': Subversive Fables and Proverbs in Edna O'Brien's *House of Splendid Isolation* and Edwidge Danticat's *Breath, Eyes, Memory*." MA thesis, University of North Carolina at Wilmington, 1999.

Braziel, Jana Evans. "Nomadism, Diaspora and Deracination in Contemporary Migrant Literatures." PhD diss., University of Massachussetts at Amherst, 2000.

Brown-Hinds, Paulette D. "Long-Memoried Women: Memory and Migration in 20th-Century Black Women's Narrative." PhD diss., University of California–Riverside, 1998.

DeLoughrey, Elizabeth Mary. "Antipodean Archipelagoes: Post-Colonial Cartographies in Caribbean and Pacific Island Literatures." PhD diss., University of Maryland–College Park, 1999.

Dismont Robinson, Kim. "Probing the Wound: Re-Membering the Traumatic Landscape of Caribbean Literary Histories." PhD diss., University of Miami, 2003.

Duvivier, Sandra Caona. "Mapping Intersections: Black Women's Identities and the Politics of Home in Transnational Black American Women's Fiction." PhD diss., University of Massachusetts–Amherst, 2006.

Francis, Aisha X. L. "Language and the Black Body Politic in Edwidge Danticat's *The Farming of Bones.*" MA thesis, Vanderbilt University, 1999.

Gerber, Nancy F. "From Shadow to Substance: The Figure of the Mother-Artist in Contemporary American Fiction." PhD diss., Rutgers University, 1999.

Kerby, Erik R. "Negotiating Identity in the Transnational Imaginary of Julia Alvarez's and Edwidge Danticat's Literature." MA thesis, Brigham Young University, 2008.

Leedham, Nicola Elizabeth. "Afrocentric Mythology and Cultural Retentions in the African American Novel." PhD diss., University of South Carolina, 1995.

Lorgia, García Peña. "Dominicanidad in Contra (Diction): Marginality, Migration, and the Narration of a Dominican National Identity." PhD diss., University of Michigan, 2008.

Ortiz, Lisa M. "Autoethnography: Genealogical, Autobiographical, and Historical Recovery in the Novels of Alvarez, Cliff, and Danticat." PhD diss., Wayne State University, 2000.

Putnam, Amanda. "Legacies and Literacies: Life Lessons from Black Grandmothers and Other Matrilineal Substitutes." PhD diss., University of Nebraska–Lincoln, 1999.

Rohrleitner, Marion Christina. "Intimate Geographies: Romance and the Rhetoric of Female Desire in Contemporary Historical Fiction by Caribbean American Women Writers." PhD diss., University of Notre Dame, 2007.

Saunders, Kristyn. "Sugar and Spice: Slavery, Women, and Literature in the Caribbean." PhD diss., Columbia University, 2003.

Zinn, Emily R. "Rewriting the Kitchen: Gender and Food in Contemporary Fiction." PhD diss., University of Pennsylvania, 2007.

INTERVIEWS

Anglesey, Zoe. "The Voice of the Storytellers: An Interview with Edwidge Danticat." *Multicultural Review* 7, no. 3 (September 1, 1998): 36–39.

Lyons, Bonnie. "Interview with Edwidge Danticat." *Contemporary Literature,* 44, no. 2 (Summer 2003).

Patterson, Christina. "A Brooklyn Bridge-Builder: Edwidge Danticat—Once a Poor Immigrant, Now a Rising Literary Star—Talks to Christina Patterson." *Independent* (London), March 13, 1999, 14.

Shea, Renee H. "Bearing Witness and Beyond: Edwidge Danticat Talks about Her Latest Work." *Journal of Haitian Studies* 7, no. 2 (Fall 2001): 6–20.

———. "The Dangerous Job of Edwidge Danticat: An Interview." *Callaloo* 19, no. 2 (Spring 1996): 382–89.

———. "Interview" [with Edwidge Danticat]. *Belles Lettres* 10, no. 3 (1995): 12.

———. "Traveling Worlds with Edwidge Danticat." *Poets and Writers* 25, no. 1 (January/February 1997): 42–51.

Wachtel, Eleanor. "A Conversation with Edwidge Danticat." *Brick* 65–66 (2000): 106–19.

Classic and Contemporary Haitian Literature

Agnant, Marie-Célie. *La dot de Sara.* Montreal: Les Éditions du Remue-ménage, 1995, 2000.

———. *Le livre d'Emma.* Montreal: Les Éditions du Remue-ménage and Éditions Mémoire, 2001; La Roque d'Anthéron, France: Vents d'Ailleurs, 2004. English ed., *The Book of Emma,* trans. Zilpha Ellis; Toronto: Insomniac Press, 2006.

———. *Le silence comme le sang.* Montreal: Les Éditions du Remue-ménage, 1997.

Alexis, Jacques-Stephen. *Les Arbres Musiciens.* Paris: Gallimard, 1957, 1984; Port-au-Prince: Les Editions Fardin, 1986.

———. *Compère Général Soleil.* Paris: Gallimard, 1955. English ed., *General Sun, My Brother,* trans. Carrol F. Coates; Charlottesville: University Press of Virginia, 1999.

———. *Dans l'espace d'un cillement.* Paris: Gallimard, 1959, 1983. English ed., *In the Flicker of an Eyelid,* trans. Carrol F. Coates and Edwidge Danticat; Charlottesville: University of Virginia Press, 2002.

———. *Romancero aux Étoiles.* Paris: Gallimard, 1960.

Bastien, Cynthia. *Les Mendiantes de soleil.* Port-au-Prince: Les Éditions des Presses Nationales d'Haïti, 2005.

Casséus, Maurice. *Viejo.* Port-au-Prince: Éditions la Presse, 1935; Nendeln, Liechtenstein: Kraus, 1970.

Chancy, Myriam J. A. *The Scorpion's Claw.* Leeds, UK: Peepal Tree Press, 2004.

———. *Spirit of Haiti.* London: Mango, 2004.

Chauvet, Marie. *Amour, Colère, Folie.* Paris: Gallimard, 1968; Paris: Maisonneuve & Larose and Emina Soleil, 2005. English ed., *Love, Anger, Mad-*

ness: A Haitian Trilogy, trans. Rose-Myriam Réjouis and Val Vinokur; New York: Modern Library, 2009.

———. *Fille d'Haïti*. Paris: Fasquelle, 1954.

———. *Les Rapaces*. Port-au-Prince: Deschamps, 1986.

Clitandre, Pierre. *Cathédrale du mois d'août*. Port-au-Prince: Fardin, 1979; Paris: Syros, 1982. English ed., *Cathedral of the August Heat*, trans. Bridget Jones; New York: Readers International, 1987.

———. *Vin de soleil*. Port-au-Prince: Éditions Mémoire, 2000.

D'Adesky, Anne-Christine. *Under the Bone*. New York: Farrar, Straus and Giroux, 1994.

Dalembert, Louis-Philippe. *L'autre face de la mer*. Paris: Stock 1998; Paris: Le Serpent à Plumes, 2005.

———. *Le crayon de bon dieu n'a pas de gomme*. Paris: Stock, 1996; Paris: Le Serpent à Plumes (Motifs), 2004; Port-au-Prince: Éditions Presses Nationales d'Haïti, 2006.

———. *Les Dieux voyagent la nuit*. Monaco: Du Rocher, 2006.

———. *Histoires d'amour impossibles . . . ou presque*. Monaco: Le Rocher, 2007.

———. *Le roman de Cuba*. Paris: Du Rocher, 2009.

———. *Rue du Faubourg Saint-Denis*. Monaco: Du Rocher, 2005.

Depestre, René. *Alleluia pour une femme-jardin*. Paris: Gallimard, 1981, 1986, 1990.

———. *Hadriana dans tous mes rêves*. Paris: Gallimard, 1988, 1990.

Desquiron, Lilas. *Les Chemins du Loco-Miroir*. Paris: Stock, 1990; Presses Pocket, 1992. English ed., *Reflections of Loko-Miwa*, trans. Robin Orr Bodkin; Charlottesville: University Press of Virginia, 1998.

Dominique, J. J. *Mémoire d'une amnésique*. Port-au-Prince: Deschamps, 1984; Montreal: CIDIHCA / Éditions du remue-ménage, 2004. English ed., *Memoir of an Amnesiac*, trans. Irline François; Coconut Creek, FL: Caribbean Studies Press, 2008.

Fignolé, Jean-Claude. *Aube Tranquille*. Paris: Seuil, 1990.

———. *Moi, Toussaint Louverture . . . avec la plume complice de l'auteur*. Montréal: Plume & Encre, 2004.

———. *Les Possédés de la Pleine Lune*. Paris: Seuil, 1987.

———. *Une heure pour l'éternité*. Paris: Sabine Wespieser, 2008.

Frankétienne. *Dezafi*. Port-au-Prince: Édision Fardin, 1975; Châteauneuf-le-Rouge, France: Vents d'ailleurs, 2002.

———. *Mûr à crever (genre total)*. Port-au-Prince: Presses port-au-princiennes, 1968; Port-au-Prince: Éd. Mémoire, 1994; Bordeaux, France: Ana Éditions, 2004.

———. *Ultravocal.* Port-au-Prince: Imprimerie Gaston, 1972; Paris: Hoëbeke, 2004.

———. *Corps sans repères.* Port-au-Prince: Spirale, 2007.

———. *Amours, délices et orgues.* Port-au-Prince: Deschamps, 2008.

Hibbert, Fernand. *Scènes de la vie haïtienne: Les Thazar.* Port-au-Prince: Impr. de l'Abeille, 1907; Port-au-Prince: Fardin, 1975; Port-au-Prince: Deschamps, 1988.

Innocent, Antoine. *Mimola ou l'histoire d'une cassette.* Port-au-Prince: Imprimerie Malval, 1906; Nendeln, Liechtenstein: Kraus, 1970; Port-au-Prince: Fardin, 1981, 1999; Port-au-Prince: Éditions Presses Nationales d'Haïti, 2006.

Laferrière, Dany. *Le charme des après-midi sans fin.* Outremont, Québec: Lanctôt, 1997. Paris: Le Serpent à plumes, 1998; oohoo.com, 1999.

———. *Je suis un écrivain japonais.* Paris: Grasset, 2008; Montréal: Boréal, 2008.

———. *L'odeur du café.* Montréal: VLB, 1991; Montréal: Typo, 1999; Paris: Serpent à plumes, 2001.

———. *Vers le sud.* Paris: Grasset, 2006; Montréal: Boréal, 2006.

Lahens, Yanick. *La Couleur de l'aube.* Paris: Sabine Wespieser, 2008; Port-au-Prince: Presses Nationales d'Haïti, 2008.

———. *Dans la maison du père.* Paris: Le Serpent à Plumes, 2000.

———. *La Folie était venue avec la pluie.* Port-au-Prince: Éditions Presses Nationales d'Haïti, 2006.

———. *La Petite Corruption.* Port-au-Prince: Éditions Mémoire, 1999; Montréal: Mémoire d'encrier, 2003.

———. *Tante Résia et les Dieux, nouvelles d'Haïti.* Paris: L'Harmattan, 1994.

Lhérisson, Justin. *La famille des Pitite-Caille (Les fortunes de chez nous).* Port-au-Prince: Héraux, 1905; Paris: Firmin-Didot, 1929; Port-au-Prince: Imprimerie des Antilles, 1963; Port-au-Prince: Éditions Presses Nationales d'Haïti, 2005.

———. *Zoune chez sa ninnaine: Fan'm gain sept sauts pou li passé.* Port-au-Prince: A.A. Héraux, 1906; Port-au-Prince: Imprimerie Dorsinville, 1953. Port-au-Prince: Éditions Presses Nationales d'Haïti, 2005.

Lespès, Anthony. *Les Semences de la Colère.* Port-au-Prince: Deschamps, 1949; Port-au-Prince: Fardin, 1983.

Marcellin, Frédéric. *Thémistocle Épaminondas Labasterre, petit récit haïtien.* Paris: P. Ollendorff / Société d'éditions littéraires et artistiques, 1901; Port-au-Prince: Fardin, 1976, 1982, 1999; Port-au-Prince: Éditions Presses Nationales d'Haïti, 2005.

————. *La Vengeance de Mama, roman haïtien*. Paris: Société d'éditions littéraires et artistiques, 1902; Port-au-Prince: Fardin, 1974, 1997.

Marcelin, Pierre, and Philippe Thoby-Marcelin. *Canapé-Vert*. New York: Édition de la Maison Française, 1944. English ed., *Canape-Vert*, trans. Edward LaRocque Tinker; New York: Farrar & Rinehart, 1944.

Mars, Kettly. *Fado*. Paris: Mercure, 2008.

————. *L'heure hybride*. La Roque d'Anthéron, France: Vents d'Ailleurs, 2005.

————. *Kasalé*. Port-au-Prince: Imprimeur II, 2003.

————. *Mirage-Hôtel*. Port-au-Prince: Imprimerie Caraïbe, 2002.

————. *Un Parfum d'Encens*. Port-au-Prince: Imprimeur II, 1999.

Metellus, Jean. *La Famille Vortex*. Paris: Gallimard, 1982. English ed., *The Vortex Family*, trans. Michael Richardson; London: Peter Owen, 1995.

————. *La Parole prisonnière*. Paris: Gallimard, 1986.

Ollivier, Émile. *La Brûlerie*. Montréal: Boréal, 2004; Paris: Albin Michel, 2005.

————. *La Discorde aux cent voix*. Paris: Albin Michel, 1986.

————. *Mère-Solitude*. Paris: Albin Michel, 1983; Paris: Le Serpent à Plumes, 1994. English ed., *Mother Solitude*, trans. David Lobdell; Ottawa: Oberon, 1989.

————. *Mille Eaux*. Paris: Gallimard (Haute Enfance), 1999.

————. *Passages*. Montreal: l'Hexagone, 1991; Paris: Le Serpent à Plumes, 2001. English ed., *Passages*, trans. Leonard W. Sugden; Victoria, BC: Ekstasis Editions, 2004.

————. *Les Urnes Scellées*. Paris: Albin Michel, 1995.

Philoctète, René. *Le peuple des terres mêlées*. Port-au-Prince: Deschamps, 1989. English ed., *Massacre River*, trans. Linda Coverdale; New York: New Directions, 2005.

Poujol-Oriol, Paulette. *Le Creuset*. Port-au-Prince: H. Deschamps, 1980.

————. *La Fleur rouge*. Port-au-Prince: Le Natal, 1992.

————. *Le Passage*. Port-au-Prince: Le Natal, 1996. English ed., *Vale of Tears*, trans. Dolores A. Schaefer; Bethesda, MD: Ibex, 2005.

Placide, Jaira. *Fresh Girl*. New York: Wendy Lamb Books, 2002.

Roumain, Jacques. *La montagne ensorcelée*. Port-au-Prince: Imprimerie E. Chassaing, 1931; Paris: Éditeurs français réunis, 1972; Port-au-Prince: Fardin, 1976; Montréal: Mémoire d'encrier, 2005.

————. *Gouverneurs de la Rosée*. Port-au-Prince: Imprimerie de l'État, 1944; Paris: La Bibliothèque Française, 1946; Paris: Les Éditeurs Français Réunis, 1961; Pantin, France: Le Temps des Cerises, 2000; Montréal: Mémoire d'encrier, 2004. English ed., *Masters of the Dew*, trans. Langston Hughes and Mercer Cook; New York: Reynal & Hitchcock, 1947; New York: Collier Books, 1971; London: Heinemann, 1978.

Saint-Amand, Edriss. *Bon Dieu Rit*. Paris: Domat, 1952; Port-au-Prince: Les Éditions du Soleil, 1978; Paris: Hatier, 1989.

Trouillot, Évelyne. *La Chambre Interdite*. Paris: L'Harmattan, 1996.

———. *Le Mirador aux étoiles*. Port-au-Prince: L'Imprimeur II, 2007.

———. *L'Oeil-Totem*. Port-au-Prince: Éditions Presses Nationales d'Haïti, 2006.

———. *Parlez-moi d'amour . . .* Port-au-Prince: Imprimerie Caraïbe, 2002.

———. *Rosalie l'Infâme*. Paris: Dapper, 2003.

Trouillot, Lyonel. *L'Amour avant que j'oublie*. Arles, France: Actes Sud, 2007; Port-au-Prince: Presses Nationales d'Haïti, 2007.

———. *Bicentenaire*. Arles, France: Actes Sud, 2004.

———. *Les Enfants des héros*. Arles, France: Actes Sud, 2002.

———. *Les Fous de Saint-Antoine: Traversée rythmique*. Port-au-Prince: Editions Deschamps, 1989.

———. *Rue des Pas Perdus*. Port-au-Prince: Editions Mémoire, 1996; Arles, France: Actes Sud, 1998. English ed., *Street of Lost Footsteps*, trans. Linda Coverdale; Lincoln: University of Nebraska Press, 2003.

———. *Thérèse en mille morceaux*. Arles, France: Actes Sud, 2000.

———. *Yanvalou pour Charlie*. Arles, France: Actes Sud, 2009.

Valcin, Cléante. *La Blanche Négresse*. Port-au-Prince: V. Valcin, 1934; Port-au-Prince: Presses Nationales d'Haïti, 2007.

Victor, Gary. *À l'angle des rues parallèles*. Port-au-Prince: Imprimeur II, 2000; Châteauneuf-le-Rouge, France: Vents d'Ailleurs, 2003.

———. *La chorale de sang*. Port-au-Prince: Mémoire, 2001.

———. *Les cloches de la Brésilienne*. La Roque d'Anthéron, France: Vents d'Ailleurs, 2006.

———. *Le diable dans un thé à la citronnelle*. Port-au-Prince: Imprimeur II, 1998.

———. *Je sais quand Dieu vient se promener dans mon jardin*. La Roque-d'Anthéron, France: Vents d'Ailleurs, 2004.

———. *Un octobre d'Élyaniz*. Port-au-Prince: Imprimeur II, 1996.

———. *Treize nouvelles vaudou*. Préface by Alain Mabanckou. Montréal: Mémoire d'encrier, 2007.

Works on Haitian Literature, History, Culture, Society

CULTURE AND LITERATURE

Alexis, Jacques-Stephen. "Du réalisme merveilleux des Haïtiens." *Présence Africaine* 8–10 (June–November 1956): 25–34.

Antoine, Régis. *La littérature franco-antillaise: Haïti, Guadeloupe, Martinique.* Paris: Karthala, 1992.

Bell, Madison Smartt. *All Souls' Rising.* New York: Pantheon Books, 1995. (novel)

———. *Master of the Crossroads.* New York: Pantheon Books, 2000. (novel)

———. *The Stone That the Builder Refused.* New York: Pantheon Books, 2004. (novel)

Berrou, Raphael, and Pradel Pompilus. *Histoire de la littérature haïtienne, illustrée par les textes.* 3 vols. Port-au-Prince: Caraïbes, 1975–77; Paris: l'École, 1975, 1978.

Carpentier, Alejo. *Kingdom of This World.* New York: Knopf, 1957; New York: Farrar, Straus and Giroux, 2006. (novel)

Chancy, Myriam J. A. *Framing Silence: Revolutionary Novels by Haitian Women.* New Brunswick, NJ: Rutgers University Press, 1997.

Coates, Carrol F. "The Haitian Intellectual Scene: Creative Writers, Essayists and Visual Artists." *Callaloo* 15, no. 3 (1992): 863–73.

Condé, Maryse. *La Parole des femmes: Essai sur les romancières des Antilles de langue française.* Paris: l'Harmattan, 1979.

Dash, J. Michael. *Culture and Customs of Haiti.* Westport, CT: Greenwood Press, 2001.

———. *Haiti and the United States: National Stereotypes and the Literary Imagination.* New York, St. Martin's Press, 1988, 1997.

———. *Literature and Ideology in Haiti, 1915–1961.* London: Macmillan Press, 1981.

———. *The Other America: Caribbean Literature in a New World Context.* Charlottesville: University Press of Virginia, 1998.

Fignolé, Jean-Claude. *Vœu de voyage et intention romanesque.* Port-au-Prince: Fardin, 1978.

Fleischmann, Ulrich. *Ecrivain et société en Haïti.* Montréal: Centre de recherches caraïbes de l'Université de Montréal, 1976.

Gardiner, Madeleine. *Visages de femmes, Portraits d'écrivains.* Port-au-Prince: Deschamps, 1981.

Greene, Graham. *The Comedians.* New York: Viking, 1966; Vintage, 2004. (novel)

Hoffmann, Léon-François. *Essays on Haitian Literature*. Washington: Three Continents Press, 1984.

———. *Haïti: Couleurs, croyances, créole*. Montréal: CIDIHCA, 1990; Port-au-Prince: H. Deschamps, 1990.

———. *Haïti: Lettres et l'être*. Toronto: Éditions du GREF, 1992.

———. *Littérature d'Haïti*, Paris: EDICEF, 1995.

———. *Le Roman haïtien: Idéologie et structure*. Sherbrooke, Québec: Naaman, 1982.

Hurston, Zora Neale. *Tell My Horse: Voodoo and Life in Haiti and Jamaica*. Philadelphia: Lippincott, 1938; New York: Harper Perennial, 1990.

Jonassaint, Jean. *Le Pouvoir des mots, les maux du pouvoir: Des romanciers haïtiens de l'exil*. Paris: Arcantère / PUM, 1986.

———. *Des romans de tradition haïtienne: Sur un récit tragique*. Paris: L'Harmattan, 2002; Montréal: CIDICHA, 2002.

Lahens, Yanick. *L'Exil, entre l'ancrage et la fuite, l'écrivain haïtien*. Port-au-Prince: Éditions Deschamps, 1990.

———. "Littérature haïtienne: Problématiques." *Notre Librairie* 132 (1997).

Laroche, Maximilien. *La littérature haïtienne: Identité, langue, réalité*. Montréal: Lemeac, 1981.

Latortue, Régine. "The Woman in the Haitian Novel." PhD diss., Yale University, 1983.

Munro, Martin. *Exile and Post-1946 Haitian Literature: Alexis, Depestre, Ollivier, Laferrière, Danticat*. Liverpool: Liverpool University Press, 2007.

Munro, Martin, and Elizabeth Walcott-Hackshaw. *Reinterpreting the Haitian Revolution and Its Cultural Aftershocks*. Barbados, Jamaica, and Trinidad: University of the West Indies Press, 2006.

Price-Mars, Jean. *Ainsi parla l'oncle*. Compiègne, France: Imprimerie de Compiègne, 1928; New York: Parapsychology Foundation, 1954; Montréal: Leméac, 1973, 1979; Port-au Prince: Imprimeur II, 1998. English ed., *So Spoke the Uncle*, trans. Magdaline W. Shannon; Washington, DC: Three Continents Press, 1983.

———. *La Vocation de l'élite*. Port-au-Prince: Edmond Chenet, 1919; Port-au-Prince: Ateliers Fardin, 1976; Port-au-Prince: Les Éditions des Presses Nationales d'Haïti, 2001.

Shelton, Marie-Denise. "Haitian Women's Fiction." *Callaloo* 15, no. 3 (1992): 770–810.

———. *Image de la société dans le roman haïtien*, Paris: l'Harmattan, 1993.

Sourieau, Marie-Agnès, and Kathleen M. Balutansky, eds. *Haïti: Ecrire en pays assiégé: Writing under Siege.* (Francopolyphonies: 1.) Amsterdam: Rodopi, 2004.

Trouillot, Hénock. *Les origines sociales de la littérature haïtienne.* Port-au-Prince, Théodore, 1962.

HISTORY AND SOCIETY

Accilien, Cecile, Jessica Adams, and Elmide Méléance, eds. *Revolutionary Freedoms: A History of Survival, Strength and imagination in Haiti.* Coconut Creek, FL: Caribbean Studies Press, 2006.

Arthur, Charles, and J. Michael Dash, eds. *Libète: A Haiti Anthology.* Princeton, NJ: Markus Wiener, 1999.

Bell, Beverly, ed. *Walking on Fire: Haitian Women's Stories of Survival and Resistance.* Ithaca, NY: Cornell University Press, 2001.

Casimir, Jean. *La Culture opprimée.* Port-au-Prince: Imprimerie Lakay, 2001.

———. *Pa Bliye 1804, Souviens-toi de 1804.* Port-au-Prince: Imprimerie Lakay, 2004.

———. *Haïti et ses élites: L'interminable dialogue de sourds.* Haïti-Poche, Éditions de l'Université d'État d'Haïti, 2009.

Dayan, Joan. *Haiti, History, and the Gods.* Berkeley: University of California Press, 1996.

Desmangles, Leslie. *The Faces of the Gods: Voodoo and Roman Catholicism in Haiti.* Chapel Hill: University of North Carolina Press, 1992.

Deren, Maya. *Divine Horseman: The Living Gods of Haiti.* London: Thames and Hudson, 1953; New Paltz, NY: McPherson, 1983.

Dubois, Laurent. *Avengers of the New World: The Story of the Haitian Revolution.* Chapel Hill: University of North Carolina Press, 2004.

———. *A Colony of Citizens: Revolution and Slave Emancipation in the French Caribbean, 1787–1804.* Chapel Hill: University of North Carolina Press, 2004.

Dupuy, Alex. *Haiti in the New World Order: The Limits of the Democratic Revolution.* Boulder, CO: Westview Press, 1996.

———. *Haiti in the World Economy: Class, Race, and Underdevelopment since 1700.* Boulder, CO: Westview Press, 1989.

———. *The Prophet and Power: Jean-Bertrand Aristide, the International Community, and Haiti.* Lanham, MD: Rowman and Littlefield, 2006.

Fick, Carolyn. *The Making of Haiti: The Saint Domingue Revolution from Below.* Knoxville: University of Tennessee Press, 1990.

Firmin, Anténor. *De l'égalité des races humaines: Anthropologie positive.* Paris: F. Pichon, 1885; Paris: l'Harmattan, 2003; Montréal: Mémoire d'encrier, 2005. English ed., *The Equality of Human Races: Positivist Anthropology,* trans. Asselin Charles; New York: Garland, 2000.

Fischer, Sibylle. *Modernity Disavowed: Haiti and the Cultures of Slavery in the Age of Revolution.* Durham, NC: Duke University Press, 2004.

Geggus, David Patrick. *Haitian Revolutionary Studies.* Bloomington: Indiana University Press, 2002.

———, ed. *The Impact of the Haitian Revolution in the Atlantic World.* Columbia: University of South Carolina Press, 2001.

Hurbon, Laënnec. *Comprendre Haïti: Essai sur l'État, la nation, la culture.* Paris: Karthala, 1989.

James, C. L. R. *The Black Jacobins: Toussaint L'Ouverture and the San Domingo Revolution.* New York: Dial Press, 1938; Random House, 1963; London: Allison and Busby, 1980; New York: Vintage, 1989; Penguin, 2001.

Labelle, Michelle. *Idéologie de couleur et classes sociales en Haïti.* Montréal: Presses de l'Université de Montréal, 1978.

Nicholls, David. *From Dessalines to Duvalier: Race, Colour and National Independence in Haiti.* London: Cambridge University Press, 1979; London: Macmillan, 1988; New Brunswick, NJ: Rutgers University Press, 1996.

———. *Haiti in Caribbean Context: Ethnicity, Economy, and Revolt.* London: Macmillan, 1985.

Plummer, Brenda Gayle. *Haiti and the United States: The Psychological Moment.* Athens: University of Georgia Press, 1992.

Renda, Mary A. *Taking Haiti: Military Occupation and the Culture of U.S. Imperialism, 1915–1940.* Chapel Hill: University of North Carolina Press, 2001.

Schmidt, Hans. *The United States Occupation of Haiti, 1915–1934.* New Brunswick, NJ: Rutgers University Press, 1995.

Trouillot, Michel-Rolph. *Haiti, State against Nation: The Origins and Legacy of Duvalierism.* New York: Monthly Review Press, 1990.

———. *Silencing the Past: Power and the Production of History.* Boston: Beacon Press, 1995.

Wilentz, Amy. *The Rainy Season: Haiti since Duvalier.* New York: Simon & Schuster, 1989.

CONTRIBUTORS

MADISON SMARTT BELL is the author of twelve novels and two collections of short stories. His eighth novel, *All Souls' Rising,* was a finalist for the 1995 National Book Award and the 1996 PEN/Faulkner Award and winner of the 1996 Anisfield-Wolf Award for the best book of the year dealing with matters of race. Born and raised in Tennessee, he has lived in New York and London and now lives in Baltimore, Maryland. A graduate of Princeton University (AB, 1979) and Hollins College (MA, 1981), he has taught in various creative writing programs, including the Iowa Writers' Workshop and the Johns Hopkins University Writing Seminars. Since 1984 he has taught at Goucher College, along with his wife, the poet Elizabeth Spires. He has been a member of the Fellowship of Southern Writers since 2003.

MYRIAM J. A. CHANCY is Professor of English at the University of Cincinnati. Her first novel, *Spirit of Haiti* (2003), was a finalist in the Best First Book Category, Canada/Caribbean region, of the Commonwealth Prize 2004. She is the author of *Framing Silence: Revolutionary Novels by Haitian Women* (1997), *Searching for Safe Spaces: Afro-Caribbean Women Writers in Exile* (1997; Choice OAB Award, 1998), a second novel, *The Scorpion's Claw* (2005) and, forthcoming, *The Loneliness of Angels.* Her work as editor of *Meridians* (2002 to 2004) garnered the CELJ Phoenix Award for Editorial Achievement (2004).

MARYSE CONDÉ was born in Point-à-Pitre, Guadeloupe, in 1937. Educated in Guadeloupe and Paris, she lived in Africa in the 1960s and early 1970s before returning to Paris in 1973. She taught in several universities and embarked on her career as a novelist. After the publication of her fourth novel, *Ségou* (1985), she returned to Guadeloupe for a short while before leaving for the United States. She was a tenured professor at Columbia University until 2005. She has published fifteen novels and many other works including literary criticism, plays, and writing for children.

J. Michael Dash, born in Trinidad, has worked extensively on Haitian literature and French Caribbean writers, especially Edouard Glissant, whose works *The Ripening* (1985), *Caribbean Discourse* (1989), and *Monsieur Toussaint* (2005) he has translated into English. After twenty-one years at the University of the West Indies, Jamaica, where he was Professor of Francophone Literature and Chair of Modern Languages, he moved to New York University, where he first was Director of the Africana Studies Program and currently is Professor of French. His publications include *Literature and Ideology in Haiti* (1981), *Haiti and the United States* (1988), *Edouard Glissant* (1995), and *The Other America: Caribbean Literature in a New World Context* (1998). He has also translated *The Drifting of Spirits* (1999) by Gisèle Pineau. His most recent books are *Libète: A Haiti Anthology* (1999) with Charles Arthur and *Culture and Customs of Haiti* (2001).

Charles Forsdick is James Barrow Professor of French at the University of Liverpool, United Kingdom. He is author of *Victor Segalen and the Aesthetics of Diversity* (2000), *Travel in Twentieth-Century French and Francophone Cultures* (2005), and *Ella Maillart, "Oasis interdites"* (2008); and co-author of *New Approaches to Twentieth-Century Travel Literature in French: Genre, Theory, History* (2006). He is also co-editor of *Francophone Postcolonial Studies* (2003) and *Postcolonial Thought in the French-Speaking World* (2009).

Mary Gallagher is Professor of French and Francophone studies at University College Dublin. She has published principally on writing from and about the French-speaking Caribbean, most notably *La Créolité de Saint-John Perse* (1998) and *Soundings in French Caribbean Writing since 1950* (2002). Her most recent publication is *World Writing: Poetics, Ethics, Globalization* (2008). She is currently working on a book about the Creole connection in the work of the Greco-Anglo-Irish author Lafcadio Hearn.

Régine Michelle Jean-Charles is Assistant Professor of African and African Diaspora Studies and Romance Languages and Literatures at Boston College. Her areas of specialization include gender and feminism, francophone African and Caribbean literature, Haitian studies, African and African diasporic women's literature, and comparative literary and cultural studies. Her current book project is on the representation of sexual violence in the works of Caribbean and African women writers. She has published several articles on the subject of black women in Africa and the diaspora including "Beneath Layers of Violence: Images of Rape in the Rwandan Genocide" and "Terre et chair: Rape, Land, and the Body in Gisele Pineau's *Macadam Dreams.*" She is also a board member, lecturer, and performer for A Long Walk Home, Inc., a nonprofit organization that uses art therapy and the visual and performing arts to document, educate, and bring about social change.

CARINE MARDOROSSIAN is Associate Professor of English at the University at Buffalo, where she teaches postcolonial and feminist studies. Her articles have appeared in *Ariel, Hypatia, Signs, Journal of Caribbean Literatures, College Literature,* and *Small Axe.* Her book *Reclaiming Difference: Caribbean Women Rewrite Postcolonialism* (2005) was published by University of Virginia Press. She is currently completing a manuscript entitled "Reframing the Victim: National Identity and Masculinity in the Contemporary United States."

NADÈVE MÉNARD teaches literature at Ecole Normale Supérieure of the Université d'Etat d'Haïti. Her research focuses on representations of history and historical events in twentieth-century Haitian literature. Her topics include the U.S. occupation of Haiti as well as the 1937 massacre of Haitians in the Dominican Republic. She is the editor of a forthcoming volume that contains both articles on contemporary Haitian literature and interviews with authors.

MARTIN MUNRO is Professor of French and Francophone Studies at Florida State University. He previously worked in Scotland, Ireland, and Trinidad and is the co-editor of two volumes on the Haitian Revolution. He is the author of *Shaping and Reshaping the Caribbean: The Work of Aimé Césaire and René Depestre* (2000), *Exile and Post-1946 Haitian Literature: Alexis, Depestre, Ollivier, Laferrière, Danticat* (2007), and *Different Drummers: Rhythm and Race in the Americas* (2010). He is a member of the Small Axe editorial collective.

NICK NESBITT is Professor of French at Princeton University. He is the author of *Universal Emancipation: The Haitian Revolution and the Radical Enlightenment* (2008) and *Voicing Memory: History and Subjectivity in French Caribbean Literature* (2003). He is the editor of *Toussaint Louverture: The Haitian Revolution* (2008) and co-editor with Brian Hulse of *Sounding the Virtual: Gilles Deleuze and the Philosophy of Music* (2010).

MIREILLE ROSELLO teaches at the University of Amsterdam in the Comparative Studies Program and the Amsterdam School of Cultural Analysis (ASCA). Her most recent publications are *The Reparative in Narratives: Works of Mourning in Progress* (2009), *France and the Maghreb: Performative Encounters* (2005), its French version *Encontres Méditerranéennes: Littératures et cultures France-Maghreb* (2006), and *Postcolonial Hospitality: The Immigrant as Guest* (2001). Together with Sudeep Dasgupta, she is also preparing a collection of essays on "What's queer about Europe."

RENEE H. SHEA is Professor of English and Modern Languages at Bowie State University, a historically black institution in the University System of Maryland. Winner of the Regents Award for Public Service in 2007, she is the coauthor of *The Language of Composition: Reading, Writing, Rhetoric* (2007) and *Literature and Composition: Reading, Writing, Thinking* (forthcoming in 2010). She has also coauthored two volumes in the High School Literature Series published by the National Council of Teachers of English on Amy Tan and Zora Neale Hurston. With expertise in writing assessment, she currently serves on the Critical Reading Development Committee for the SAT and has been a member of the development committee for the Advanced Placement English Language and Composition Examination. She publishes widely on contemporary women authors, including Danticat in *Poets & Writers Magazine, Journal of Haitian Studies, The Caribbean Writer,* and *Callaloo.*

ÉVELYNE TROUILLOT, born in Port-au-Prince, Haiti, traveled with her family to the United States at a very young age. Since her return to Haiti in 1987, she has been working in the field of education. Her first book of short stories was published in France in 1996, while her first novel, *Rosalie l'infâme,* appeared in 2003 and was awarded the Soroptimist Prize for a francophone novel. In 2004, her first piece for the theater, *Le bleu de l'île,* received the Beaumarchais Prize for Etudes théâtrales de la Caraïbe. She has also published one book of poetry in French and one in Kreyòl, as well as two other books of short stories and two other novels. Her latest novel, *Le mirador aux étoiles,* was published in Haiti in November 2007. She is the author of an essay on childhood and human rights entitled *Restituer l'enfance* (1998). She also writes for children.

LYONEL TROUILLOT was born in Port-au-Prince, Haiti, in 1956. He has collaborated on various journals in Haiti and the diaspora. He teaches literature at the Institut Français and the Université Caraïbe in Haiti. As a poet, essayist, and novelist, he is one of Haiti's most important contemporary writers. His works include *Les Fous de Saint-Antoine* (1989), *Rue des pasperdus* (1998), *Bicentenaire* (2004), and *Yanvalou pour Charlie* (2009).

Kiera Vaclavik is Lecturer in French Studies and Comparative Literature at Queen Mary University of London. She is the author of several articles on nineteenth-, twentieth-, and twenty-first-century children's literature in French and English as well as a monograph entitled *Uncharted Depths,* which explores the descent into the underground in works for young readers (2010). Her current project examines issues of authenticity and self-recognition in children's literature of Haiti and the Haitian diaspora. The study will examine the implications of writing for a diasporic, multilocational readership and of consuming texts that originate elsewhere and may circulate widely.

INDEX

creolization, 28, 49
Cronin, Michael, 109
Cudjoe, Selwyn, 40, 49n3

Dadié, Bernard, 100
Dalembert, Louis-Philippe, 9
Dash, J. Michael, 101, 102
Davies, Carol Boyce, 40
Davis, Rocio, 75
Dayan, Joan, 108, 138–39
Depestre, René, 26, 103, 107–8, 111
Derby, Lauren, 145
Deren, Maya, 145
De Rivera, Jenesha, 116n39
Des Rosiers, Joël, 3, 4
Dew Breaker, The (Danticat), 6, 7,
    22, 23, 26, 29, 36, 42, 58, 59–60,
    64, 65, 82, 104, 109–10, 113, 144,
    147–60, 165
diaspora, 5, 6, 27, 29, 37, 39, 66–67,
    103, 110
Didier-Urbain, Jean, 116n37
Dominican Republic, 36; 1937 mas-
    sacre in, 7, 22, 30, 31, 34, 47–48,
    57–58, 59, 130–44, 178
Dominique, J. J., 62
Dupuy, Alex, 85n6
Duvalier, François, 14, 15, 29, 32, 33,
    102, 103, 148, 165, 178

Edmondson, Belinda, 41
education, 15, 16, 19
Equiano, Olaudah, 100
exoticism, 2, 101

Fanon, Frantz, 44
Farming of Bones, The (Danticat), 7,
    23, 24, 26, 29–30, 33, 34–35, 36,
    47, 57–58, 59, 74, 79, 103, 104, 107,
    108, 115n18, 130–44, 147, 148, 154,
    166, 176–77, 181
Ferguson, James, 142, 145n2
Fido, Elaine Savory, 40
Fignolé, Daniel, 14–15
Fish, Cheryl J., 114n4
Francis, Donette, 127
Frankétienne, 9, 165

Friedman, Susan Stanford, 50n6
Fulani, Ifeona, 49n3

Gates, Henry Louis, Jr., 59
gender, 5, 40, 47, 48, 49, 54, 57–58,
    99–101, 118, 144
Girard, Philippe, 101
Glissant, Édouard, 32, 46, 104, 133–
    34, 163
globalization, 8
Gourdine, Angeletta K. M., 99, 106,
    109, 113
Gracchus, Fritz, 50n8
Greene, Graham, 102, 109
Griffin, Farah J., 114n4

Hall, Derek, 114n5
Hall, Stuart, 45
Hallward, Peter, 85n6
Harper, Frances, 54
Henderson, Mae Gwendolyn, 65
history, 16
Holloway, Karla, 54
hooks, bell, 134–35
Hurston, Zora Neale, 21, 56, 61, 62

indigenism, 27

Jacmel, 99, 102, 104, 105, 106–10
Jaeckle, Jeffrey Allan, 128–29
Jamaica, 108
Jansen-Gruber, Marya, 88, 93
Jean, Wyclef, 105
Johnson, Mark, 129n3
Jonassaint, Jean, 103

Kincaid, Jamaica, 41, 48
Kinnaird, Vivian, 114n5
Kpomassie, Tété-Michel, 100
Kreyòl. *See* language
Krik? Krak! (Danticat), 6, 22, 27, 33,
    55, 56–57, 58, 62, 63, 73, 74–82,
    169, 170, 175

Laclau, Ernesto, 85n11
Laferrière, Dany, 2–3, 9, 32, 36–37,
    67, 103, 115n19